A SHORT HISTORY OF CAMBRIDGE

RICHARD TAMES read History at Pembroke College, Cambridge, and took his postgraduate degree at the University of London. He has taught for the London programmes of several US universities, including Syracuse University and the University of Maryland, and is a qualified Blue Badge guide. He is also the author of *A Traveller's History of Oxford*, *A Traveller's History of Bath*, and *A Traveller's History of London*.

A Short History of Cambridge

Richard Tames

First published in Great Britain in 2013 by
Haus Publishing
4 Cinnamon Row
SW11 3TW

Email: *haus@hauspublishing.com*
Tel: +44(0)20 3637 9729

This edition published in 2025

A CIP catalogue record for this book is available from the British Library

ISBN: 978-1-914979-16-3
eISBN: 978-1-914979-17-0

Typeset in Garamond by MacGuru Ltd
Printed in the UK by Clays Ltd (Elcograf S.p.A.)

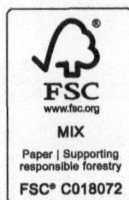

Contents

Introduction

The Cambridge moment

Once a year, millions of people around the world – almost 200 million by one count – focus their attention for an hour or so on an East Anglian market town at the edge of the Fens. There, in an iconic building which has come to represent the place itself, the silence of expectation is magically broken by the soaring voice of a boy soprano proclaiming *Once in Royal David's City*. Thus begins, every Christmas Eve, the Festival of Nine Lessons and Carols at the chapel of King's College, Cambridge, where the singing and the setting combine in excellence and resonance to create in the mind's eye a scene of solemn joy.

The Festival is, in fact, a rather recent tradition, dating only from 1918. It was the creation of the Dean of King's College, Eric Milner-White, DSO, a battlefront padre, who adapted an existing format some 40 years old, devised by a bishop of Truro. *Once in Royal David's City* was not even in the first service but was added in 1919. The Festival was first broadcast in 1928 and has been every year since – except for 1930 – even during the Second World War, when the chapel was unheated and the glorious stained-glass windows had been removed and secreted away, safe from bombing, to an undisclosed location.

The Christmas carol service at King's is not, however, 'typical' Cambridge. Nor is mid-winter the most choice time to contemplate the city, which is then notoriously chilly, damp and windswept. At Christmas the city is almost empty of students, undergraduates at least. Nostalgic reminiscences of Cambridge, by contrast, bathe it in perpetual summer sunlight, as the American novelist Henry James did in 1883 in *English Hours*:

> Six or eight of the colleges stand in a row, turning their backs to the river; and hereupon ensues the loveliest confusion of Gothic windows and ancient trees, of grassy banks and mossy balustrades, of sun-chequered avenues and groves, of lawns and gardens and terraces, of single-arched bridges spanning the little stream, which is small and shallow and looks as if it had been turned on for ornamental purposes. The scantily-flowing Cam appears to exist simply as an occasion for these brave little bridges – the beautiful covered gallery of St John's or the slightly-collapsing arch of Clare.

He went on to rhapsodise about the city at large:

> In the way of College-courts and quiet scholastic porticoes, of grey-walled gardens and ivied nooks of study, in all the pictorial accidents of a great English university, Cambridge is delightfully and inexhaustibly rich. I looked at these one by one and said to myself always that the last was the best.

The year after celebrating its 800th anniversary, Cambridge was voted the best university in the world; the year after that it was voted to the first rank again. But whether or not it remains number one, the university will continue to command the affectionate reverence of a faithful global gathering, who honour not only its intellectual eminence, but also its power to evoke a moment of transcendence.

What is Cambridge for?

In the words of a former editor of the *Cambridge Evening News,* Cambridge is both 'a relatively small East Anglian town' and 'a world city'. The German travel writer Peter Sager opines that 'even more so than with Oxford, the history of Cambridge is the history of its university'. Not quite; Cambridge as a town had existed for more than a millennium before the university began to take it over, like a clerical cuckoo in a thriving commercial nest.

When the university emerged eight centuries ago, its fundamental purpose was to produce literate servants for the Church and state. It has never ceased to do this, but later acquired the additional function of preserving a heritage of learning. Later still it served to mould the outlook not just of the governing elite but of the influential classes as a whole. In his *Letters from England* (1807) the poet Robert Southey, adopting the literary persona of a foreign traveller, explains in 'Letter 45' that Cambridge is there to impart not so much general knowledge as 'a knowledge of the world'; that it is essentially a place of acculturation rather than of culture. Perhaps that is what the historian G M Trevelyan meant a century later when he declared breezily, 'As far as I can make out the Cambridge people are intellectual but not serious'. Nowadays most Cambridge types would regard it as a serious place, teaching cutting-edge, serious subjects that make a difference in the world. Even the members of Footlights want to be seriously good entertainers.

One way to illustrate the significance of Cambridge might be to look at the people it has produced, starting with what one might call 'The Westminster Abbey Test'. In Scientists' Corner there are memorials to Newton, Darwin, Clerk Maxwell and Dirac, in Poets' Corner to Spenser, Milton, Gray, Dryden, Wordsworth, Byron, Tennyson, Housman and Sassoon, and in Musicians' Aisle to Orlando Gibbons and Ralph Vaughan Williams. F W Maitland has the distinction of being the first historian to be honoured with an Abbey memorial, and looming over all is the statue of Britain's youngest-ever Prime Minister, William Pitt.

A more contemporary version might be 'The Television Test', yielding such public members of the Clever Club as Bamber Gascoigne, Stephen Fry, Jeremy Paxman, Sebastian Faulks, Clive James, Germaine Greer, Andrew Roberts, Simon Schama, David Frost, Neal

Ascherson, John Simpson, Roger Scruton, Claire Tomalin and David Starkey. 'The Top Job Test' gives a dozen British Prime Ministers, two Prime Ministers of India; Jawaharlal Nehru and Rajiv Gandhi, former Prime Minister of Singapore Lee Kuan Yew and Fernando Cardoso, former President of Brazil. For a wider perspective one might look over the pages of the *Dictionary of National Biography* to register the interlocking Cambridge dynasties bearing such names as Arnold, Adrian, Butler, Huxley, Stephen, Macaulay, Trevelyan, Darwin, Gurney, Fry, Gaskell and Hodgkin.

For the quintessential Cambridge character it would be difficult to surpass John Maynard Keynes (1883–1946). Born in Cambridge, the son of academics, he was an undergraduate at King's, where he rowed, played golf, won an English essay prize and served as President of the Union. He was initially anything but overwhelmed by the university – 'I've had a good look round the place and come to the conclusion that it's pretty inefficient'. As an undergraduate, Keynes bought an *original* copy of Newton's *Principia,* then went on to write a book that revolutionised the discipline (and practice) of economics, serve as a brilliant bursar of King's, make a personal fortune out of shrewd speculations, marry a Russian ballerina, organise the financing of Britain's war effort in World War Two, create the Arts Council, and design the monetary institutions of the post-war world. Significantly, the plaque commemorating his life-long commitment to Cambridge is to be found, not at the faculty of economics, but above the entrance to the Arts Theatre, which he founded and funded. The last word, however, goes to Roy Jenkins, former Chancellor of Oxford, who observed sardonically of Keynes that 'he soon became too fond of the trains to London to be a strict Cambridge man'.

Some were destined never to live out their promise as Keynes did. Frank Ramsey (1903–30), son of a Magdalene don and a protégé of Keynes, translated Wittgenstein's *Tractatus* at 19 and made distinguished contributions to economics, logic, the philosophy of language and probability theory. He only ever published eight pages in his official discipline, mathematics, but these pages nevertheless spawned a whole new field – 'Ramsey theory'. Ramsey died at the age of 26 of jaundice; a militant atheist, he was spared seeing his brother become Archbishop of Canterbury.

Part of the charm of the Cambridge story is, however, its capacity not just to throw up the occasional genius but also to tolerate the spectacularly eccentric. A E Housman knowingly called Cambridge 'an asylum in more senses than one'. R V Laurence, a bachelor tutor at Trinity, complained that living in college left him 'always exposed, weekdays and Sundays alike, to pupils and their parents'; his solution was 'to take the train to London, simply to have a little snooze at the club'. Habitually swathed in his dressing-gown, the medieval historian G G Coulton inhabited rooms of medieval inconvenience at St John's, using a wash-stand as a writing desk and subsisting on specially imported cocoa which took ten hours to prepare. The gastronome and world-class name-dropper Oscar Browning habitually pronounced 'very interesting' as 'veynsing'. J E Nixon was similarly given to such compressed elisions, 'temmince' meaning ten minutes, 'hairpin' for 'high opinion' and 'official sources' coming out as 'fish sauce'. Economist A C Pigou affected 'an extraordinary burlesque jargon, part Victorian, part home-made ... often accompanied by an indefinable foreign accent'.

Walter Headlam, 'one of the finest of all interpreters of Greek thought and language',

> seemed to have only a frail contact with reality. Travelling was
> difficult because he could not take the right train ... Letters were
> difficult because he chose his stamps only for the beauty of the
> colours ... pupils' work was usually lost ...

Mathematician G H Hardy, who was 'meticulously orderly in everything but dress', refused ever to use either a watch or a fountain pen and loathed the telephone so much that he habitually communicated by telegram or pre-paid postcard. Violently anti-clerical, but with many clerical friends, Hardy also conceived of God as a personal enemy with a particularly malevolent interest in the vagaries of the weather during the cricket season. Philosopher John McTaggart was an atheist who nevertheless supported the Church of England and believed in immortality but devoted a lengthy treatise to the argument that time itself was a delusion. His pupil and successor C D Broad, living in Newton's former rooms at Trinity, rejected McTaggart's philosophy but spent most of the 1930s on a two-volume analysis of it.

Frederick Arthur Simpson was the archetype of the eccentric bachelor don. The first of four projected volumes on Napoleon III gained him a fellowship at Trinity (1909). The long-delayed second volume (1923), was so brutally trashed in reviews that Simpson effectively gave up and devoted his life to pruning. Roaming through college gardens, stooped and shuffling, 'Snipper Simpson' would create a trail of branches and leaves by which he could be tracked back to his rooms in Great Court. A sore trial to generations of college gardeners, Simpson hung onto his fellowship for 62 years, dying aged 90. Simpson's Latin memorial in Trinity's chapel tactfully refers to his *magnum opus* as 'happily begun' but not completed and notes that 'he took assiduous care of the shrubs around the college gardens.' You couldn't make it up.

The University and the colleges

Cambridge is not a 'campus' university, although it has begun to acquire a campus of sorts. The buildings of the university and its constituent colleges are dispersed throughout the city, and the relationship between the university and the colleges is similarly diffuse. It can be described as a sort of semi-federal system of shared and divided powers and functions, though doubtless Cambridge insiders might regard any attempt to reduce it to a concise formulation as hopelessly naïve or misleading.

Suffice to say that a college provides its undergraduates with accommodation, food, individual tuition, pastoral care, entertainments and a framework for taking part in team sports. Colleges also have their own libraries and sports facilities. University departments organise lectures, seminars and 'practicals' and are grouped into faculties, which co-ordinate the curriculum, set examinations and monitor research submitted for higher degrees.

Degrees are granted by the university rather than the colleges and awarded at a ceremony held in the Senate House. The standard undergraduate degree is the BA, Bachelor of Arts – even for non-humanities degrees.

Each college has – and certainly believes it has – a distinctive character, the complex product of its history and heritage, size and location, wealth and connections. Trinity College is far richer than any other, allegedly Britain's third greatest landowner after the Crown and the Church of England, hence a pacemaker of change in many ways. St John's comes second, but a long way second, with perhaps a quarter of Trinity's estimated wealth. Except for the theological institutions like Ridley Hall, individual colleges are not usually associated with individual disciplines, although Trinity Hall has long been associated with lawyers and its neighbour Caius with medicine.

The look of the place

Cambridgeshire has abundant clays for brick-making but, unlike Oxford, no good building stone. The gault clay from the west bank of the Cam yields a yellow-grey brick, the Jurassic clays of the north of the county a rich red. The soft local limestone, known as 'clunch' is, however, good for carving and local craftsmen have made abundant use of it for decorative purposes. The nearest good building-stone comes from Ketton in Northamptonshire, to the north-west. Importing its stone from various locations has given Cambridge a visual variety of greys, creams, golds, browns and reds, in contrast to the honey colours prevalent at Oxford, which is well supplied locally. Lacking ready supplies of good stone nearby, Cambridge turned to brick far earlier than Oxford. Thus the Old Court of Queens' College was economically built of Flemish red brick around an inner core of clunch rubble (1448–9). When the Classical Revival of the 18th century made Gothic brick look 'barbarick' many colleges undertook a cosmetic process of 'ashlaring', re-facing facades, particularly those facing onto streets, with stone, as at Christ's on St Andrew's Street and Pembroke on Trumpington Street. Another by-product of the local shortage of stone has been a recurrent impetus to recycle materials from redundant or demolished buildings.

Connoisseurs of architecture can find in Cambridge Sir Christopher Wren's earliest completed work, the chapel of Pembroke College, plus work by James Gibbs, Sir George Gilbert Scott, Alfred Waterhouse, G F Bodley, Sir Giles Gilbert Scott, Basil Spence, Denys Lasdun, James Stirling and Norman Foster. The city has probably the finest collection of sculpture outside the capital, with works by Michael Rysbrack, Louis-François Roubiliac, Joseph Nollekens, Sir Francis Chantrey, Sir Richard Westmacott, Dame Barbara Hepworth, Oscar Nemon and Maggi Hambling. College chapels and halls offer a panorama of five centuries of the art of making stained glass. In the city's 120-odd libraries there are more than 3,000 illuminated manuscripts, a treasure trove only surpassed by the collections of the Vatican.

And everywhere there are inscriptions, on gateways and gravestones, on libraries and laboratories, from the World War Two graffiti on the ceiling of the back bar of the Eagle pub in Bene't Street to the lettering of the supreme master of the art, Eric Gill, whose work can be seen around the pond at Newnham's Sidgwick Hall, at the entrance to the Pitt Building on Trumpington Street and around the war memorial at Trumpington. Gill's legacy was continued by his former apprentice David Kindersley (1915–95) through the workshop he established in 1945. Kindersley's projects included the World War Two memorial in the ante-chapel at Trinity, where an entire wall of 382 names was carved *in situ,* the Churchill College Archives Centre, where a list of benefactors runs for 13 ½ metres along an exterior wall, and the foundation stone of Darwin College. Kindersley, like Gill, was also a typographer and devised the letters used on modern

Cambridge street signs. Recent rarities from the workshop now run by his widow include a four-panel glass window with quotations in three languages in Corpus Christi's Taylor Library, and at Girton the only example of a Kindersley painted sign, marking the site of the last College laboratory to remain in use.

The plethora of Cambridge inscriptions is a reminder of how densely textured the past has become. The bollards outside Magdalene are shaped liked fountain pens in tribute to the literary tradition of that college. At Newnham the shape of the Rare Books Library recalls that of a medieval book chest. Nevile's Court at Trinity may stand as an extended examplar. Named after its scholarly builder, it was completed at the same time as Wren's local masterpiece, the college library. Isaac Newton experimented in the north cloister of Nevile's Court by stamping his foot and using gunshots to produce echoes in a failed attempt to measure the speed of sound. In 1712, in his room adjacent to the library, Henry Sike, a brilliant German orientalist who had been head-hunted for the college, gave way to depression and hanged himself with the cord of his dressing-gown. Lord Byron had splendidly furnished rooms here when he was an undergraduate and kept a bear as a pet. In 1864, on the occasion of a visit of the Prince and Princess of Wales, a grand ball was given in a marquee. The guests of honour stayed for five hours and 'during the whole of that time, the Prince, who is an indefatigable dancer, never sat down, except at the supper table' – which he was also quite capable of occupying for five hours. Leonard Woolf, future husband of Virginia, reminisced how at the turn of the century he, her brother Thoby Stephen, Lytton Strachey, Clive Bell and other future members of the 'Bloomsbury Group' of metropolitan intelligentsia, would, after a meeting of the 'Apostles', late on a summer's night 'sometimes walk through the Cloisters of Nevile's Court and looking out through the bars at the end on to the willows and water of the Backs, ghostly in the moonlight, listen to the soaring song of innumerable nightingales' and then 'sometimes as we walked back through the majestic Cloisters we chanted poetry. More often than not it would be Swinburne'.

During the First World War the cloisters became a temporary field hospital for wounded soldiers. In Virginia Woolf's experimental third novel *Jacob's Room* (1922) Jacob Flanders lives in Nevile's Court. Philosopher Bertrand Russell and Nobel Laureate and scientist Lord Adrian really did.

And then there's the 'lost' Cambridge beneath. There was once an iron foundry where the Master's Lodge of St John's College now stands and another on the site of Marks & Spencer's. There were breweries in Magdalene Street and in Trinity Street; but then, in the 1880s, there were 40 more scattered throughout the town. Where Murray Edwards College now stands there was once a coprolite mine. The superb lawn stretching between the Gibbs' Building at King's College and the Cam covers the main commercial quarter of medieval Cambridge, entirely razed to the ground on the orders of a demented monarch.

The other place

> There are also in this Island two famous Universities ... excelling all the Universities in Christendom ... let this suffice, not to enquire which of them is superior, but that neither of them have their equal; neither to ask which of them is the most ancient, but whether any other be so famous.
>
> – John Lyly, *Euphues and his England* (1579)

The medieval historian F W Maitland once observed that the oldest inter-varsity contest between Oxford and Cambridge universities was lying about their origins. Oxford's famous antiquary, Anthony Wood, didn't even bother with evidence, simply stating in 1674 that Oxford was 'a famous place before this present town of Cambridge in all probability was built'. The most distant claim – both in terms of time and plausibility – was that Cambridge had been established by Athenian philosophers under the patronage of Prince Cantaber, the Spanish son-in-law of Gurguntius Brabtruc, King of the Britons, in

375 BC. Oxford merely claimed to have been founded by King Alfred the Great of Wessex (d.899), so that put them in their place. Prince Cantaber's initiative, endorsed by charters supposedly issued by King Arthur, the Saxon King Edward the Elder and the Welsh warrior Cadwallader, was invoked by Robert Hare in his *Privileges of the University of Cambridge* in 1590 and repeated by Francis Brackyn, Recorder of Cambridge, in a speech delivered before James I when he visited in 1615, noting that the town 'was builded before Christ's incarnation with a castle, towers and walls of defence'. The Athenian philosophers were 'lovinglie lodged' by local citizens in their own homes until *ostles* (hostels) were built for them and then the 'materials of the castle, towers and walls' were recycled into Colleges, 'beautifying this famous university'. None of these preposterous claims was, of course, true but a strict adherence to verifiable evidence and to consistent chronology were no part of the antiquarian's skills set. What would one day be called 'Oxford history' – getting the dates right – would come later.

The monk and poet John Lydgate (c.1370–1451), not even a Cambridge man, though admittedly from neighbouring Suffolk, claimed that Julius Caesar

Tooke with him clarks of famouse renowne
Fro Cambridg and ledd theim to rome towne,
Thus by procese remembred here to forne
Cambridg was founded longe or Chryst was borne.

Dr John Caius also believed that Cambridge existed before the Romans, attributing its foundation to the ancient priestly caste of Druids. Writing in 1694, James Brome, a Kentish vicar, argued that, as one of 28 cities in Britain founded by the Romans, Cambridge inevitably had its 'Schools of Learning, wherein the several Professors of Arts and Sciences did instruct both the Roman and British youth'. Forged papal bulls were used in the 15th century to claim that the 7th-century popes Honorius I and Sergius I had granted the university autonomy from ecclesiastical supervision. Sigeberht, a 7th-century King of the Angles, with the support of St Felix, was another candidate for the Founding Fathers, commended in the university's annual Commemoration of Benefactors until 1914.

The poet Matthew Arnold experienced a mild sense of disorientation visiting Cambridge, writing to his wife in February 1853 'it seems so strange to be in a place of colleges that is not Oxford'. William Morris, another Oxford man, was similarly brusque: 'rather a hole of a place and can't compare for a moment with Oxford'. The 1887 edition of Karl Baedeker's celebrated guide book to Britain, a bible for Continental tourists, was equally dismissive in its advice: 'Oxford is on the whole more attractive than Cambridge to the ordinary visitor; and the traveller is therefore recommended to visit Cambridge first, or to omit it altogether if he cannot visit both.' It is doubtful if such a well-seasoned travel trade professional would make that judgment nowadays. Oxford attracts more than five million visitors a year, Cambridge almost four. But many Oxford visitors will be day-trippers dashing through – via Stonehenge or Salisbury – to Blenheim or Stratford. Visitors to Cambridge have come to visit Cambridge; in terms of tourism it isn't perceived as being on the way to anywhere else, though the Visits outlined at the end of this book may change your mind about that. As far as looks go, let the last word go to the scholarly Lord Norwich: 'Cambridge ... in its ensemble is even lovelier than Oxford, thanks in large measure to the way it uses its river, an invaluable asset which Oxford seems virtually to ignore.'

As for intellect, the verdict of the diarist, diplomat and dilettante Harold Nicolson is irresistible: 'I am reading Roy Harrod's book on Keynes which I find entrancing. Really that Cambridge set were more gifted than anything we have seen since. They make Balliol look like an old cart-horse.'

By the book

The estimable Herr Sager asserts that 'in the literary Boat Race Cambridge is several shelf lengths ahead of its rival' – a bold claim, even an arrogant one, but consider, 'Dear Reader', some of the titles which have issued from the pen of Cambridge authors – *The Book of Common Prayer*, John Foxe's *Martyrs*, *Principia Mathematica*, *Tristram Shandy*, *Vanity Fair*, *On the Origin of Species*, *A Passage to India*, *Lolita*, *Under the Volcano*, *The Cruel Sea*, *Empire of the Sun*, *Birdsong* and *Midnight's Children*, not to mention *Winnie-the-Pooh*, *The Sword in the Stone*, *The Female Eunuch* and *The Hitchhiker's Guide to the Galaxy*. Stephen Hawking's *A Brief History of Time* became a global publishing phenomenon, remaining on the *New York Times* bestseller list for a year and a week and on *The Sunday Times* list for more than four years, as well as being reinterpreted as a film and an opera, and selling over 10 million copies in 40 languages. Other bestselling contemporary Cambridge authors include Robert Harris, Nick Hornby, Howard Jacobson, Peter Ackroyd, Alain de Botton, A S Byatt, Margaret Drabble, Iris Murdoch and Zadie Smith.

Name games

Discussing the origins of the name of Cambridge as a town, Recorder Brackyn in 1615 argued that

> ... the Towne being situated and united with a bridge upon the river then called Canta, was denominated Cantabridge; and in tract of tyme the name of the River being altered to Granta, the town likewise to Grantabridge; and after it was called Cam, and the Towne Cambridge, which yet remaineth.

Pioneering architectural historian John Willis Clark (1833–1910) offered a contrary chronology:

> The river was originally called the Granta ... The earliest form

of the town's name was Grantabrycge or Grentebrige, which in process of time became Cantbrigge and Caumbrege. Lastly, in the Sixteenth and Seventeenth centuries, when it became necessary to find a name for the river, the old name of the town having been forgotten, Cam was adopted from Cam-bridge, the shortened form of Caumbridge. Thus the river derived its name from the town, and not the town from the river, as was formerly supposed.

In Brackyn's day, the Cam, as he well knew, was not the endlessly photographed picture postcard 'landscape feature' of today but a vital economic artery – 'this river is current through the heart of the Shire, with navigation to the Sea, and is the life of the trafficke of this Towne and countie; and no bridge is over the same but at Cambridge'. Frederic William Maitland asserted in 1898 that what is now Magdalene Bridge was nothing less than 'the most famous bridge in England: the one bridge that gives its name to a county'.

Both Cambridge and Oxford universities have colleges called Trinity, St John's, Jesus and Pembroke. But at Oxford one talks about (strictly speaking The) Queen's College, whereas at Cambridge it's Queens' – note the respective positioning of the apostrophes, indicating that the Oxford institution is associated with a single queen, and its Cambridge counterpart with a plurality. There is also a Magdalen College at Oxford – its Cambridge equivalent is spelt Magdalene, with an 'e' on the end – though both cling to the medieval pronunciation 'Maudlin'. And at Oxford it's St Catherine's College, at Cambridge St Catharine's. At Oxford, moreover, it is more customary to say 'College' after the name of a specific institution, whereas at Cambridge this is often omitted.

A few more linguistic distinctions: Cambridge colleges are built around Courts, Oxford colleges around Quadrangles or 'Quads'. At Cambridge the traditional male student servant/bed-maker was a 'gyp', at Oxford a 'scout'. Both have been superseded by mostly female 'bedders'.

At Cambridge an undergraduates' weekly one-to-one teaching

session is a 'supervision', at Oxford a 'tutorial'. Heads of Oxford colleges have many different titles. Heads of Cambridge colleges are usually called the Master except for King's (Provost); Queens', Murray Edwards, Wolfson, Lucy Cavendish and Clare Hall (Presidents); Girton (Mistress); Newnham (Principal) and Robinson (Warden).

Verdicts

The distinguished English literary historian Professor Sir Frank Kermode once wrote that 'the thing I remember with greatest pleasure of my time at Cambridge is the year I spent at Harvard.' Mary Lamb, co-author of the famous children's *Tales from Shakespeare*, wrote in 1815 'in my life I never spent so many pleasant hours together as I did at Cambridge. We were walking the whole time – out of one College into the other ... I liked them all best.' The intention of this book is to put you in the Lamb camp.

1

Before the Scholars Came

The river

Cambridge was only raised to the status of a city as recently as 1951, although unbroken human occupation dates from the Anglo-Saxon period. Before that there were what cautious scholars would call 'extended settlement episodes' on either side of the ford now crossed by Magdalene Bridge. The bridge, flanked by three boats, is the central feature of the coat of arms granted to the town of Cambridge in 1575, a reminder that because the River Cam was navigable to the small boats of pre-modern times, Cambridge remained a significant inland port until the 18th century.

The source of the Cam is at Ashwell in Hertfordshire, 16 miles south-west of the city. It rises through chalk as a spring, surrounded by ash trees, generating an average flow of about 1,300,000 gallons a day, depending on the previous winter's rainfall. This feeds the river Rhee, the principal element of the Cam, which rises near Saffron Walden in Essex and joins the Granta near Trumpington, just south of Cambridge. The united streams flow through the city until 10 miles to the north, near Ely, they join the Great Ouse. This major river becomes a tidal estuary feeding into the North Sea via the Wash in north-east Norfolk, some 65 miles from the Ashwell source.

The Romans

At the northern end of Arbury Road, in the north of the city, off the road to Ely, once stood what antiquarians came to call Arbury Camp, an undefended Iron Age site, consisting of a circular bank and ditch 100 metres across, probably used as a compound to protect livestock from predators. There is also evidence of Roman settlement – a 4th-century house with painted walls, a tessellated floor, a tiny bath, burial sites and a mausoleum. Variously rendered in medieval times as Herburg or Ertburg, Arbury simply means 'earthwork'. Out at Wandlebury, however, three miles south-east of the present city, was a rather more impressive hill-fort, the ruins of which are still visible to picnickers. At Cherry Hinton some defensive war ditches remain today.

The Catuvelluani, an Iron Age Celtic people, settled on the hillside above and west of the ford but left before the Romans created a camp there, soon after their conquest began in AD 43. The Roman camp's position became a key junction in their strategic road system. A route branching off from Ermine Street near present-day Wimpole Hall ran north-east to Cambridge, where it crossed the Via Devana (now the A604) from Colchester to Chester, before passing via Landbeach and Ely to reach the coast at Brancaster. Until the draining of the impenetrable Fens in the mid-17th century, other routes from the east had to skirt their southern edge, leading them also to converge at Cambridge.

By the 2nd century AD the Roman camp above the Cam ford was the nucleus of a town standing on the site of the present-day Shire Hall. By the year 300 this settlement covered perhaps 25–30 acres, protected by earthen ramparts, surmounted by a wall of Northamptonshire limestone. The river crossing was probably a paved ford, not a bridge, so that when James Essex built the predecessor to the present Magdalene Bridge he noted that the river bed 'very plainly shewed itself in the year 1754 as a firm pavement of pebbles'. The settlement established by the Romans declined following the departure of their legions in c.410 AD. As for other Roman remains, there's little to show for almost four centuries of occupation. St Peter's Church next to Kettle's Yard incorporates reddish Roman *tegulae* (roof tiles) in its outer walls, the only remaining visible evidence of Cambridge's Roman past. Less visibly, the line of Mount Pleasant follows two sides of a Roman wall and ditch. Chesterton Lane takes its name from the Anglo-Saxon *ceastre*, meaning the site of a former *castrum* or Roman camp.

Anglo-Saxons and Danes

The discovery of Anglo-Saxon cemeteries on the sites of Girton and Newnham Colleges and St John's cricket ground imply a pattern of straggling hamlets, rather than a compact settlement, established by Germanic newcomers in the 5th century.

In 634 Penda (c.575–655), King of powerful Mercia, destroyed the settlement on Castle Hill following victory over the East Angles. In 679 St Etheldreda died at Ely. According to the Northumbrian chronicler Bede (672–735), by c.695 when Ely monks were seeking stone for a shrine in her honour, Cambridge was '*civitatula quondam desolata*' – a little town *formerly* desolate.

In the 8th century the Cam marked the frontier between East Anglia and Mercia, and it is possible that the first bridge was built by Offa the Great, ruler of Mercia from 757 to 796. The *Anglo-Saxon Chronicle* entry for 875 refers to Cambridge as Grantabrycge, probably the first use of the word 'bridge' in written English, for what was quite possibly the first bridge built in England since the Romans left. (As the *Chronicle* was probably not begun until the 890s this reference is recently retrospective, rather than exactly contemporary.)

A significant Anglo-Saxon village then developed on a dry ridge now covered by Market Hill, Peas Hill and St Andrew's Hill; 'hill' in Cambridge meaning an open space rather than a conspicuously elevated location. The market has never moved since and remains, therefore, the single most enduring feature of Cambridge as an urban settlement.

As the river was navigable right through to King's Lynn and thus to the open sea, by the 9th century Cambridge had become an inland port. This maritime aspect of town life was strengthened by more than half a century of rule by sea-faring Danes. The church at Bridge Street, dedicated to St Clement, patron saint of Danish sailors, is a reminder of this period, which was ended by the re-incorporation of Cambridge into the Anglo-Saxon realm under Edward the Elder (c.870–924) in 921. He recognised the town's commercial importance by establishing a royal mint. By 960 Cambridge was recognised as the county town of its shire, ranked by the contemporary *Liber Eliensis* (*Book of Ely*) alongside Norwich, Ipswich and Thetford. Outside the town proper were outlying hamlets at Newnham, Barnwell and Chesterton, the latter under royal control and not formally incorporated into Cambridge until 1912.

Built c.1025, the tower of St Bene't's church still stands, the oldest surviving stone structure not only in Cambridge, but in the county of Cambridgeshire. Named for St Benedict (480–543), founder of western monasticism, this church served for three and a half centuries as the chapel of Corpus Christi College.

The Normans

The Norman Conquest was consolidated at Cambridge with a castle, built in 1068 by Picot de Say (c.1022–90), sheriff of Cambridgeshire, whom the local chronicler dubbed 'a hungry lion, a ravening wolf, a filthy hog'. 27 houses were destroyed to clear the site, although John Willis Clark would characterise its construction as more symbolic than strategic, noting disparagingly that it 'was never more than a third-class fortress which may have lent a certain dignity to the town but could not have afforded it any serious protection'. Picot's wife, Hugolina, is credited with founding the church of St Giles and a house of six Augustinian ('Austin') canons in 1092 as a thank-offering for recovery from an illness.

Cambridge Castle did serve as a base for the anti-guerrilla campaign waged by the Normans against the last leader of Anglo-Saxon resistance, Hereward the Wake (c.1035–72). Hereward took refuge in the fens of the Isle of Ely, where the heavily-armoured knight – like a modern tank – would be at a clear disadvantage. Undeterred, the Normans built a causeway and chased Hereward out of his refuge and into legend. Cambridge Castle was extensively rebuilt between 1283 and 1307 and later plundered for building stone, so that by 1606 only the gatehouse survived intact. In 1610 topographer William Camden (1551–1623) noted that the 'large and ancient Castle ... seemeth now to have lived out his full time.' All that now survives is the motte (earth mound), 12 metres high and 60 across, parts of curtain walls and two bastions from the Civil War period.

The Domesday survey of 1086 confirmed that 'Cantebrigie' had 373 dwellings, including some 50 ruinous ones, suggesting a population of perhaps 2–3,000. The Millpond at the end of Mill Lane, where visitors now hire punts from Scudamore's boatyard, is mentioned. Although the demolition of 27 houses and the existence of 50 in ruins suggests the Norman impact was initially destructive, Cambridge still benefited from the general economic expansion of the 12th century. By 1201 it was wealthy enough to gain a charter recognising a Guild Merchant to regulate its commerce. In 1207 arrangements were confirmed for electing a provost to act as its spokesman and supervise local administration.

Piety, prosperity, philanthropy

The economic life of early medieval Cambridge flourished most visibly between Market Hill and the Cam, where there were riverside 'hythes' – landing-places named after what they handled, for example corn, coal, salt and flax. This commercial quarter was bisected by the major thoroughfare, Milne Street, and lined with the substantial residences of substantial merchants. By the 15th century it would be demolished to make way for colleges.

In 1109 Ely became the seat of a new bishopric, with Cambridge in its jurisdiction. In 1112 the canons of Castle Hill were moved eastwards by a crusading knight, Pain Peverell (c.1060–1113), to the well-watered and more spacious setting of Barnwell, where their new priory had a church 60 metres long. Barnwell Priory benefited from the profits of a fair, confirmed by charter in 1229, held on Midsummer Common (then Greencroft) for four days from 23 June, the feast of St Etheldreda. Also known as 'Pot Fair' due to the crockery sold there, it survived the dissolution of the priory itself. The 13th-century church of St Andrew the Less, built for local peasants, not the priory, still survives. To the south in Abbey Road is the picturesque, timber-framed Old Abbey House, a Tudor structure, refronted and extended in brick in 1678; its garden wall may be its only link with the former priory.

The founding of new parishes and building of new stone churches for an expanding population confirm the prosperity of early medieval Cambridge, mostly financed by the benefactions of laymen rather than aristocrats or royalty. Apart from the aforementioned St Peter's, St Clement's, St Bene't's and St Giles, the churches of St Mary the Less, St Edward, St Botolph and Holy Trinity were all in existence by 1200. What has since 1351 been known as Great St Mary's, the university church, was built in 1205. St Mary's-by-the-market was destroyed by fire in 1291; the construction of the present church dates essentially from 1475 to 1519, although its tower was not completed until 1609.

Churches dedicated to the Anglo-Saxon Botolph, patron saint of travellers, were nearly always sited near city gates, in this case Trumpington Gate, where wayfarers could seek a blessing on departure or offer thanks for a safe return. 13 churches founded before the Black Death of 1349 still survive; only three have disappeared. The former site of the church of St John Zachary lies under the chapel of King's College. All Saints by the Castle was torn down after the Black Death, when its parish was absorbed into St Giles. Of All Saints in the Jewry only the churchyard survives, opposite St John's College. Its craft market is now a popular attraction.

The Church of the Holy Sepulchre on Bridge Street is one of only five surviving round churches in all England and a major modern Cambridge visitor attraction. Built around 1130 by a local 'fraternity of the Holy Sepulchre' (in Jerusalem), of which little is known, its site was donated by Reinald (Reginald), Abbot of Ramsey between 1114 and 1133. In the 15th century, a battlemented polygonal bell-tower was added and most of the original windows altered. In 1815 'the Round Church' was featured in Ackermann's celebrated print series of views of Cambridge. In 1841 part of the vault of the east aisle collapsed – as it might after 700 years. Led by Anthony Salvin (1799–1881), early Victorian restorationists, in the form of the Cambridge Camden Society, set about restoring it to what they thought it ought to look like, destroying most of the 15th-century work, including the belfry and Gothic windows, and replacing it with 'correct' 12th-century features. Today's visitor to 'the second oldest building in Cambridge', in return for a modest admission charge, can see not only the building, but also an illustrated exhibition on 'The Impact of Christianity in England' and a video presentation, 'Saints and Scholars', telling the history of Cambridge and the university.

Between 1133 and 1138, a Benedictine nunnery, initially dedicated to St Mary, later to St Radegund (a 6th-century French saint buried at Poitiers) was established on the northern edge of the city. Jesus College Chapel now incorporates parts of the former St Radegund's church. Two walls of the north transept have round-headed windows and shafted arcades from c.1160; the chancel has Early English lancet windows, blank arcades with trefoil heads, a double sedilia with stepped seats and a double piscine. Later, around 1230, a chapter-house was added. These are the most important and extensive monastic remains in Cambridge. From around 1150 the nuns benefited from the proceeds of an annual Garlic Fair, held on the 14th and 15th of August, the Festival of the Assumption of the Virgin Mary; however, the house was never wealthy and was dissolved in 1496.

A hospital, dedicated to St John, stood where St John's College stands today. Founded c.1135 by a burgess, Henry Frost, it was staffed by Augustinians pledged to tend the sick and poor.

At outlying Stourbridge, on the Newmarket road, a leper hospital dedicated to St Mary Magdalene was founded. Its chapel from c.1125 survives as 'one of the finest examples of Norman architecture in the county', featuring the zig-zag chevron patterns beloved of Norman stone-carvers. The building survived the dissolution of religious houses thanks to its periodic use in association with Stourbridge Fair, not for worship but as a store for lumber, a victualling house, a drinking booth, a stable and a barn. In 1816 it was bought by Rev Thomas Kerrich (1748–1828) and given to the university. Restored in 1843–5, it was used as a place of worship by navvies building the Eastern Counties Railway. In 1867 Victorian England's most eminent architect, Sir George Gilbert Scott, inserted the present west window. Restored again by the university in 1949, in 1951 it was handed over to the Cambridge Preservation Society, together with Chapel Close, the six-acre field in which it stands. Standing a mile and a half from the city centre, it is best viewed from the south-west.

Stourbridge Fair

A major annual fair of international, rather than merely regional, significance was already well established at Stourbridge by 1211 when King John confirmed its legality and the use of its profits for the benefit of the leper hospital. Although the main traded product was English wool, merchants also brought tin from distant Cornwall and lead from Derbyshire. Flemings came with linens, Mediterranean traders with wines, silks and spices, and representatives of the Hanseatic League with Baltic timber, amber and furs. Stourbridge Fair by the 16th century had expanded from a small-scale affair of a couple of days to what some claimed was the largest fair in all Europe, lasting four to five weeks. Garlic Lane, Cheddars Lane and Oyster Row in the area where it was once held recall the clustering of specialised traders.

Medieval memories

Cambridgeshire's oldest surviving house, known by the 16th century as the 'School of Pythagoras', was built from stone around 1200. It was never a school and seems to have had nothing to do with the university – or at least the local one. Now it stands in the grounds of St John's College, and in around 1250 it was home to the Mayor of Cambridge, Hervey Fitz Eustace Dunning. In 1270 it became the property of Merton College, Oxford and in the 16th century a manor house, Merton Hall, was attached to it. This was at one point briefly a boys' school and an early (1872–4) home to the young ladies of Newnham. Both properties remained in the possession of Merton College until 1959. The School of Pythagoras has been used as a theatre by St John's Dramatic Society and in 2013 became the home of the College Archives, while Merton Hall is occupied by graduate students.

A major defensive work for the city, known as the King's Ditch, was constructed, probably in the 11th century though possibly even earlier, enclosing the south and east sides of the town along the line of Mill Lane, Pembroke Street, Lion Yard, Hobson Street and Park Parade. Like the great common fields lying either side of the town until their enclosure by Acts of Parliament in 1803 and 1807, the ditch constrained the expansion of the urban area for centuries to come. It was re-cut and cleaned out in 1267–8. Used for sewerage more than defence, it became over succeeding centuries a major health hazard. As the theologically flexible Andrew Perne observed during a plague outbreak in 1574, 'our synns is the principall cause ... The other cause I conjecture is the corruption of the King's Ditch.' The conduit built in 1610 by Thomas Hobson was in part intended to tackle this noisome nuisance. All that now remains of the King's Ditch is a depression running through the Fellows' Garden of Sidney Sussex College.

The names of surviving open spaces recall the lives of Cambridge folk who lived as much in the surrounding country as in the medieval town. Donkey's Green and Sheep's Green testify to the importance of communal rights to graze livestock, Laundress Green of when common land was used to dry washing, and the two Butts Greens of the days when all able-bodied men were required by law to attend regular archery practice for the defence of the realm. Pound Hill was near the former Pound Green, where stray animals were impounded;

Haymarket Road was conveniently nearby. Downing Street was once Bird-Bolt Lane, a reference to the ammunition used in crossbows for hunting small game. Plague victims were buried under Coldham's Common, near the present-day football ground of Cambridge United. Its Abbey Stadium is a misnomer – a tribute to Barnwell Priory.

Despite its importance as a communications hub by both road and water, medieval Cambridge did not enjoy easy access to London. Between the two lay bands of dense forest, heavy clays all but impassable in bad weather, and stretches of higher ground, optimistically known as the East Anglian Heights, which would have presented a far more formidable obstacle to a pedlar or pilgrim than to a modern motorist, who would barely notice them beyond the occasional gear change. Consequently the journey between Cambridge and capital was literally far from straightforward – which may explain why, unlike so many other English towns, Cambridge has no London Road.

KING'S COLLEGE CHAPEL: AN ICONIC INTERLUDE

The outline of the roof of King's College Chapel is to Cambridge what the Tyne Bridge is to Newcastle and the Eiffel Tower to Paris – a symbol of the city itself. At least the City Council thinks so, using it to adorn both its website and its dustbins.

The diarist and dilettante John Evelyn (1620–1706) disparaged almost everything he saw at Cambridge – but he was an Oxford man. The one great exception was King's College Chapel, which 'altogether answered expectation, especially the roof all of stone, which for the flatness of its laying and carving may, I conceive, vie with any in Christendom.' Evelyn's friend, Sir Christopher Wren (1632–1723) was equally impressed by the sheer technical brilliance of its construction, saying that he could show how the second stone was laid – if someone could show him how the first one was.

'Cambridge makes no appearance at a distance. King's-college chapel is the only object which presents itself with any dignity, as we approach.' This grudging praise came from the (posthumously published) pen of William Gilpin (1724–1804), vicar, schoolmaster, prolific author and self-appointed expert on 'the picturesque', who had toured East Anglia in 1773. His approach would have been across the vast open fields of farmland which then hemmed Cambridge in but have long since been built over with suburban streets. He didn't like the inside of the chapel at all – 'tho it is an immense and noble aisle, presenting the adjunct idea of lightness and Solemnity; yet its disproportion disgusts. Such height and such length, united by such straitened parallels, hurt the eye.' He also disliked 'the tedious repetition of roses and portcullises, which are at best but heavy and unpleasing ornaments.'

The Romantic novelist Maria Edgeworth (1768–1849), by contrast, was overwhelmed – 'on the first entrance I felt silenced by admiration. I never saw anything at once so beautiful and so sublime ... no engraved representation can give an idea of the effect of the size, height and continuity of grandeur in the whole building.' The wayward Samuel Taylor Coleridge was likewise exhilarated by the chapel's 'marvellous sublimity and transcendent beauty ... it is quite unparalleled.' When the landscape painter Joseph Farington (1747–1821) was shown round by the indefatigable preacher Simeon he found that his guide had his own distinctly idiosyncratic approach to the marvels of the architecture –'He told me that he had lately compared the size of it with the dimensions of Noah's Ark as given in the Scripture, and found that the Ark was twice the length, and twice the breadth and two-thirds the height of the Chapel'. So that will give you something novel to conjure up in your mind's eye when next you look at it.

Henry James (1843–1916) endorsed Maria Edgeworth's impression:

... the single object at Cambridge that makes the most abiding impression is the famous chapel of King's College – the most beautiful chapel in England. The effect it attempts to produce within is all in the sphere of the sublime. The attempt succeeds ... after you have looked about you for ten minutes ... you perceive

the chapel to be saved from being the prettiest church in England
by the accident of its being one of the noblest.

James was similarly enchanted by the choir; spellbound for a quarter
of an hour one Sunday morning as he listened to them rehearse for
Evensong:

> ... the beautiful boy-voices rose together and touched the splendid
> vault; they hung there, expanding and resounding, and then like
> a rocket that spends itself, they faded and melted towards the end
> of the building. It was positively a choir of angels.

In Wordsworth's Ecclesiastical Sonnet No 43, *Inside of King's College
Chapel, Cambridge,* the poet praised the unstinting expenditure
behind the creation of the building and touched on some crucial
aspects of its history:

> Tax not the royal saint with vain expense,
> With ill-matched aims the Architect who planned –
> Albeit labouring for a scanty band
> Of white robed Scholars only – this immense
> And glorious Work of fine intelligence!
> Give all thou canst; high Heaven rejects the lore
> Of nicely-calculated less or more:
> So deemed the man who fashioned for the sense
> These lofty pillars, spread that branching roof
> Self-poised, and scooped into ten thousand cells,
> Where light and shade repose, where music dwells
> Lingering – and wandering on as loth to die;
> Like thoughts whose very sweetness yieldeth proof
> That they were born for immortality.

The 'scant band of white robed scholars' was in fact the largest body of
such in the medieval university. The 'glorious Work of fine intelligence'

represents not the creative power of a single architect but the combined efforts of teams of masons, sculptors and glaziers working in discontinuous phases over the best part of a century. And if the 'royal saint', Henry VI, was lavish in his initial funding, the project still required further generous donations from the next four occupants of the throne of England. Each did so to emphasise that he was the legitimate successor to the murdered king. (It was the supposedly villainous Richard III who transported Henry VI's body from its original resting place at Chertsey in Surrey to St George's Chapel, Windsor.) In 1507, John Fisher delivered an Oration, more than half a century after the still-unfinished chapel had been begun, aiming squarely at the most distinguished members of the congregation before him, the redoubtable Lady Margaret Beaufort and her son, King Henry VII, successfully persuading that notoriously stingy monarch to donate £5,000 for the completion of the building. The King also left money in his will towards the cost of stained-glass windows. His son, Henry VIII, paid for the oak screen housing the organ, which bears his initials and those of his ill-fated Queen, Anne Boleyn.

A brief tour

The foundation stone of 'The King's College of Our Lady and Saint Nicholas in Cambridge' was laid on Passion Sunday, 1441. Henry VI, the King in question, was the only monarch ever crowned King of both England and France, and the chapel at King's may well have been inspired by Sainte Chapelle, where his French coronation had taken place. He was believed to have been anointed with oil given to St Thomas Becket by the Blessed Virgin Mary and grew up a man of intense religiosity, planning to have Mass celebrated at King's seven times every day. Henry intended the college to outshine every other in Cambridge or Oxford and left detailed instructions for its building; yet only the chapel was finished as he envisaged it, and the projected 'Great Court' was never even begun. The chapel is 88 metres long, 12 metres wide and 24 metres high. The apparent architectural unity of the exterior obscures the fact that it was built in three phases as funding and commitment faltered: note the change from white (magnesian) limestone, hauled all the way from Yorkshire, to a brownish (oolitic) one, drawn from Rutland – a much shorter journey. The breathtaking fan-vaulted ceiling – the largest of its kind in the world – was completed between 1512 and 1515. The glaziers then took more than 30 years to make and install 26 sets of stained-glass windows.

Inside, the visual legacy of the various patrons is keenly felt: as you enter via the North Porch the ante-chapel is festooned with triumphalist Tudor motifs. The double rose symbolises the reconciliation of the dynastic houses of York (white) and Lancaster (red); the portcullis and the greyhound are emblems of the Beaufort family; the *fleur-de-lys* refers to the English monarchs' claim to the throne of France and the dragon of Cadwallader to the Tudors' Welsh ancestry. The chapel in the south wall contains the imposing marble tomb of John Churchill (1685–1702), only son of the Duke of Marlborough (1650–1722), ancestor of Sir Winston Churchill and victor of the landmark battle of Blenheim (1704). The boy died of smallpox while a teenage student at King's, his grief-stricken parents at his bedside. The chapel also contains a memorial brass to Robert Hacomblen (1455–1528), composer and Provost (Master) of the college from 1509–28. Other notable Kings' characters buried elsewhere in the chapel include prolific preacher Charles Simeon, world class name-dropper Oscar Browning, murdered explorer Alexander 'Sandy' Wollaston and theatrical guru George 'Dadie' Rylands.

Beyond the dark wooden screen, carved in an elaborate Renaissance manner, the austere decoration of the choir contrasts with the flamboyance of the ante-chapel, reflecting the simplicity which Henry VI had preferred and offsetting the exuberance of the carving of the choir-stalls. In the centre of the choir is a brass lectern, topped with a miniature statue of Henry VI, the gift of Robert Hacomblen. On the Sanctuary Altar, underneath the huge East Window, is Peter Paul Rubens's *Adoration of the Magi*. Originally painted in 1634 for the Convent of the White Nuns at Louvain in Belgium, its donation in

1961 provoked controversy as the altar had to be lowered and the east end of the chapel restructured to accommodate it. Others objected on the grounds that, whatever its merits as a painting, its style just didn't 'fit' with its setting.

To the right of the altar is the Chapel of All Souls, now a memorial chapel for members of the college and its associated Choir School killed in the two World Wars. One sequence of names runs in alphabetical order; the other does not, but both are divided into categories: Fellows, Scholars, Choral Scholars, Choristers, Pensioners, Boys at the Choir School and College Servants. Look out for the name of Rupert Brooke, second on the list of Fellows in World War One and, carved alone on the north side of the door, Ferenc Békássy, who fought on the other side but is still remembered as a former member of the college. The seat is in memory of Eric Milner-White who inaugurated the Festival of Nine Lessons and Carols.

Running through the former side chapels along the north wall is a fascinating exhibition about the history of the chapel and the college. Exhibits include the Foundation Charter of 1446; a scale model of the college as it had been planned by Henry VI set against a map of Cambridge in 1445, showing how an entire riverside district was razed to make way for its construction; a biographical sketch of the life of John Argentein (1443–1508), a Fellow of King's who became royal physician to the ill-fated 'Princes in the Tower'; a display illustrating the posthumous cult of Henry VI and the miraculous cures and pilgrimages associated with him; and models and exhibits explaining the techniques which made possible the vaulting of the ceiling and illustrating the work of Flemish glaziers and French carvers.

The windows

The windows illustrate a scheme attributed to Bishop Richard Fox (1448–1528), executor of Henry VII's will, narrating the interlocking stories of the Blessed Virgin Mary, Christ and the emergence of the early church. In each window the upper panels depict incidents and personalities from the Old Testament which prophesy or foreshadow the scenes beneath them, taken from the New Testament. However, Sir Nikolaus Pevsner considers that 'the design of the glass and the making do not help ... so much was only painted on the glass and the leads cut across so confusingly, that all that those in the chapel can enjoy is the general effect of strong colour and busy action.' As it is hard to make out the upper panels without expert knowledge and the good fortune of a bright day outside, the following sequence refers – except for the East Window above the altar – to the lower (New Testament) panels, running first from the west end of the church (to your right as you enter) along the north side and then from the east along the south side:

West window
Last Judgment (made by Clayton and Bell, 1879)

North windows

1. Joachim and Anna (parents of the Virgin Mary)	Birth of the Virgin
2. Presentation of Mary in the Temple	Marriage of Joseph and Mary
3. The Annunciation	The Nativity
4. The Circumcision of Christ	The Adoration of the Magi
5. Christ in the Temple	The Flight into Egypt
6. Egyptian idols fall before Christ	Massacre of the Innocents
7. Baptism of Christ	Temptation of Christ
8. Raising of Lazarus	Christ's Entry into Jerusalem
9. The Last Supper	The Agony in the Garden
10. The Betrayal of Christ	Christ blindfolded and mocked

11. Christ before the High   Christ before Herod
    Priest
12. Flagellation of Christ   Christ Crowned with Thorns

East window
1. Christ Nailed to The Crucifixion   The Deposition
   the Cross
2. Ecce Homo   Pilate washes his   Christ bearing the
                     hands   Cross

South windows
1. Naomi lamenting   The Lament over the dead
   Abimelech   Christ
2. The Burial of Christ   Christ in Limbo
3. The Resurrection   Christ appears to Mary
4. The Three Mary's at the   Mary Magdelene sees Christ
   empty tomb
5. Christ appears to two   The Supper at Emmaus
   disciples
6. Doubting Thomas   Christ Blesses the Apostles
7. The Ascension   Descent of the Holy Spirit
8. St Peter going to the   Ananias struck dead
   Temple
9. Worship of SS Paul and   St Paul stoned
   Barnabus
10. St Paul's farewell at   St Paul before Nero
    Miletus
11. Death of the Virgin   Burial of the Virgin
12. Assumption of the Virgin Coronation of the Virgin

2

Colleges by the Cam

Oxford origins

Cambridge had been a successful settlement for centuries before the university came into being. Quite how that happened is not entirely clear. According to the St Albans chronicler Roger of Wendover (d.1236) – cautiously endorsed by university historian Elisabeth Leedham-Green as 'an unreliable but in this instance plausible contemporary source' – in 1209 two Oxford scholars were hanged by the town authorities following the killing of a townswoman, possibly a prostitute, possibly by accident. Normally, the offenders, who were clerks in minor orders, would have been dealt with by the ecclesiastical authorities, who would have protected them against the harsher secular law of noble or civic courts – clerical status was a privileged standing. But 1209 was not a normal year. All England was under interdict because King John, who ruled from 1199 to 1216, refused to accept the domineering Pope Innocent III's nominee, Cardinal Stephen Langton (c.1150–1228), as Archbishop of Canterbury. This meant the closure of churches and suspension of 'normal service' by the clergy. John himself was also personally excommunicated, and therefore not inclined to intervene on behalf of the Church. Thus the two clerks felt the full weight of the secular courts' judgement – their schools in Oxford closed and the occupants dispersed, some to Reading, others to London, Lincoln, Northampton or Stamford. A significant cohort settled in Cambridge, including one John Grim, a Cambridge man by birth, formerly Master of the Schools (senior administrator) at Oxford from 1201–3. Like several significant persons who follow in this chapter, he remains a shadowy figure, of whom neither the dates of his birth nor death are known.

Cambridge was a flourishing market town and port in a fertile region, with a prosperous Jewry. All Saints' Passage was once the *Vico Judaeorum*, or irreverently, Pilat's Lane. Limited by law to money-lending and a few skilled professions, such as medicine and gold refining, Jews were evidence of urban sophistication. Further proof of the region's economic diversity lay in the existence of 30-plus guilds for different trades or crafts. A dozen miles from Cambridge was the great cathedral at Ely, where Bishop Eustace had graduates on his staff and looked kindly over the infant academic community. By 1225 Cambridge had a Chancellor, with powers delegated to him by the Bishop. In 1233 Pope Gregory IX (1170–1241) granted further legal privileges, recognising Cambridge as a *studium particulare*, which could draw its intake from its locality, rather than the international community.

These developments overlapped with the arrival of other newcomers, both religious and academic. Around 1224 the Franciscan friars established themselves; by 1238 they had been joined by their Dominican rivals, who were then followed by Carmelite Friars at Newnham, the Friars of the Order of Bethlehem, the Friars of the Sack/Penitence, the Gilbertine Canons of Sempringham in Trumpington Street and, in 1290, by Augustinian (Austin) friars. Unlike monks, friars were bidden not to live in seclusion but to be active in the community, exemplifying the gospel in their lives and fighting heresy. In 13th-century Cambridge they may have accounted for a third of all teachers. At their best they also represented a model of orderly and studious collegiate existence. In 1325 the Franciscans laid down the pipelines for the town's first water supply.

Royal regard

In 1229, Henry III (r.1216–72), enthusiastic for all things ecclesiastical, offered asylum to scholars from Paris, some of whom went to Cambridge. In 1231 he warned the Mayor of Cambridge against overcharging students for rent, emphasising the value of the university:

> ... a multitude of scholars from divers parts, as well as from this
> side the sea as from overseas, meets at our town of Cambridge for
> study, which we hold a very gratifying and desirable thing, since
> no small benefit and glory accrues therefrom to our whole realm;
> and you, among whom these students personally live, ought
> especially to be pleased and delighted at it.

Turbulent teenagers

'Pleasure and delight' may have been optimistic – a large body of students gave excellent cover for youths more devoted to crime than study. Writing in the 1630s, the first great historian of the university, Thomas Fuller (1608–61) of Queens', noted that in that very same year, 1231, there also existed 'a crew of pretenders to scholarship,' who 'did much mischief' and 'lived under no discipline', claiming to be scholars if arrested but, if taken before the Chancellor's court, claiming to be laymen and beyond his jurisdiction.

Not that genuine students, mostly teenagers, weren't also capable of causing mayhem. Becoming a student meant being entered on the roll (*matricula* – hence matriculate) of a recognised teacher. Canon law set 14 as the minimum age for taking the associated oath. Some undergraduates might be in their twenties but the average was probably around 17. The monastic heritage of the learned professions of the Church, law and medicine required their aspirants to live in an exclusively masculine society. Women figured only in the background as landladies, stallholders, cooks, cleaners, laundresses, seamstresses, tavern-keepers and prostitutes.

The architecture of the oldest college chapels supplies a telling indicator of the university's monastic past. Whereas most parish churches have pews or chairs arranged north to south across the nave, monastic chapels which later became collegiate have stalls arranged east to west, allowing an unobstructed view of the altar and encouraging antiphonal singing from one side and then the other. Nor do they have a pulpit since the preaching is not *de haut en bas* but among clerical equals. King's College and St John's maintain the monastic tradition of all-male choirs. Jesus has it both ways, with one choir male and one mixed.

Few aristocrats became students, and those that did were mostly younger sons, without prospect of land or title. Instead the student body was drawn or, rather, in the absence of formal entrance procedures, drew itself, from a wide social range. Even former serfs, the illegitimate and the handicapped were not disbarred, unless afflicted by incurable disease or gross deformity, since these could not take holy orders. With no uniform or centralised admissions policy the 'wastage' rate was high by modern standards. Inability, idleness, illness or poverty meant probably less than half of students completed their degree. Graduation was expensive compared to the penny-a-day cost of 'commons' (food and drink). Some students were helped out by relatives, godparents or patrons; others worked part-time as gardeners, labourers, waiters or scriveners, copying texts. By the 15th century, inventories show some students owning more than clothes and bedding: having cutlery, lanterns, musical instruments, even chests to keep them safe in. But, before the advent of printing presses, almost none would own a book. Even college libraries, established from the 15th century, held at most 300 volumes, and almost all of those were donated as gifts, rather than bought.

Far from father and family, crowded into often squalid hostels and exposed to the usual urban temptations of drink and women, students were combustible material. In 1261 a fight between a student from the north of England and one from the south became a general affray, giving townsmen the chance to vent their frustrations on the persons, property and, most significantly, the records of the university, which embodied its privileged standing. 16 townsmen and 28 scholars were found guilty of offences. The scholars received the King's pardon; the townsmen were hanged. In the endless friction of 'Town versus Gown' over subsequent centuries the university would repeatedly use royal and court connections as trump cards.

Students were banned from keeping bad company, indulging in disorderly and insulting behaviour, possessing weapons, vandalising university property, taking unauthorised absences, gambling and heresy, and were liable to punishment for minor infractions such as breakages, lateness or lewd speech. The ultimate punishment was expulsion, although serious offences were usually punished with fines, and trivial ones with denial of daily rations. Younger offenders could be flogged. However, despite the fights between 'town' and 'gown' and students fighting each other, the masters' authority was never confronted collectively by the student guilds that emerged in the universities of Italy, Spain and France as a counterweight to the academic establishment.

In 1970 manuscript 401 in Rome's Angelica Library was identified as a compilation of Cambridge University regulations dating from around 1250. If they represent an official code of statutes then they are the earliest in Europe. The manuscript might, however, be a privately commissioned administrative handbook, combining formal statutes with recorded working practices, known as ordinances. Together the regulations defined the functions of university officers, including the Chancellor, rectors (later proctors) and bedells, outlined rights of jurisdiction and judicial procedures and established rules for dress, discipline, hostels, rents and public ceremonies like the commemoration of benefactors. Regent Masters – graduates with a Master of Arts degree – were obliged both to teach and to take part in university administration. Chancellors were chosen by Regent Masters but confirmed in office by the Bishop of Ely, to whom they swore obedience; this lasted until 1401, when the tradition was quashed by papal bull.

Latin learning

Teaching was in the international language of learning, Latin, the key to the intellectual heritage of Christendom and the passport to profitable employment. Students had to have competent Latin to be accepted for study and had to speak it outside the classroom as well as during lectures and debates, although some institutions with members aspiring to courtly or diplomatic careers permitted social conversation in French. Speaking Latin, together with their dress and demeanour, made scholars of all ages sharply distinguishable from local English-speaking townsfolk.

The initial three-year course of study, the Trivium (whence the debased term 'trivia' for unfocused knowledge), equipped the student with the basic tools of study – Logic, Grammar and Rhetoric – Logic being regarded as the most important, Rhetoric the least. Success in an oral examination – the normal procedure until the 18th century – led to the degree of Bachelor of Arts. Four more years were required for the Quadrivium, covering Arithmetic, Geometry, Astronomy and Music, which was conceived as a branch of mathematics rather than the performing arts – a dim echo of the divine harmonies of Heaven. This led to the degree of Master of Arts, which provided the graduate with a licence to teach as a Regent Master. Masters could also seek royal or ecclesiastical employment or further studies in Medicine, Law or, the supreme field of study, Theology. A late medieval illustration of 'The Tower of Learning' depicts it being approached via the Alphabet, followed by Grammar. Its first floor consists of Logic, Rhetoric and Poetry and Arithmetic; the second houses Music, Geometry and Astronomy; the third, Physic (Medicine) and Ethics; and the fourth Theology and Metaphysics.

At all levels and for most subjects the works of Aristotle and scholarly commentaries on them were the core texts and canon of authority. Worthwhile knowledge was in effect a fixed quantum, based on the Bible, the heritage of Greece and Rome and some infusion of Islamic learning; extending its frontiers was less important than ensuring its survival and reproduction. The medieval university was emphatically about teaching, not 'research'.

The teaching faculty would seem youthful to modern eyes, few being over 40. Graduates were usually required to teach for a year or two as a condition of their new status. Teaching was therefore, in the words of Alan Cobban, 'a degree requisite rather than a career prospect'. Only a tiny fraction of 'academics' could aspire to a high-flying and remunerative career as administrative bigwigs. Few teachers owned books, although they usually had preferential rights of borrowing. Without salaries most relied on fees and gifts from students.

The rise of universities had meant a change in the nature of books. Those made at huge expense as objects of veneration and display, like the missals used in worship by aristocrats, were increasingly outnumbered by much smaller, more portable volumes geared to practical use, with lists of contents and numbered pages for easier access to the information they contained. In the production of written documents there was likewise a trend towards the use of cursive scripts for easier note-taking and for more closely packed writing to economise on expensive parchment. Reeds gave way to quills. Chests of books gave way to libraries, usually located at first-floor level and orientated north-south. This made them lighter, with less need for candles and the attendant risk of fire. They were also safer from flooding and rats.

Given the scarcity and price of books before printing, there was constant demand for repetitive lectures on the 'core curriculum', largely provided by graduates anticipating higher study or employment elsewhere. Even later, when college fellowships brought teachers some economic security, they were often burdened with having to say masses in remembrance of benefactors or distracted for weeks by rural forays to college holdings to collect or audit revenues, appoint or remove staff or settle disputes. Recurrent epidemics of plague and 'sweating sickness' caused further unwanted career breaks.

Hostels into Colleges

Around 1278, land adjacent to the Market Square, where the Senate House and Old Schools buildings now stand, was given to the university by a doctor, Nigel de Thornton. This area would be occupied from around 1350–1400 by buildings devoted to teaching – a Regent House, a chapel, and schools and libraries devoted to Civil Law, Canon Law and Divinity. Teaching and administration took place around St Mary's Church and the market, and by 1280 there were 34 student hostels scattered throughout town. Eventually they reached a peak of around 60, then gradually disappeared through suppression, demolition or incorporation into colleges proper as they in turn emerged. Today only the names of Garret Hostel Lane and Bishop's Hostel in Trinity College recall the plethora of early student residences.

While some hostels were simply common lodging-houses, others were inhabited by a Master and his students. Lectures and disputations took place in the college – often initially known as a Hall – which also housed communal facilities such as a dining hall and chapel. Later features included a library, a garden and, as an expression of corporate pride, an imposing lodging for the Master. To free its members from domestic chores it also employed gatekeepers, porters, cooks, bakers, brewers, barbers, laundresses and gardeners. As they multiplied, prospered and expanded, the colleges became the dominant driver of the town's economy, thanks to their demand for fuel, food and drink, building materials and writing materials and the specialised services of masons, glaziers, carpenters, carriers, messengers and physicians.

Founded and endowed by a benefactor, the college was an autonomous society, independent of any religious order and – most importantly – with the legal right to hold property in 'mortmain': literally 'dead hand', i.e. in perpetuity. Benefactors unable to bequeath whole estates donated individual buildings, cash, books, vestments or silver plate. So a college could simply go on accumulating wealth over the centuries – subject to the vagaries of its own managerial competence, arbitrary royal interference, economic recession or civil war.

Peterhouse, the university's oldest college, was founded in 1284 by Hugh of Balsham, Bishop of Ely, for scholars who had, since 1280, been in the Hospital of St John the Evangelist, an Augustinian charity, sited where St John's College now stands. This had proved unsatisfactory, so the bishop bought two hostels near St Peter without Trumpington Gate (now St Mary the Less / Little St Mary's), which would serve as the college chapel. (Visiting Americans may note, just inside the church entrance, on the left, the monument to Godfrey Washington (1670–1729), the first President's great-uncle, bearing the family crest of stars and stripes.) Bishop Balsham also donated enough money to buy the land where Peterhouse now stands and erect a new building on it. The Hall at Peterhouse was built in 1286 and is therefore the oldest surviving collegiate structure in Cambridge. An extensive Victorian restoration features the original 1861 *Daisy* tile design by William Morris around the fireplace, and stained glass in the bay-window made by Morris & Co from designs by Ford Madox Brown (1821–93) and Edward Burne-Jones (1833–98).

Nearby, roughly where the Fitzwilliam Museum now stands, the House of the Friars of the Sack had been erected in 1258. When they were suppressed in 1307 Peterhouse incorporated their former property. The statutes organising the structure and running of the college were lifted wholesale from those formulated by Walter de Merton (1205–77) for the college named after him at Oxford; these became the template for other Cambridge colleges. Students were required to attend lectures, take part in disputations, stay in lodgings at night and dress appropriately. The foundation of Peterhouse, separate from a monastic establishment, was an implicit acknowledgment that university education was no longer just for those intended for the Church. Peterhouse had fewer than 20 members – but it was the principle that counted.

University autonomy

In 1303 the university clarified its most important procedure for internal legislation – 'it is ordained that in making statutes, which concern the common advantages of the said University, that alone shall be accounted a statute which shall have been enacted, by decree, with the consent of the greater and more discreet part of the aforesaid regents, and with the consent of the non-regents.' Regents meant the rank-and-file of active teachers, non-regents their academically qualified elders and betters. If this wasn't exactly academic democracy it at least meant a participatory mode of governance as a check on the abuse of authority and a guard against unwanted external interference.

A charter of 1317 decreed that the mayor and the bailiffs of the city should swear annually before the Chancellor to respect the privileges of the university. In 1318 Pope John XXII (d.1334) confirmed Cambridge as a *studium generale* – a university that attracted students from abroad, which meant that it might now also look to the Pope for protection, in addition to the Chancellor. When the migration from Oxford occurred in 1209 it was one of only eight *studia generale* in Europe; two more were in France, and the remaining five in Italy: Oxford's standing in this respect was never formally confirmed by the Vatican. In 1433 a bull issued by Pope Eugenius IV (1383–1447), confirmed the autonomy of Cambridge by recognising its exemption from the jurisdiction of any bishop or archbishop. In the words of Elisabeth Leedham-Green 'as so often Cambridge had started after Oxford and finished first.'

The coming of the colleges

Eight colleges were founded between 1324 and 1352, despite the preceding decades of disaster. England was farmed extensively during the 1300s, which drove marginal populations into fens, forests and moorlands. There were costly and damaging wars with Scotland and France. Appalling weather devastated crop yields and spread animal diseases, creating a general European famine in 1315–17. In 1349 Europe was ravaged by an epidemic later known as 'the Black Death', killing at least a third of the population and an even higher proportion of the literate, since the professionally religious were amongst those most at risk. Priests staying with their flocks had a higher risk of infection, and likewise monks were highly vulnerable if the contagion breached their seclusion. The result was a manpower crisis for church and state, aggravated by the recurrence of 'the great pestilence' in 1361, 1369, 1374, 1379 and 1390.

The gloomy doctrine of purgatory, formalised at the Second Council of Lyon in 1274, taught that individual souls would endure an unpleasant period of purgation before finally proceeding to heaven, but also that this passage could be accelerated by the saying of masses for their benefit. The wealthy built chapels and endowed priestly stipends specifically for this purpose. Originally associated with cathedrals, after the onset of the Black Death and its recurrent outbreaks, the number of chantries increased rapidly and they became attached to ordinary churches, monasteries and hospitals. Colleges were a form of secular chantry, a commitment to the sacred business of learning, to offset the sins of their founders.

Michaelhouse was founded in 1324 by Hervey de Stanton (1260–1327), Chancellor of the Exchequer to Edward II (r.1307–27). The nearby, still existing, church of St Michael served as the college chapel.

University Hall was founded in 1326, uniquely by the university itself, at the initiative of the Chancellor, Richard Badew (d. 1361), who converted two houses on the west side of Milne Street. But it was insufficiently endowed and the university made it over to Lady Elizabeth de Burgh (1295–1360), a member of the Clare family, who had married – and buried – three rich husbands. (Her coat of arms featured 12 silver tears.) As patroness she refounded and endowed the institution as Clare Hall (from 1856 Clare College).

King's Hall, founded by Edward III (r.1327–77) in 1337, was also to be re-founded as part of Trinity College. It was already in effect a re-foundation. In 1317 the King's father, Edward II, had established King's Hall to train 32 scholars from his own household, but the Hall had remained more of an under-funded programme than an institution, so the title of founder is usually given to his son. King's Hall, recruiting its scholars by royal nomination, became the only one of these foundations with a sizeable student population and in time the largest college in Cambridge, with prestigious leadership. John

Gunthorp (d.1498), Master from 1468–77, prefigured the versatile, upwardly mobile men of the Tudor era, for whom the university was the launching pad for a career in the service of Church or state, often both.

Pembroke Hall stood just opposite the Trumpington Gate, adjacent to Peterhouse. The college was founded in 1347 by a fabulously wealthy, childless French widow, Countess Marie de St Pol [St Paul] (c.1303–77), as the Hall of Valence Marie. Her much older husband, Aymer de Valence (Audomare de Valentia), Earl of Pembroke, had died in 1324 on a diplomatic mission to Paris, possibly from overdoing lunch. (Thomas Fuller's version was that he was 'unhappily slain tilting at her nuptials', making her 'maid, wife and widow all in a day.') The house endowed by the Countess was for 30 students, barred in perpetuity from 'drunkenness, taverns, contentiousness, lechery and notable viciousness.' Preference in admissions was to be given to Frenchmen, presumably because they were free from such shortcomings.

Gonville Hall was founded in 1348 by Edmund Gonville (d.1351), a Norfolk parson. After Gonville's death in 1350 his executor, Bishop Bateman of Norwich (c.1298–1355), exchanged the original site, a house in what is now Free School Lane, for properties owned by the religious Guild of Corpus Christi, where the present Gonville and Caius College now stands. The college's Old Court, built between 1352 and 1377, is the oldest surviving quadrilateral court in Cambridge.

Trinity Hall, or to give it its full name The College of Scholars of the Holy Trinity of Norwich, came into existence in 1350. Immediately to the north of Clare Hall, it was another foundation of Bishop Bateman. From its earliest days it was associated with the training of lawyers, a tradition that has been maintained ever since. It still possesses 350 manuscripts from its medieval library, including two donated in 1351 by one of the founding fellows.

Licensed by Edward III in 1352, Corpus Christi, originally Bene't College, was unique in that it was founded by the people of Cambridge, as represented by the guilds of Corpus Christi and St Mary.

As this was immediately after the Black Death its foundation may have been motivated by a sudden shortage of priests and a rise in the charges they made for baptisms, weddings and funerals. Certainly graduates were expected to serve in the local community churches before moving on.

Whatever the varying motives for their creation, the establishment of colleges profoundly altered the nature of the university, creating what university historian Christopher Brooke has called 'the subtle alchemy of the Cambridge colleges – all eager to preserve their separate characters while constantly imitating one another'. This imitation could take many forms – attracting the most learned scholars and best students, building the most handsome halls and chapels, accumulating the best-stocked libraries and wine-cellars, excelling on the sports field or cultivating friends in high places. In pursuit of these aims colleges came to complement, and at times to rival and even outshine, the university itself as a provider of teaching and sponsor of learning.

Revolt!

There were 'Town versus Gown' affrays involving loss of life and property damage in 1249, 1260, 1304, 1322 and 1371, but none matched the destructiveness of 1381, when the people of Cambridge joined in the misleadingly named Peasants' Revolt. Peasants did revolt, against oppressive taxation, and demanded an end to serfdom, but many rebels were from the propertied classes. Urban violence was directed against institutions deemed oppressive and abusive of privilege – notably the universities of Cambridge and Oxford and the religious houses in Bury St Edmunds and St Albans. In Cambridge the mob's aim was not to loot but to destroy documents which recorded the rights of those in power who lorded their wealth over them. At Corpus Christi they carried off 'all the books, charters, writings and effects' they could find and at Great St Mary's 'they broke open the common chest of the University and burnt and destroyed the bulls, charters and muniments therein.' They also seized another university chest lodged at the Carmelite Friary. The following day the 'mayor, bailiffs, burgesses and commonalty ... compelled the masters and scholars, by menace of death, to deliver up their charters and letters patent, and publicly burnt the statutes, ordinances and other evidences of the University in the market-place, amidst the rejoicing of the populace'. The day after that, Monday 17 June, a royal proclamation was read out, prohibiting public gatherings on pain of death – which entirely failed to prevent the mob from sacking Barnwell Priory the very same day.

Disorders continued until the arrival of Henry le Spencer, Bishop of Norwich (d.1406), along with a small retinue of armed men, who set about restoring the status quo by killing or imprisoning its challengers. The royal backlash gave the university commercial privileges – legal powers to regulate the quality and prices of bread, wine and beer, to control the sale of fish and flesh and to approve the weights and measures used in the market – which had an immediate and lasting impact on the daily lives of the townspeople.

Locations and livelihoods

Ronald Gray and Derek Stubbings, authors of the fascinating *Cambridge Street-Names: Their Origins and Associations* (2000), emphasise that 'almost every street in the medieval town had a different name from the one now used.' King's Parade has only been known as such since about 1850. Six centuries before that it was Magna Strata (Great Street), later Heighe Warde, Heyestrete, High Street and then Trumpington Street.

One can only regret the loss of Creeper's Lane, Pisspot Lane and Le Endelesweye (the 'Endless Way'). Many street names denoted concentrations of particular trades, clustered together to ease the task of regulation and possibly limit noxious smells. Thus there were 'Rows' named for Butchers, Shoemakers, Cutlers, Pewterers and Lorimers (makers of small metalwares, like harness-fittings and buckles). Market Street was Cordewanaria, the home of 'cordwainers', craftsmen in fine leather prepared in the style of Córdoba. Other street names indicated specific types of retailer. The 'Chesemarketh' was separate from both 'Botry Rowe' and the Milk Market. Smearmongers Row was for dealers in tallow and lard. Le Dudderey was where woollen cloth and clothes ('duds') were sold – not to be confused with 'The Shraggery', for second-hand garments. The Crowne Plaza Hotel occupies the former site of the Hog Market, so Downing Street was once Hog Hill. Only the name remains of nearby Petty Cury. Recorded in 1330 as 'parva Cokeria' and in 1344 as 'le Petitecurye', this was originally noted for its fast-food stalls.

Religion was the other major factor in the naming of locations. As Gray and Stubbings note, the only personal names attached to streets in the medieval city centre were those of saints or other religious figures – though these are not necessarily the names they bear today. St Andrew's Street was once Hadstock Way, then Black Friars Lane and then Preacher's Lane. Emmanuel Street was once Praise-Be-To-God Street.

Renewal

After Corpus Christi no more new colleges were founded for three-quarters of a century. In 1385 a severe fire in the town centre destroyed over 100 properties, leaving many homeless.

In 1428 Abbot Litlyngton of Crowland was granted a site by the Cam for a hostel for Benedictine monks. Because Henry, second Duke of Buckingham (1455–83), is credited with building the Chapel and Edward, third Duke, the Hall, this became known as Buckingham College. Other parts of what is now Magdalene's First Court are attributed to Litlyngton's successor, Abbot Wisbech, c.1476. The south range (for example staircase E) is of particular interest for its almost intact arrangement of medieval scholars' rooms. Thomas Cranmer (1489–1556), creator of the Church of England's *Book of Common Prayer*, was a lecturer until marriage obliged him to resign his fellowship. Declining as a result of Henry VIII's hostility to religious houses, the institution was virtually defunct by 1539 but in 1542

Thomas, Lord Audley (1488–1544), whose mother had been a benefactor, was granted permission to refound the hostel as Magdalene College, as a recognition of a lifetime of pliant service to the King. An opportunist *par excellence*, Audley had managed the legislation for the King's divorce and the dissolution of the monasteries and presided over the disgracing of discarded royal servants Cardinal Wolsey, Sir Thomas More and Thomas Cromwell. Henry made Audley Baron of Walden and a Knight of the Garter. Audley was, however, dogged by ill health and died at 56 without issue. He was buried in a magnificent tomb at Saffron Walden, leaving none of his vast wealth to 'his' college. The real credit for Magdalene's salvation should go to a Welsh scholar, John Hughes, Chancellor of Bangor Cathedral, who, in 1543, made over lands and tenements in Caernarvonshire to fund the maintenance of a scholar – a modest gesture but a precedent, nonetheless, although Magdelene would never become a wealthy college.

Around 1436–42 William Byngham (c.1390–1451), rector of the tiny parish of St John Zachary in London, established God's House, a small college to teach grammar. It was originally south of Clare Hall but within a decade this site was required for King's College Chapel and in 1446 God's House was moved to just outside Barnwell Gate, on what is now St Andrew's Street. A foundation charter was granted by Henry VI (r.1422–71) in 1448 and a new charter ratified by Henry VII in 1505 when the college was re-founded as Christ's College by his mother, Lady Margaret Beaufort, who financed the completion of the building of First Court and its showpiece gateway between 1505–11.

Note the apostrophes! King's and Queens'

King's College was the pet project of the periodically deranged but sincerely religious Henry VI, who made an annual grant of £1,000 from the Duchy of Lancaster for the venture. Its realisation involved flattening an entire riverside neighbourhood – much of the commercial and industrial heart of the city – including a riverside quay, a parish church, the recently-founded college of God's House, two inns, two cottages, three gardens, four student hostels and nine dwelling houses. Cambridge would never look – or be – the same again.

Henry founded his 'King's College of St Nicholas' (Henry's patron saint) on his birthday in 1441, a few months after establishing Eton College near Windsor Castle. By 1443 the new foundation had become 'the King's College of the Blessed Mary and St Nicholas', and recruited solely from Eton, a tradition continued for the next five centuries. Henry's 'wille and entente' were set out in detail in 1448, although only the world-famous chapel was to be completed as envisaged. Statutes granted in 1453 provided for 70 fellows and scholars, 10 chaplains, 6 clerks and 16 choristers, an establishment of a size unprecedented in Cambridge.

Queens' College has the unusual distinction of being founded three times over. In 1446 Andrew Doket (or Duckett) (d.1484), the Rector of St Botolph's, founded a college dedicated to St Bernard, with himself as President. Perhaps recognising the threat implied by the relocation of God's House, in 1448 Doket skilfully enlisted the support of Henry VI's formidable teenage wife, Margaret of Anjou (1430–82). Flattered and proud to be the first queen associated with founding a Cambridge college 'to laud and honneure of sexe feminine', she agreed to become the patroness of 'the Queen's College of St Margaret and St Bernard'. However, Margaret's contribution remained nominal: she lent her name but neither issued statutes nor provided any money, leaving the compliant King to come up with £200. When Margaret's faction foundered, Doket adroitly appealed to the queen consort Elizabeth Woodville (c.1437–92), wife of Margaret's enemy, Edward IV (and incidentally the model for the queen on packs of playing cards) to perfect the foundation and become 'foundress by right of succession'. Under her auspices the first college statutes were issued in 1475. Doket, having successfully guided his foundation through 38 years of uncertainty, died in 1484, doubtless well satisfied that the college had already built what would become Old Court and part of Cloister Court, and also acquired from the town further land on the west bank of the Cam. The four fellows he originally envisaged had, moreover, already become 17.

In 1473 Dr Robert Woodlark (d.1479) founded a Hall dedicated to 'the Honour of God, the most blessed Virgin Mary and St Catharine' (of Alexandria). His intention seems to have been to create a chantry rather than a college, as the master and three fellows were to pray for their benefactor and study theology and philosophy. A charter was granted in 1475 by Edward IV (r.1461–83). To survive the Reformation, St Catharine's was obliged to perform some teaching, but the hall remained tiny. In 1564 the total body of fellows and students was only 21. None of the original medieval buildings remains.

Jesus College was founded in 1496 by John Alcock (1430–1500). A clever Yorkshire grammar-school boy, Alcock became Lord Chancellor and Bishop successively of Rochester, Worcester and Ely. As Comptroller of the Works to Henry VII (r.1485–1509) he also gained real professional expertise in architecture and property development. Alcock suppressed St Radegund's nunnery and took over its site, adapting it for collegiate life, and justifying his action by citing 'the dissolute conduct and incontinence of the prioress and nuns'. Actually there were only two nuns at the time – one of them, admittedly, held to be '*infamis*' – so it was another case of appropriating an institution already virtually defunct. Formally known as 'The College of the Blessed Virgin Mary, St John the Evangelist and the Glorious Virgin Saint Radegund, near Cambridge' – note that *near* – the new foundation lay beyond Barnwell Gate and was thus blessed with spacious grounds. Alcock marked his creation with a grand gatehouse with diapered brickwork and stepped battlements, placing his rebus, a carved cockerel, above the central niche. This motif appears throughout the college as a ubiquitous reminder to future generations of the identity of the founder.

Medieval Cambridge attracted students from eastern and northern counties and areas where its institutions – friaries and hostels, later the colleges – owned estates. Oxford drew its intake from the South-West and the Midlands, also attracting more Scots, Irish and Welsh; in Cambridge Celts accounted for just one student in 100. At around 1,500 in the mid-14th century, Oxford's student population was twice, perhaps three times, as large as that of Cambridge, though they were roughly even a century later. Medieval Cambridge was therefore more of a regional, less of an international institution than its rival. It produced no scholar of European reputation. Indeed, as the most relevant authority, Professor Emeritus of Medieval Theology and Intellectual History Gill Evans has concluded, at the close of the 15th century Cambridge had 'nothing world-shattering to show for its efforts as yet.'

'The flower of all the University'

However, the meteoric career of John Fisher (c.1469–1535) precipitated great change in the university, and saw him rise from fellow to proctor, then to Vice-Chancellor, President of Queens' College and, from 1514, Chancellor for life – as well as simultaneously holding the post of Bishop of Rochester. An ascetic who wore a hair shirt, slept on straw and lived on gruel, Fisher's only luxury was his library, which, when seized at his disgrace, filled 32 huge barrels. An enthusiast for 'the new learning', at 50 Fisher began to tackle both Greek and Hebrew. A zealot for old standards, he banned card-playing – except among fellows at Christmas. Fisher was also, crucially, chaplain and personal confessor – in effect 'life coach' – to Lady Margaret Beaufort (1443–1509), Countess of Richmond and Derby. Fisher channelled Lady Margaret's philanthropy into the establishment of a Chair of Divinity in 1502 (of which he was the first occupant), a University Preachership in 1504 and two entire colleges.

'The Lady Margaret', as she is always known in Cambridge, was a formidable woman, married at 12, and by 14 mother of the future Henry VII. Devout, learned and a stickler for etiquette, she survived years of imprisonment and outlived four husbands. Tough, resourceful and worldly, she recovered debts owed to her grandfather more than a century previously. A sponsor of the new art of printing, she was also herself a translator (with some help) and patron of church music. Erasmus hailed her as a 'holy heroine' and paid her the backhanded compliment of having 'a mind most unlike a woman's'. A portrait, based on her superlative effigy in Westminster Abbey, was painted in around 1598, long after her death, showing her, despite arthritis and rheumatism, kneeling at prayer. Dressed with the simplicity of a nun, the Lady Margaret is shown in a private oratory, gorgeously gold, its ceiling adorned with the red rose of Lancaster, its walls and stained-glass window bearing the portcullis badge of the Beaufort family, now the official badge of the Houses of Parliament.

Of the two other colleges funded by the Lady Margaret, Christ's (1505) was a re-foundation of the former God's House, inadequately established by Henry VI. St John's (1511) was founded after the death of the Lady Margaret, whose fulsome funeral sermon was preached by Fisher. It was, moreover, Fisher who persuaded her to bequeath her bounty to Cambridge rather than to Oxford or to Westminster Abbey and who outwitted Henry VIII in his attempts to grasp his grandmother's money by having her will confirmed by a papal bull, which the King – at that stage of his reign – dared not flout.

Fisher himself contributed the enormous sum of £1,000 to the founding of St John's, framed its statutes, chose its first fellows and installed his own chaplain, Nicholas Metcalfe (c.1475–1539), as the first Master. St John's was built on the site of a decayed hospital, the inmates of which were despatched to Ely. The chapel was retained for the use of the new foundation. Destined to become a key centre of Renaissance learning, St John's was required to recruit half its intake from the northern counties, where Fisher believed educational and ecclesiastical standards were lowest.

Fisher also became confessor to Henry VIII's first queen, Catherine of Aragon (1485–1536), and was ultimately brought down by his loyalty to her. When, in 1533, Henry VIII tried to annul their marriage, Fisher was imprisoned and then executed in the Tower of London for denying the King's supremacy over the Church. His corpse was interred in the Tower and his head displayed on London Bridge and then tossed into the Thames. On the 400th anniversary of his death, in 1935 John Fisher was canonised by Pope Pius XI.

Europe's greatest scholar and England's greatest teacher

It was almost certainly Fisher who head-hunted Desiderius Erasmus (1466–1536) to succeed him as Lady Margaret Professor of Divinity in 1511. For the next three years the great Dutch scholar was at Queens' – when not seeking refuge from the college in London or from the plague in isolated Landbeach. Europe's leading intellectual suffered from gallstones and was socially limited by his inability to speak English. His correspondence was all complaints – about his miserly income, the idleness of his academic colleagues, the foulness of the beer and poor quality of the wine, the closeness of the atmosphere, the noise, the continual rain, the rapacious shopkeepers and the lack of an amanuensis to copy documents for him. But he did successfully establish the study of Greek, encourage the teaching of mathematics and promote a reassessment of the canonical writings of Aristotle.

Even as an undergraduate Roger Ascham (c.1515–68) was so good at Greek he taught his fellow students. His handwriting was so elegant he wrote the University's official letters. He also became University Orator. In 1538 St John's appointed him Reader in Greek. But Ascham was no study-bound scholar. A lover of music and chess (and cock-fighting), in 1545 he published *Toxophilus*, 'Lover of the Bow', the first English treatise on the longbow, composed as a dialogue between two Cambridge students and consisting of 'Englishe matter in the Eng-lishe tongue for Englishe men'. *Toxophilus* won Ascham a pension of £10 a year from Henry VIII. As tutor to the intellectually gifted Prin-cess Elizabeth, Ascham successfully gave her a lifelong love of Greek. After her accession as Queen in 1558 he was both her tutor and Latin Secretary, conducting her international correspondence. In urging Cambridge to teach more languages and sciences Ascham was ahead of his time. In 1570 Ascham's widow published *The Scholemaster*, a handbook of teaching, in which he denounced the beating of pupils, explained the best way of teaching Latin and put forward the first pedagogic plea that sport was an essential part of education.

'Little Germany', big consequences

In 1521 Cardinal Wolsey (1473–1530) came in person to supervise the public burning of the heretical works of Martin Luther (1483–1546) – for which Erasmus's Greek translation of the New Testament had formed the basis – outside the university church of Great St Mary's. Free ale was distributed to ensure a good turnout of onlookers, but the message was largely ignored. A blue plaque on King's Chetwynd Court building, at the junction of King's Parade and Bene't Street, marks the site of the former White Horse tavern, a discreet gathering-place of early enthusiasts for the teachings of Martin Luther and Erasmus's translations from the New Testament. The martyrologist John Foxe noted decades later that 'this house especially was chosen because many of them of St John's, the King's college and the Queens' college, came in on the back side.' Their numbers included William Tyndale (c.1492–1536) and Miles Coverdale (c.1488–1569), who would both produce English translations of the Bible, and Matthew Parker and Thomas Cranmer (1489–1556) of Jesus, the first Protestant Archbishop of Canterbury and the 'intellectual father of the English Reformation', who would manage Henry VIII's divorce and his assumption of supremacy over the Church in England. Under Edward VI (r.1547–53) Cranmer would be responsible for defining the worship of the new Anglican Church by issuing two editions of the *Book of Common Prayer* (1549 and 1552), and himself composing 84 of the pithy Collects.

The White Horse is long gone, but a minute's walk away, backing onto Peas Hill, still stands the historic church of St Edmund, King and Martyr, whose signboard proclaims it as the 'Cradle of the Reformation'. A site of worship since Saxon times, the present building dates from around 1400; the side aisles were added in 1446 for use as chapels by Clare College and Trinity Hall. Here other members of the White Horse clique, Thomas Bilney (c.1495–1531), Robert Barnes (1495–1540) and Hugh Latimer (c.1487–1555), preached the earliest sermons in England critical of the state of the Roman Catholic Church – and not to fellow academics but to townsfolk. All three would eventually be burnt at the stake for their Protestantism. The pulpit from which they preached still stands in St Edmund's.

Reformation

Henry VIII's search for a divorce led him to consult university experts and, having recognised them as a national resource, in 1535 he imposed a series of reforms in line with the general evolution of his religious policy. The teaching of canon law was suppressed. All colleges were to provide a daily Greek lecture, and the university was to provide for the teaching of Hebrew. Theology was to be taught directly from the Bible, not from the traditional schematic commentaries of the medieval schoolmen. Later there would be encouragement for arithmetic and the use of contemporary medical texts alongside Galen and Hippocrates. However, these reforms merely sped up changes that were already underway.

Henry VIII's enforcer, Thomas Cromwell (c.1485–1540), the ultimate roughneck careerist, was no university man but sent a son to Pembroke and was an enthusiast for 'the new learning'. Destined to follow More to the block, Cromwell left a lasting legacy in the establishment in 1540 at both universities of five prestigious Regius Professorships – in Greek, Hebrew, Divinity (Theology), Civil Law and Physic (Medicine) – to be appointed at the King's pleasure.

Henry VIII's dissolution of religious houses and confiscation of their assets brought him a massive windfall, mostly squandered in less than a decade. When in 1545 an Act was passed empowering him to dissolve any chantry, corporation or college, a combination of apparent compliance, skilful string-pulling and nifty obfuscation enabled Oxford and Cambridge to thwart the greatest threat ever to hang over them. Rather than incur the expense and delay of sending outsiders to survey college assets, the King was persuaded to trust local experts. At Cambridge this meant John Redman (1499–1551), one of the King's own chaplains, Public Orator, Lady Margaret Professor of Divinity and Master of King's Hall; William Meye (d.1560),

President of Queens'; and Matthew Parker (1504–75), Vice-Chancellor and Master of Corpus. Redman had also been tutor to the tutors of the heir to the throne, Thomas Smith (1513–77), recently Vice-Chancellor, and John Cheke (1514–57), the first Regius Professor of Greek, and through them enlisted the active support of the last of Henry VIII's six wives, Catherine Parr. They also lobbied William Paget (1506–63), a former Trinity Hall lawyer, now Secretary of State. Through such contacts they learnt that the danger came less from the King himself than from greedy courtiers looking for pickings. In the event the wily dons trounced their would-be predators.

The colleges presented returns of holdings and incomes, which showed them all barely struggling along. The King observed sceptically that 'he thought he had not in his realm so many persons so honestly maintained in living by so little land and rent'. Pressed to explain, the colleges pleaded constant recourse to expedients such as selling off timber and jacking up tenants' entry charges for new leases. Oxford also came up with a very shrewd proposal. Cardinal Wolsey's pet project, to found an enormous new college, had foundered with his fall from grace. If the King took it over he would gain continual prayers for his soul, a source of able servants for both Church and state, and a monument to his own liberality and learning. Thus was Christ Church, Oxford, born. Redman suggested a similar scheme for Cambridge: the enlargement of his own institution, King's Hall, by merging it with Michaelhouse and Gonville Hall's appendage, the conveniently adjacent Physwick Hostel. These three would become one – hence Trinity College. Henry took the bait – 'I judge no land in England better bestowed than that which is given to our universities, for by their maintenance our realm shall be well governed when we be dead and rotten'. Trinity would have 60 fellows, far more than any other college at either university. Henry granted its foundation charter on 19 December 1546 – and died on 28 January 1547.

LONG TO REIGN OVER US: A ROYAL INTERLUDE

When England's medieval monarchs lived in the saddle Cambridge was occasionally called upon to provide temporary hospitality as a royal residence. A late echo of this ancient custom occurred in 1912 when George V (r.1910–36) was entertained at Trinity while overseeing the army's summer manoeuvres.

James I (r.1603–25) was an academic *manqué*, the author of treatises on subjects varying from the evils of tobacco to the perils of witchcraft. Periodically wishing himself a 'university man', exchanging the burdens of kingship for the tranquillity of the study, James regarded university staff as courtiers at one remove and similarly at his beck and call. In 1607 he ordered that, providing candidates were duly qualified, Westminster School should henceforth supply the bulk of the undergraduate intake at Trinity. This proposal was met by a spirited rebuttal, probably written by the Master, Thomas Nevile, informing the meddling monarch that the college was managing quite nicely as things stood, having produced among its living alumni 60 doctors, 11 deans, 10 professors, both archbishops and 7 other bishops 'such a demonstrative instance as we think no other College in either University can afford the like – and not one of these chosen out of Westminster School.' Furthermore, anything that looked like a preference in selection would both guarantee an intake of 'Droanes and Loyterers' and 'do a grave injustice to other students who might be men of great abilities.'

James finally visited Cambridge in 1614–15. Knowing his aversion to the substance the authorities decreed a temporary tobacco-free zone around the person of the monarch, offenders risking 'payne of finall expellinge the Universitie'. James was entertained with plays and a programme of debates in divinity, law, physic and philosophy. Based on personal experience, his terse advice was to 'pray at King's, dine at Trinity, study and sleep at Jesus', adding as an afterthought, 'stool at Magdalene'. James was often crude but he was no philistine and praised Nevile's beautification of Trinity, personally raising the palsied old man from his knees to tell him that he was 'proud of such a subject'.

When the University Chancellor, Lord Suffolk, died in 1626 the new king, Charles I (r.1625–49), nominated as his successor the grossly over-promoted and widely loathed Duke of Buckingham. Deference narrowly overcame defiance and Buckingham squeezed in by 108 votes to 103. He visited the university in March 1627 and was loyally entertained, but the news of his assassination in August 1628 doubtless came as a welcome relief. In 1629 Charles intervened again, requiring Pembroke College to elect one Jasper Chomley of Corpus Christi to a fellowship. The Master replied emolliently on behalf of his colleagues that 'we wish with all our hearts that his fame were as really sweet in Cambridge as it was charitably conceived in Whitehall' but no one in Corpus had a good word to say for him – besides which he had 'once in a sudden passion (which they say haunteth him often) upon very slender provocation' stabbed a man in the guts. Therefore, having 'little hope of safe converse with a man of his morosity' and fearing that 'the College would be rent in pieces with brawls at home and law-suits abroad', on this occasion the Master felt constrained to decline the opportunity of obliging his Majesty.

Informed that many students, 'not regarding their own birth, degree and quality, have made diverse contracts of marriage with women of mean estate and of no good fame in that town', in 1629 Charles I issued decrees – targeting especially the daughters of taverners, innholders and victuallers – requiring identifiable temptresses 'to remove out of the University and four miles of the same'. When civil war between King and Parliament broke out in 1642, the university sided with the monarch – and the town did not.

The Restoration of King Charles II (r.1660–85) was proclaimed in Cambridge on 12 May 1660, 17 days before the King's triumphal entry into London. Appropriately, the ceremony took place at King's College, where 'all the soldiers were placed round the top of their chapel from whence they gave a volley of shot.' When Charles came in person in 1671 the 'Conduit ran claret wine when his Majesty passed by, who was well pleased with it.' The King, although cultured, was, however, usually more interested in the Newmarket races than in the University.

In 1674 the office of Chancellor was conferred on Charles II's eldest illegitimate son James, Duke of Monmouth. In 1685, following the King's death, Monmouth's coup to seize the throne failed, and he was subsequently executed. The Senate ordained a prompt about-face and unanimously approved the public burning of the late Chancellor's portrait 'On Commencement Day'.

James II (r.1685–8) was to prove even more high-handed in his dealings. When monarchs demanded honorary degrees for 'Ambassadors or foreign princes', Cambridge invariably obliged, even granting one to the secretary of the Moroccan ambassador. The unspoken understanding was that such honours were given only 'to strangers, who intended not to live among them'. When James sent a letter of *mandamus* (literally 'we order') requiring the degree of Master of Arts to be conferred on 'an ignorant Benedictine Monk' this was rejected 'with great unanimity, and with a firmness, that the Court had not expected.' Cambridge could, apparently, swallow the occasional Muslim, but would choke on a Catholic. The Vice-Chancellor was sacked from his – unpaid – post. The subsequent deposition of James II rendered the monk's non-degree a non-issue.

In 1705 Queen Anne (r.1702–14), another racing obsessive, travelled over from Newmarket for the day to knight Sir Isaac Newton. The Vice Chancellor ordered all students to kneel as the sovereign passed by and forbade anyone to stand on 'Benches or Seats, or look over the Partition of ... Houses, or gather together in Companies'. This was clearly appreciated, as he was knighted, too.

Queen Victoria (r.1837–1901) made the first of several visits to Cambridge in 1843 when her new husband Prince Albert (1819–61) was to receive an honorary degree of Doctor of Civil Laws. The British are supposed to be very good at the ceremonial, but even they benefit from rehearsal and on this occasion there was none. Most unusually, the Queen and Prince kept to their scheduled timing, arriving at Senate House ten minutes early – 'so that there were no oaths ready, and the Vice-Chancellor administered the oaths from memory, and of course forgot half and boggled the rest.' And there was no Bible to swear on, so they used 'a little Church service' book a courtier had in his pocket.

A subsequent occasion demonstrated that the university was sometimes capable of brilliant improvisation. In the 19th century even wealthy Trinity emptied its lavatories directly into the Cam. As the Queen crossed over the river she turned to the Master, the omniscient Dr Whewell, and asked 'What are all those pieces of paper floating down the river?' To which he instantly replied, 'Those, ma'am, are notices that bathing is forbidden.'

Albert returned in unhappier circumstances in November 1861 to confront the errant Prince of Wales (1842–1910) over rumours of misconduct. The Prince, supposedly studying hard, was isolated at Madingley Hall in a vain attempt to keep him from the temptations of the town. For privacy they walked the country lanes until a rain-soaked Albert was reassured, and father and son reconciled. The already weakened Albert allegedly took a chill, and died within a month. For the rest of her life the Queen blamed her son for the premature death of her beloved Albert. As Edward VII (r.1901–10), the former Prince of Wales returned in good-natured pomp in 1904 to open important additions to the university's central facilities. Thirty years later George V came to open the new University Library.

What can truly be called a unique royal visit occurred in 1905 when the Mayor received a hasty telegram warning him of the imminent arrival at Cambridge station of the Sultan of Zanzibar. The train was met by the town clerk, and the Sultan and his attendants were driven to the Guildhall and formally received by the Mayor. The visitors then descended unannounced on a charity bazaar before undertaking a tour of the principal colleges. Courteously returned to the station by the Town Clerk, the Sultan and his companions suddenly plunged into the crowd, jumped into cabs and disappeared in the distance, leaving the dignitaries of Cambridge to discover that they had been completely hoaxed by two Cambridge undergraduates and an Oxford friend, decked out in exotic clothing by a London theatrical costumier.

In 1920 the future George VI (r.1936–52) spent a year studying in Cambridge, nominally at Trinity, though he did not live in college and took no examinations. He returned in 1922 to unveil the city's war memorial.

Enrolled at Trinity College in 1967 under the watchful eye of the Master (former Conservative Home Secretary R A Butler (1902–82)) the former Prince of Wales undertook a regular Bachelor degree in Archaeology and Anthropology, although his circumstances were scarcely those of a regular undergraduate. Charles had his own key to the Master's Lodging and was allowed to keep his MGB sports car in college, in flagrant violation of the normal rules. He also acquired his first girlfriend, the Master's research assistant, Lucia Santa Cruz, daughter of the Chilean Ambassador. Although the Prince took part in amateur dramatics and the musical life of the university, his social circle remained exclusively upper-class. The Prince passed his degree examinations with a respectable II:II.

From 1977 to 2011 the Prince's father, the Duke of Edinburgh, served as Chancellor of the University. Prince Edward, Duke of Wessex, followed in his elder brother's footsteps to become an under-graduate at Jesus and also participated enthusiastically in local the-atrical life. In April 2011, on the occasion of the marriage of Prince William to Catherine Middleton, Her Majesty Queen Elizabeth II was pleased to confer upon the royal couple the title of Duke and Duchess of Cambridge – an unanticipated boost to the name recogni-tion of both city and university worldwide.

3

From Reformation to Civil War

Civic progress

By the mid-16th century, Cambridge had begun to look more than just a modest market town. A Paving Act in 1544 gave promise of less muddy streets and a memorable visit by Queen Elizabeth I in 1564 prompted a general sprucing up. In the same year the Chancellor was empowered to license alehouses, cutting their number from 80 to around 30. In 1573 the university was granted its own coat of arms. The town followed suit two years later, with a design featuring Magdalene (Great) Bridge, the ancient castle, three ships and the rose and *fleur-de-lys*, indicating royal favour. Pointedly, there are no references to the presence of the university. The ruined remains of former religious houses were replaced by new colleges – Emmanuel and Sidney Sussex – and the decayed Gonville Hall was revived. In 1604 the university was invited to send two Members to Parliament. The town meanwhile campaigned for promotion to the status of city but the university, fearing the 'power and authority which the very bare title of a city will give unto them' scotched that by backstairs appeals to its friends and alumni in high places. Both Town and Gown remained, however, vulnerable to capricious Nature in the shape of plague, with more than 400 dying in 1610, and another very severe outbreak in 1630. In 1666, the year after London's Great Plague, more than 800 were carried off, one in eight of the town's population.

Fires of faith

Henry VIII repudiated the authority of the Pope to become head of *the* Church *in* England, yet died believing himself a good Catholic. His three children set the country on a religious switch-back, which ultimately created *a* Church *of* England, basically Protestant in its doctrines but, for Puritans, still too Catholic in governance and worship.

Henry's precociously pious son Edward VI pushed England towards Protestantism. In 1549, when the first edition of Archbishop Cranmer's *Book of Common Prayer* came into use, Cranmer invited the German Protestant theologians Martin Bucer (1491–1551), an ex-friar married to an ex-nun, and Paul Fagius (1504–49), to Cambridge as Regius Professor of Divinity and Regius Professor of Hebrew, respectively. Providence, however, had other plans. Fagius died of plague almost immediately. Bucer died in 1551 and was buried in the chancel of Great St Mary's. None of this had been good for university recruitment. Bishop Latimer warned Edward VI that 'there be none but great men's sons in colleges and their fathers look not to have them preachers'.

Passionately Catholic Mary (r.1553–8) led a sustained campaign to reinstate Catholicism. Mass was re-established, all but three Cambridge heads of houses dismissed, Protestant activists driven into exile and searches made for suspect writings and incriminating letters. Visitors to Oxford now orientate themselves from the Victorian Gothic 'Martyrs' Memorial', honouring the deaths in 1555 of Bishops Latimer and Ridley (c.1500–55) and Archbishop Cranmer, burnt for refusing to renounce their Protestant convictions. These 'Oxford Martyrs' were, all three, Cambridge men.

In 1557 Fagius and Bucer were posthumously tried and condemned for heresy and their coffins dug up and burnt in the market place, while heretical books were flung on the flames. However, following Elizabeth I's accession in 1558 their degrees and titles were restored and Bucer's memory was honoured with a second funeral in 1560, memorialised with a floor plaque to the right of the altar of Great St Mary's.

Caius College

What is now the fourth largest college is usually referred to as Caius (pronounced 'Keys'), the Latinised form of the name of its re-founder Dr John Keys or Kay(e) (1510–73). Caius went to Gonville Hall as a fount of the new 'Greek learning'. Intended as a theologian, by 23 he was Principal of Fiswick's (Physwick) Hostel but left in 1539 to study abroad. In Padua, Europe's leading centre of medical education, he qualified as a doctor under the founder of modern anatomy, Andreas Vesalius (1514–64). Returning, Caius lectured on anatomy, became royal physician to Edward VI, Mary and Elizabeth and served nine times as President of the Royal College of Physicians. The leading expert on the Roman medical authority Galen, Caius also wrote a definitive account of sweating sickness and as London's leading practitioner became very rich.

In 1557 Mary authorised Caius to re-found his old college, Gonville Hall, which, crippled by the royal confiscation of Physwick Hostel, was in danger of being swallowed up by the cuckoo Trinity. Curiously for a medical man, Caius' articles of governance at Gonville excluded 'the deaf, dumb, deformed, chronic invalids and Welshmen.' The last may have been the result of a clerical error – 'Wallicum' rather than perhaps the intended 'Gallicum' – i.e. Frenchmen. In that same year, Caius conducted, at Gonville Hall, Cambridge's first recorded dissection of a human body.

In 1559, following the death of the Master of what was henceforth Gonville and Caius College, Caius was persuaded to succeed him. Autocratic and cantankerous, Caius sacked several fellows and was accused of being a crypto-Catholic. As adjudicator, Archbishop Parker found 'both parties ... not excusable from folye', criticising Caius for 'overmoche rashness for expelling felowes so sodonly'. He conceded that 'the contemptuose behaviour of these felowes hath moch provoked him' and concluded realistically that 'founders and benefactors be very rare in these days ... Scholars controversies ... many and troublouse'. A prolific, and respected, medical author, Caius ventured into history to prove Cambridge more ancient than Oxford.

Ecclesiastical historian Professor C N L Brooke has dismissed Caius's *De Antiquitate Cantabrigiensis Academiae* (1568) as 'a miracle of perverted learning, based on a magnificent list of irrelevant authorities.'

Caius's commitment to the college manifested itself in a substantial building programme, enlarging the Master's lodging and creating Caius Court (1565–7) as student accommodation. Its design drew on his medical expertise to pioneer the three-sided courtyard, an open side deemed essential for air circulation against damp, infectious vapours. This novel idea was to be taken up at Emmanuel and Sidney Sussex, Trinity, Trinity Hall (Library Court), Peterhouse (Entrance Court), Pembroke (Ivy Court) and Jesus (First Court). Much later it was applied to the main court at King's (1824–8), Gisborne Court at Peterhouse (1825–6), New Court at St John's (1826–31), Memorial Court at Clare (1923–4), North Court at Jesus (1963–4) and the Wolfson Flats at Churchill (1965–8).

Caius's major architectural legacy was, however, the construction (to his own designs) of a sequence of fantastical gateways symbolising the successful progress of a model student: he would enter via the modest Gate of Humility (1565), pass through the Gate of Virtue (1565–7) and emerge through the triumphal arch of the Gate of Honour (1573–5) to proceed to the Old Schools and take his degree. (A fourth gate in Tree Court, opening onto a lavatory, is referred to unofficially as the Gate of Necessity.) The original Gate of Humility was removed to the Master's garden. On Trinity Street its 19th-century replacement still bears the injunction '*Humilitatis*'. The Gate of Virtue, linking Tree Court to Caius Court, is Gothic on one side, classical on the other. The extravagant Gate of Honour now leads rather incongruously into constricted Senate House Passage. Pevsner observes that this gate, smallest of the three, is absurdly out of scale for the complexity of its design and decoration – 'illustrations make one expect a building twice the size'. See what you think of one of the most photographed architectural details in Cambridge.

Caius's memorial in the college chapel carries an epitaph as terse as even Latin gets – *Fui Caius* ('I was Caius') – complemented by *Vivit*

Post Funera Virtus ('Virtue Lives Beyond the Grave') – the very words chosen by Caius for Thomas Linacre (c.1460–1524), first President of the Royal College of Physicians, whose tomb in St Paul's Cathedral he paid to refurbish.

Caius was succeeded by the lawyer Thomas Legge (1535–1607). Another Norwich man, Legge also fell out with his juniors and was accused of favouring Yorkshiremen and Catholics, embezzlement, and disturbing students with rowdy music, none of which stopped him from serving as Regius Professor of Civil Law, Vice-Chancellor (twice) and Justice of the Peace for Cambridge. He also wrote a play in Latin about Richard III.

Parker's principles

An early but cautious Protestant, learned scholar, potent preacher and conscientious educator, Matthew Parker (1504–75) was successively chaplain to the ill-fated Anne Boleyn (1501–36) and then to Henry VIII, who ordered his election in 1544 as Master of his old college, Corpus Christi. Parker immediately reordered its affairs, organising inventories of assets and properties and commissioning a college history. Scrupulously conscientious, he yet remained, like his close friend John Caius, a loyal member of the Norwich and Norfolk university mafia, endowing scholarships and fellowships limited to candidates from his own city and county and giving them preference in the allocation of rooms, the reservation of books and even bedding.

Despite his Protestantism, Parker was sufficiently traditionalist to keep the college as Corpus Christi, despite the Papist overtones of the name. Even so, he was one of Mary's victims, forced to live on the run until her death in 1558. Parker then pleaded with Elizabeth to allow his return to Cambridge, but loyal to the memory of her mother, Anne Boleyn, the Queen instead persuaded him to become the second Protestant Archbishop of Canterbury in 1559, tasked with enforcing the beliefs, worship and Bible of the new 'Church of England'.

However, Parker remained devoted to both Corpus and Cambridge. In 1568 Elizabeth authorised him to recover library holdings scattered by Henry's dissolution of religious houses. Ostensibly the aim was to copy precious documents but hundreds were never returned, and the bulk of the collection, 433 manuscripts, went to Corpus. The manuscripts form an invaluable historical record. Almost 40 pre-dated the Norman Conquest, with highlights including the earliest extant editions of the Dark Age chronicler Gildas, Asser's biography of Alfred the Great, a 9th-century dictionary defining more than two thousand Anglo-Saxon words, and autographed letters of Luther, Calvin, Anne Boleyn and Edward VI. The Parker Library, now with 550 manuscripts, went online in 2010 (parker.stanford.edu/parker). Visit the site to see the oldest illustrated Latin Gospel in existence – the 6th-century Augustine Gospels on which the Archbishops of Canterbury still take their oath of office. It has been in England longer than any other book.

In 1570 Parker endorsed the new statutes which would govern the university until the reforms of the mid-Victorian period. Largely with a view to curbing Puritan extremism, these enhanced the powers of the Vice-Chancellor and Heads of Colleges, enabling them to influence most appointments, and in effect, authorising them to interpret the university's statutes as they chose. These changes were highly unpopular with the radical element amongst the junior fellows, but were enforced despite their resistance.

One of Parker's last gifts to Cambridge was one of its earliest pieces of town planning – the creation in 1574 of University Street, running from the Old Schools to the west door of Great St Mary's. Cutting through a jumble of alleys, houses and hostels, this impressed contemporaries but has now completely disappeared. The re-naming of Emmanuel Back Lane to Parker Street in the 18th century *may* be a tribute to the Archbishop – but Parker's Piece has nothing to do with him; in 1613 Trinity College swapped the 25 acres it owned in Barnwell Field for the area, then owned by the town and known as Garret Hostel Green, where Trinity would expand its buildings. At that time

Trinity's Barnwell holding was leased to college cook Edward Parker – hence Parker's Piece.

Perne's pragmatism

In the theological maelstrom of the 16th century, few proved more buoyant than Andrew Perne (1519–89). A fellow of St John's and Queens', Master of Peterhouse, canon of Windsor and Dean of Ely, Perne, serving five times as Vice-Chancellor under Protestant Edward VI, Catholic Mary and Anglican Elizabeth, was variously both for and against the adoration of images, the doctrine of transubstantiation and the authority of the Pope. He also organised the desecration of the bodies of Bucer and Fagius, then presided over their reinstatement, inspiring a new verb, 'to perne', meaning to have a threadbare garment turned. Perne seems to have shared the joke, commissioning a weathervane for St Peter's church marked with his initials, AP – variously interpreted to mean A Protestant, A Puritan or A Papist. Miserly but hospitable, sycophantic but eloquent in repartee, Perne was constant in loyalty and generosity to the college and the university, building Peterhouse library and bequeathing to it and the University Library the contents of his own fine collection.

Printing and publishing

The first printer in Cambridge was Johann Lair of Siegburg, who anglicised his name to John Siberch. Arriving in 1521 with his own press, he printed 10 different titles, but whether for professional or personal reasons, returned to Germany in 1522. In 1534 Henry VIII granted the university the right to print books, but it was not until 1584 that university printer Thomas Thomas published the first titles – treatises on the Holy Communion, a Latin dictionary and an edition of Ovid. A volume by the Puritan preacher, Walter Travers (c.1548–1635) of Trinity, put forward Presbyterian views critical of the new Anglican church settlement. Archbishop Whitgift wrote a weary 'I told you so' letter to William Cecil, the Chancellor of the university – 'Ever since I heard that they had a printer at Cambridge, I did greatly fear that this and such like inconveniences would follow.' Whitgift ordered all copies of the offending volume destroyed and as a further precaution, banned the printing of any book not authorised by himself or the Bishop of London. In 1586 the Court of Star Chamber grudgingly agreed that Cambridge and Oxford might each have one press only, with all other printing to be concentrated in London, under its watchful eye. Despite these less than encouraging origins, Cambridge University Press now claims to be the oldest publishing house in continuous existence in the world. Its most important early production was the 'Geneva Bible' of 1591, used by Shakespeare and the early Puritan settlers of New England. Later titles included the works of Milton and Newton.

Out of ruins

Emmanuel College was founded by Sir Walter Mildmay (1523–89), whose Essex family had done well out of the dissolution. Mildmay attended Christ's, leaving without a degree, but as a Gray's Inn lawyer he specialised in property and auditing, later becoming Treasurer of Elizabeth I's household and Chancellor of the Exchequer. In 1583 Mildmay paid Cambridge's former Dominican friary £550 for a new college to be erected (1584–8), not, its founder warned, to provide 'a perpetual abode for fellows', but to breed men of learning for ordination to go out into the world and change it. The founding statutes bade members to avoid idle gossip and to watch over and, if necessary, reprove each other's behaviour.

Laurence Chaderton (c.1536–1640) was almost 50 when he became Emmanuel's first Master, forced into accepting the task (and a miserly stipend of £15 a year) by Mildmay's insistence that 'If you won't be Master, I won't be Founder.' Chaderton held the post for 38 years. His grave in the college chapel claims he eventually died in his 103rd year.

When the Queen remarked challengingly, 'Sir Walter, I hear you have erected a puritan foundation', Mildmay replied with studied ambiguity – 'No, madam, far be it from me to countenance anything contrary to your established laws but I have set an acorn, which when it becomes an oak, God alone knows what will be the fruit thereof.' Half a century later the financial legacy of one of Mildmay's 'fruit' founded Harvard College.

As the first new college in Cambridge since the Reformation, Emmanuel paved the way for the foundation of Sidney Sussex College in 1596, established on the former site of the Franciscan friary. The college was established with the £5,000 legacy of Frances Sidney, Countess of Sussex, who died in 1589 before her project could be realised. Her executors, John Whitgift (c.1530–1604), Archbishop of Canterbury, and Sir John Harington (1561–1612), battled through financial complications to bring it to fruition. Harington – wit, charmer and godson of Elizabeth I – was twice banned from court for his risqué writings and is now remembered as the inventor of the flushing toilet. He once wrote that Cambridge was 'the Nursery of all my good breeding' – tongue in cheek?

Sidney Sussex was the first Cambridge college to open its fellowships to Scotsmen and Irishmen, though not, as it were, fresh from the branch. Celtic candidates had to have been in Cambridge for at least six years. And if Emmanuel was an acorn, Sidney Sussex was initially little more than a seed, consisting of a Master, three fellows and four scholars.

The topographer William Camden acknowledged the significance of 'the other University of England' and more particularly its 16 colleges – 'sacred mansions of the Muses, wherein a great number of learned men are maintained and wherein the knowledge of the best arts and the skill in tongues so flourish, that they may rightly be counted the fountains of literature, religion, and all knowledge whatsoever, who right sweetly bedew and sprinkle, with most wholesome waters the gardens of the Church and Commonwealth'. Camden made his general point firmly, not to say floridly, enough but he could not know that by 1640, 2.5 per cent of the male population was attending university, a figure not to be exceeded until the 1930s.

The undergraduate population, like the society from which it came, was hierarchical in composition. As the Renaissance made a veneer of learning a social necessity among the aristocracy, the proportion of young noblemen attending – rather than studying at – Cambridge increased. In return for hefty fees they usually dined with fellows and were relieved of the squalid obligation to take examinations. However, most undergraduates were 'pensioners', obliged both to pay fees and take exams. At the bottom of the heap were 'sizars' working their way through college by waiting on their better-off fellows at table, clearing the chamber pots in their rooms, helping out in the library or labouring in the college grounds.

Cambridge and Court

Elizabeth I built up something of a reliance on Cambridge men, and her favourites came to include the Archbishops Edmund Grindal (c.1519–83) and John Whitgift; Dr John Dee (1527–1608), her personal astrologer; Sir Francis Walsingham (c.1532–90), her self-appointed head of security; his master code-breaker and forger, Thomas Phelippes, alias Peter Hollins (1556–1625); the poetic courtier Edmund Spenser (c.1552–99); her fated favourite, Robert Devereux, Earl of Essex (1566–1601); Sir Walter Mildmay; Sir Thomas Gresham (1519–79), her financial guru and most trusted adviser; and William Cecil (1520–98), Lord Burghley, Chancellor of the University for almost 40 years.

The career of Thomas Nevile (c.1548–1615) illustrates the interaction between academic and ecclesiastical advancement and royal patronage. Initially at Pembroke Hall, Nevile became Master of Magdalene, a chaplain to Elizabeth I and Vice-Chancellor, also enjoying incomes from appointments at the cathedrals of Ely, Peterborough and Canterbury, as well as country rectories where the actual parish duties were performed by a curate as his deputy. Appointed Master of Trinity College – a post created by royal decree – Nevile undertook a dramatic building programme, which is his chief legacy. The surviving buildings from Kings Hall, Michaelhouse and the Physick Hostel were demolished in 1597 to make way for the Great Court (1597–1605), which is the largest in either Cambridge or Oxford. Nevile himself stumped up £3,000 a year over seven years (1602–8) to pay for a complementary new hall, big enough to stage plays in. The largest in Cambridge, it is exactly the same size as Middle Temple Hall in London (103ft × 40ft × 50ft). He then paid for what is now Nevile's Court (1614), which featured the novelty of two parallel cloistered ranges – and still had enough left over to bequeath to the college 'a bachelor's bounty'.

The Marlowe mystery

Playwright Christopher Marlowe (1564–93) was not yet 30 when he died, stabbed above the eye in a tavern brawl in Deptford. Whether he was deliberately 'eliminated' on the order of the government remains unclear. Marlowe was probably recruited into Walsingham's secret service while still at Corpus Christi, which he entered in 1581. After taking his BA in 1584 Marlowe was absent for such prolonged periods it became uncertain whether he would proceed to MA – until the Privy Council directed the university authorities to grant the degree as Marlowe had been employed 'on matters touching the benefit of his country', possibly infiltrating circles of English Catholics abroad or liaising with Protestant rebels in the Netherlands.

Marlowe may well have begun writing *Dido, Queen of Carthage*, and possibly even the first part of *Tamburlaine the Great*, while still at Cambridge. Mixing in criminal as well as theatrical and courtly circles in London, Marlowe enjoyed brief but brilliant success with *The Jew of Malta*, *Dr Faustus* and *Edward II*. A professed atheist and homosexual with a penchant for violence, he was probably protected by Walsingham until the latter's death in 1590, after which Marlowe's dissolute lifestyle virtually guaranteed his untimely end. The only generally acknowledged portrait of Marlowe, painted by an unknown artist in 1585, was rediscovered in 1952 among a pile of builder's rubble during renovation work on the Master's Lodge at Corpus. The baby-faced genius stares out, half-smiling, beneath an enigmatic motto – *Quod Me Nutrit Me Destruit* (What Nourishes Me Destroys Me).

A Cambridge character

Thomas Hobson (c.1544–1631) inherited a cart and eight horses and went on to build a fortune from his stable by operating a carrier's service to London and hiring out horses. Hobson ensured that each of his mounts was properly rested and fed. His insistence that they were only available in strict rotation faced clients with accepting 'Hobson's Choice' – or none. As a carrier Hobson provided wheeled transport essential for those who could not ride (women, children, the aged and infirm) and for bulky baggage, like scholars' books and trunks. He also had a prestigious sideline conveying 'great vessels of fish' (tanks in which live fish were kept fresh) 'for provision for his Majesty's household.'

Hobson's business acumen also brought him extensive properties, including no fewer than five manors. His public spirit led him to serve as mayor and in 1628 to give the city the site for 'Hobson's Workhouse', more notoriously known as the 'Spinning House', where the indigent were set to spin yarn in return for their keep. Located on the south side of St Andrew's Street, it was demolished in 1901. Hobson House now marks its site.

Between 1610 and 1614 the Cambridge New River was built, at the joint expense of town and university, to bring fresh water from Nine Wells near Trumpington – a parallel to the exactly contemporary New River project to supply London. Hobson's will provided for the perpetual maintenance of this work. A handsome hexagonal stone conduit, with shell niches, strapwork ornamentation and an ogee cupola, originally stood on Market Hill in 1614, but is now on Trumpington Street, opposite Scroope Terrace. Hobson was buried in his own parish church, St Bene't's, sufficiently renowned for Milton to write two humorous epitaphs in his honour. He is also remembered in the names of Hobson's Passage and Hobson Street.

Legacies of learning

A Caius man from the age of 17 until his death, Stephen Perse (1548–1615), as a physician and financier, built up a Cambridge property portfolio sufficient to endow six fellowships and six scholarships at Caius and help fund part of what is now Tree Court. The rooms of the original Perse Building (1617–18) were each built with a 'convenient Studdie', an early recognition that scholarship might require silence and solitude. The bulk of Perse's estate, however, was for a grammar school for 100 pupils, initially housed in former buildings of the Austin Friars, in what is now appropriately called Free School Lane. Decayed by 1800, the Perse School's main room was used as a picture gallery before the school was successfully revived in the 1840s and transferred to Hills Road in 1888. The university bought its original site for £12,500 for an engineering laboratory, and it is now the location of the Whipple Museum of the History of Science: the original Jacobean hall, with its hammerbeam roof, survives. Distinguished Perse alumni include Reuben Heffer and F R Leavis. The monument to Perse in Caius' chapel has been attributed to Maximilian Colt (d.1641), sculptor of the monument to Elizabeth I in Westminster Abbey. Another statue of Perse, holding a model of his school, can be seen in Tree Court at Caius. Perse also paid for the road now known as Maids' Causeway, and almshouses in Newnham Road.

John Harvard (1607–38) was born in Southwark, by London Bridge; his mother, having married three times, accumulated considerable property, to her son's ultimate benefit. After attending Emmanuel College from 1627–35, Harvard married in 1637 and migrated, settling at Charlestown, Massachusetts, where his wealth and learning immediately made him a man of standing and influence. He died, however, in 1638, childless, leaving half his considerable estate to a proposed college for which £400 had already been pledged, and also bequeathing his library of 329 volumes, probably the largest in the colonies at that time. Harvard's bequest prompted construction to begin and in 1639 the college was named in his honour and its site, Newtown, renamed Cambridge. John Harvard is commemorated by a stained-glass window in the chapel of Emmanuel College. As there was no surviving portrait the Victorian designers were told to make him look like John Milton but with longer hair.

Puritan pioneers

John Harvard was one of tens of thousands who left England in the 'Great Migration' of the 1630s, fleeing the rule of Charles I, who governed without Parliament and supported the anti-Puritan regime of his Archbishop of Canterbury, William Laud (1573–1645). Cambridge men provided the intellectual core of this colonising movement. William Brewster (c.1560–1644), who had studied at Peterhouse, led the way as one of the original *Mayflower* 'pilgrims' in 1620, followed by William Blackstone (1595–1675) an alumnus of Emmanuel, who in 1623 founded what became Boston. Thomas Hooker (1586–1647), a graduate of Queens', established the first church in Cambridge, Massachusetts and founded Hartford, Connecticut. Of the 140 graduates known to have emigrated to the American colonies before 1645, 102 came from Cambridge. 35 of these were from Emmanuel College alone, outnumbering the entire Oxford contingent of 32. A further 13 were from Trinity, including the first 'Overseer' of Harvard, John Cotton (1585–1652). The president-designate, Nathaniel Eaton (1610–74), another Trinity man, was sacked for thrashing students and embezzling funds, but the situation was rescued by the first actual holder of the office of President, learned, pious Henry Dunster (1609–59) a graduate of Magdalene. John Eliot (c.1604–90), the 'apostle to the Indians', was a Jesus man, as was, much later, East Apthorp (1733–1816) a signatory to the Declaration of Independence. (Another signatory was Thomas Lynch of Caius.) Peter Bulkeley (1583–1659) of St John's was a founder of Concord, New Hampshire. John Robinson (c.1576–1625), pastor to the Pilgrim Fathers, studied at Corpus. Pembroke contributed Roger Williams (1604–83), founder of Rhode Island. In 1654 Pembroke received John Stone, the first American to become a fellow at a British university.

One of the earliest Harvard graduates was George Downing (1623–84), who became a spy for Cromwell, then a turncoat to the Royalists and a secret agent against the Dutch. He received some land as a reward, on which he built Downing Street in Whitehall, where British prime ministers reside at No 10. The dubious fortune he amassed ultimately went to found Downing College.

Creeping classicism

Cambridge buildings of the early 17th century combined creativity with confusion as old-fashioned late Gothic oriels and ogees were thrown together with pediments and balustrades inspired by the models of the Classical world.

When St John's decided to build a new library it opted for a 'retro' Gothic look which initially bemused John Williams, Bishop of Lincoln (1582–1650), Lord Keeper of the Great Seal, who was paying for it. Bishop Carey (d. 1626) reassured him on behalf of the college that 'men of judgment liked the best the old fashion of church windows, holding it the most meet for such a building.' Pevsner notes the significance of this deliberate historicism – 'here for the first time Gothic forms were used self-consciously ... There can be few examples of a true Gothic Revival in the country (or, indeed, any country) earlier than this.' 100 feet long, the library, built in 1624, did feature one recognisable novelty – bookcases attached to the walls, rather than freestanding. At the top of the oriel gable of the river elevation are the initials ILCS – Iohannes Lincolnensis Custos Sigilli – John of Lincoln, Keeper of the Seals.

The new chapel at Peterhouse, by contrast, built between 1628 and 1632, during the Mastership of Matthew Wren (1585–1667), uncle of Christopher Wren, featured a mixture of motifs, including a classical pediment. Rawle considers it 'one of the finest buildings of its date in Cambridge and certainly the most striking at Peterhouse.' The classical cloisters at the west end were a later addition.

At Clare the rebuilding of what became the Old Court began in 1638 but ended abruptly in 1642 with the outbreak of civil war, by which time only the east and south ranges had been completed. Rebuilding was not recommenced until 1669 and only completed in 1715, with balustrades added in 1762. Despite taking 77 years to accomplish, Pevsner, who devotes more than two entire pages to it, considered it 'more of one style than any other 17th-century work in Cambridge'; the first totally classical court in the university. The south range, viewed from the lawns of King's and the west range, viewed from across the river, are breathtaking in their repetitive orderliness. In 1639–40 Clare also built the first bridge in Cambridge in a classical mode.

Pevsner's palm is, however, reserved for the 'New' (now Fellows') Building at Christ's (1640–3), as 'the boldest building of these years ... one of the most original of its date in England'. Rawle likewise judges it the first 'almost purely' classical building in Cambridge, notably for pioneering a new style of cross window, later much imitated. Lacking a munificent benefactor, the college wrote – in Latin – a circular letter to alumni in which it expressed itself 'confident that you will not let down the honour of those buildings in which you drew the seeds of that virtue and erudition that still adorn you as a man.' It evidently worked, with alumni raising some two-thirds of the budget of more than £3,600. Three, rather than the normal two, storeys high, with dormers inserted in the roof space and fronted by a balustrade, it was built quite independent of the previous court and featured alternating triangular and segmental pediments above its principal windows. Strongly symmetrical, it encapsulated what the Oxford-educated dilettante John Evelyn crisply called 'exact architecture'.

CAMBRIDGE GARDENS: A HORTICULTURAL INTERLUDE

The gardens of the religious houses of medieval Cambridge provided herbs for kitchen and sanatorium, fruit for the table and space for quiet contemplation. The monks of the Benedictine house which stood where Magdalene College now is were expected by the rules of their Order (*Ora et Labora* – Pray and Work) to labour daily in its gardens. The gardens of Emmanuel and Sidney Sussex are also on land once tilled and tended by monks. Peterhouse, King's Hall and Pembroke all cultivated the saffron crocus, a highly valued crop, used for both cooking and dyeing – 4,000 blooms were required to produce a single ounce. As the university spawned overcrowded lodging houses and the town was interlaced with squalid alleys, college gardens became refuges for informal teaching and recreation. As colleges developed their individual identities and a parallel sense of rivalry, gardens became objects of pride – and expenditure. In 1532 Queens' decided that its President should have his own garden 'for frute' and 'to walk in'. In 1575 the same college built a framework for a vine in the Fellows' garden and bought in 1,000 honeysuckles.

David Loggan's views of Cambridge show Pembroke had a bowling green and sedate walks but that most of its gardens were given over to productive purposes – an orchard with espaliered fruit trees, ponds for carp and pike, hives for bees and beds for fruit, vegetables and herbs. By then college gardens were being enjoyed by visitors as well as residents. Celia Fiennes remarked that 'St John's College Garden is very pleasant for the fine walks, both close shady walks and open rows of trees and quickset hedges, there is a pretty bowling green with cut arbours in the hedges ... Clare Hall is very little but most exactly neat; in all parts they have walks with rows of trees and bridges over the river and fine painted gates into the fields'.

Generations of undergraduates have exploited college gardens as potential weak points in the systems of security and surveillance. In 1754 the future Rev Dr John Trusler (1735–1820), strolling round Emmanuel College 'perceived a key left in the gate ... through which the gardener was wheeling dung'. Trusler seized his chance, paid a nearby smith to make a template of it, returned the original undetected, and had his own duplicate made, after which 'everyone wished to become my friend,' so that they could evade the normal evening curfew of 9:00 p.m. in summer, or 6:00 p.m. in winter.

The 18th-century 'Grand Tour' exposed English gentlemen to

continental gardening, and the emerging cult of 'the picturesque' awakened an appreciation of natural landscape. Botany likewise emerged as a science and an essential study for the aspiring doctor or apothecary. Familiarity with plants and garden design became therefore one of the accomplishments expected of the educated. By implication therefore, a place of education should have gardens; well-ordered by the dictates of art and the insights of science.

In 1772 St John's employed Lancelot 'Capability' Brown (1716–83), doyen of English landscape designers, to revamp their Fellows' Garden. In 1779 he presented a master-plan for reordering the Backs as a single unified parkland, sweeping away existing avenues of trees and – more importantly – overriding boundaries between different college properties. This proved several steps too far. Thanked politely for his efforts with a silver presentation plate, he was sent on his way.

The Botanic Garden

Oxford, although no great friend to science, had acquired a Botanic Garden for teaching purposes by the 1620s, belatedly following the Continental examples of Pisa, Padua and Heidelberg. Cambridge had to wait more than another century to do so. William Heberden (1710–1801) of St John's in April and May 1747 gave a course of 31 lectures – with a week's break for the Newmarket races – on the medicinal uses of local plants. Alas for Cambridge, Heberden soon afterwards qualified as a member of the Royal College of Physicians and left for profitable private practice in the capital – 'much lamenting the want of a Public Garden.' This loss rankled with the Master of Trinity, Richard Walker (1679–1764), who had his own personal patch of 'exotics' like pineapples, bananas and coffee. A passionate 'florist', he was astonished when a fellow enthusiast shot himself dead one spring, bursting out 'Good God! Is it possible? Now, at the beginning of tulip time!' In 1760 Walker at his own initiative and expense bought land for a university Botanic Garden (on the future site of the Cavendish Laboratory), conveying it in trust to the university.

The expansion of the town in the early 19th century made it essential to remove Walker's bequest to a more spacious location. This was achieved by the Rev John Stevens Henslow (1791–1861), Professor of Botany and mentor of Darwin. Henslow was also curate at St Mary the Less, whose churchyard is now an explorer's delight for children. The Botanic Garden finished moving to its new 20-acre (since expanded to 40-acre) site in 1846. Henslow's other major contribution was to extend the Garden's purposes beyond a purely medicinal remit so that plants might be collected and studied for their economic potential. He is memorialised in the name of Henslow's Walk.

Originally open to all 'respectably dressed strangers', the Botanic Garden was a much-favoured refuge of former Pink Floyd star Syd Barrett (1946–2006) after he had renounced rock 'n' roll for abstract painting. Major features now include rock gardens of limestone and sandstone, a Scented Garden, Dry Garden and Winter Garden, more than 20 specimens of trees of record dimensions and nine national collections, including those of geraniums, fritillaries and tulips. The Garden now modestly describes itself as 'particularly good in July-August; particularly interesting in winter.' It is also still home to the Faculty of Plant Sciences. Its architectural features include the iron gates of its predecessor on Free School Lane and a Director's House (1924) by Mackay Hugh Baillie Scott, rhapsodically described by Pevsner as 'a rare example of what perfection the neo-Georgian or neo-Colonial style could attain.' In 2011 the Sainsbury Laboratory was opened for 120 researchers in the Department of Plant Sciences, also providing a new home for the University Herbarium, which houses 1,000,000 plant specimens, including those collected by Darwin during his voyage on HMS *Beagle*.

College Gardens

The college gardens at Sidney Sussex date from the 18th century. University historian George Dyer, writing in 1814, was effusive in his praise – 'an admirable bowling-green, a beautiful summer-house, at the back of which is a walk, agreeably winding, with a variety of shrubs intertwining and forming ... a fine canopy ... with nothing but singing and fragrance and seclusion: a delightful summer retreat; the sweetest lover's or poet's walk, perhaps, in the University.' The main lawn is now split by a bank, a surviving vestige of that ancient defensive moat, the King's Ditch, and dominated by a beech and a horse chestnut tree, both huge. Herbaceous borders are hemmed in with low box hedging. Beyond an arch in a high yew hedge lies an unexpected hidden garden of lawns and shrubs. A small rock garden is easily missed. The flowers of a formidable wisteria overhang the garden wall at the junction of Green Street and Sidney Street.

George Dyer was more measured about the gardens at Jesus – 'though they contain but little of shrubbery, they are, at least, the best fruit gardens in the university ... in the fellows' garden is a good proportion of flowers and plants, which, to assist the botanical student, are marked with their scientific names, according to the system of Linnaeus.'

At Emmanuel a surprisingly spacious garden features an ornamental pond once stocked with fish when the Dominican friary stood here. Now ducks hold sway and even have their own page on the college website. Wendy Taylor's statue 'A Jester' marks the site of a 16th-century tennis court. The majestic Oriental plane tree is more than two centuries old, grown from seeds gathered at Thermopylae of ancient fame. In the 1960s a Tudor-style knot-garden was created in New Court.

Pembroke's tranquil garden features rich herbaceous borders. Arthur Benson spoke of it as 'a beautiful, embowered, bird-haunted place'. The elegant oasis of Peterhouse is similarly tucked away behind the Fitzwilliam Museum. From the 1860s until the interwar years the area contained a deer park, whose inhabitants periodically provisioned the dons' table.

Henry James thought Trinity Hall's riverside retreat was 'the prettiest corner of the world ... narrow and crooked; it leans upon the river, from which a low parapet, all muffled in ivy, divides it; it has an ancient wall adorned with a thousand matted creepers on one side, and on the other a group of extraordinary horse-chestnuts. The trees are of prodigious size; they occupy half the garden'. The don showing him round agreed that it was 'the most beautiful *small* garden in Europe.'

The Fellows' Garden at Christ's College is famous for a mulberry tree traditionally associated with Milton and held to be the survivor of 1,000 Cambridge mulberries planted at the behest of James I as part of an ill-managed attempt to establish a native British silk industry. Unfortunately the King's mulberries were the kind silk-worms don't eat – *Morus nigra*, not *Morus alba*. (Jesus also has a sole survivor of this initiative, though there are none at Emmanuel, which also pandered to the royal whim.) The cypress trees at Christ's were raised from seeds gathered around the tomb of Shelley in Rome. (Unlike Milton, Shelley has no direct connection to Cambridge but went to University College, Oxford until they threw him out.) The nearby 18th-century plunge pool at Christ's is now more picturesque than inviting, perhaps because the water is third-hand, having come underground from Emmanuel, which takes it from the Botanic Garden. Christ's also has a memorial to C P Snow, of 'Two Cultures' fame.

The Fellows' Garden at Magdalene College includes a Victorian pets' cemetery. When Rudyard Kipling was made an Honorary Fellow in 1932 he wrote to his daughter that, apart from having free use of a Guest Room, 'my other privilege is to walk on the grass of the Quads and in the Fellows' Garden. Undergrads are crucified for doing this.' Kipling's poetic licence may be granted, but the 1958 edition of the Blue Guide made a similar point with equal succinctness – 'Cambridge lawns are sacred to the feet of resident Fellows.'

The poet A E Housman once wrote:

Loveliest of trees, the cherry now,
Is hung with bloom along the bough
And stands about its woodland ride
Wearing white for Eastertide.

Housman, an assiduous member of the Trinity College gardening committee, is appropriately commemorated by an avenue of cherries planted along the Backs.

Selwyn College gardens reflect the High Victorian delight in huge flowerbeds, a reaction against the 'natural' look of the previous century with its emphasis on trees and shrubs. Appropriately, the planting of one bed celebrates the college connection with New Zealand, for whose first bishop the college is named.

The Newnham College website, apparently without intending a pun, describes the development of its gardens as 'organic', by which it means that a plan devised by the eminent Gertrude Jekyll was not adopted, except for the notion of extensive herbaceous borders. The oak opposite Clough Hall was a gift from Prime Minister Gladstone (1809–98). Newnham's first principal, Anne Jemima Clough, promoted gardening to expose young ladies to fresh air and exercise – as well as valuing it as a provider of wholesome food. Clough's successor, 'Nora' Sidgwick was memorialised with a summer house in 1914. Unusually among Cambridge colleges, no grassed area of Newnham's 17 acres is out of bounds to undergraduates.

During both World Wars Cambridge college gardens were sacrificed to grow food rather than flowers. Blessed with 46 acres of grounds and conveniently near ample supplies of manure from the university farm, Girton set a praiseworthy example under Chrystabel Procter (1894–1982), then one of the few female head gardeners in Cambridge. The Fellows' Garden at Girton was created by one of its graduates, a doyenne of modern English gardeners, Penelope Hobhouse.

New gardens

Intriguingly for a university which habitually thinks in centuries, several of the most outstanding college gardens are essentially postwar creations. The Fellows' Garden at Clare, arguably the most consistently admired in Cambridge, was recreated by a college fellow, biologist Professor Nevill Willmer (1902–2001), whose landscape 'pictures' reflect his passions for plants, painting and optical science. Willmer's celebrated herbaceous borders demonstrate his theories about how human perceptions of colour change with changing light, blues becoming lighter at dusk, as yellows simultaneously deepen. The planting of white flowers only along the walk between Garret Hostel Lane and the old kitchen garden wall exaggerates its perceived length. A curving lawn running down to the Cam provides a perfect setting for garden parties and balls, and a sunken water garden makes an equally suitable backdrop for outdoor theatricals in summer. The lily pool enclosed on three sides by a clipped yew hedge was inspired by a garden at Pompeii. In front of Memorial Court stands a DNA double helix symbol, commemorating James Watson's link with the college. Fortunately for non-members, the gardens at Clare are among the most accessible, open daily from Easter until September.

The 13 acres of grounds at Robinson College skilfully stitch together 10 former gardens of surrounding Victorian and Edwardian properties, absorbed into the college fabric. Mature trees and an ornamental lake with a wooden bridge and elevated walkway are complemented by a croquet lawn, a purpose-built outdoor theatre and an outdoor teaching area. Shrubs, borders and waterways welcome pheasants, woodpeckers, kingfishers, grass snakes and freshwater mussels. Nicholas Chrimes interprets this creation as a nod to William Kent and Capability Brown, the fathers of English-style landscape gardening in which 'nature was both humoured and tweaked.'

Lucy Cavendish College features an Anglo-Saxon herb garden created in the 1980s by Lady Jane Renfrew, whose special field of archaeology was palaeoethnobotany and who sourced her selection from a 10th-century work by the Benedictine monk Aelfric. Woads and pimpernels and other plants from before the Norman Conquest flourish there, showing how the first English made medicines, perfumes and dyes and flavoured food.

At Murray Edwards College head gardener Jo Cobb has rejected the generally favoured 'country house' look in favour of 'non-traditional' planting schemes. The gardens are, however, geared to the university's very traditional calendar. Newcomers are welcomed at the beginning of the academic year in October by a blaze of bright colours, and graduates can expect their great day, 30 June – graduation day – to coincide, not at all by chance, with a peak of floral glory.

4

Rebellion and Restoration

Royalist Gown, Puritan Town

When civil war broke out in August 1642, Charles I, fleeing London, established his capital in Oxford, where many Cambridge men rallied to him. The university itself sent the King neither cash nor kind, but five Cambridge colleges did. From Queens' and Peterhouse more was sent by individuals than by the colleges as institutions, while Emmanuel's entire contribution came from its Master, Dr Richard Holdsworth (1590–1649), who was also the Vice-Chancellor.

Cambridge, whose own Member of Parliament, Oliver Cromwell (1599–1658), would become Parliament's supreme war leader, was deep in Puritan country and became the headquarters of the Eastern Association – an alliance of the five East Anglian counties which provided Parliament's core support. At Cromwell's direction Cambridge townsfolk were armed, and the city fortified with ditches. The Cam's wooden bridges were dismantled to tighten control over traffic, and the decayed castle was re-occupied and re-fortified. Colleges were ordered to quarter troops and had their property plundered under the blanket justification of 'sequestration'. King's College Chapel was used as a stable and barracks. The remains of charred chicken bones, cards and dice uncovered during alterations in the 1960s suggest that the soldiers of 'the godly' weren't worthy of the name in their off-duty hours.

Royalist heads of houses were dismissed, and some imprisoned – those of St John's, Jesus and Queens' were sent to the Tower of London. John Cosin (1594–1672), Master of Peterhouse, fled abroad. By 1643, 11 heads of colleges had been forced out. When the Commonwealth was established after the execution of the King in 1649 three more went for refusing to pledge allegiance to it. No fewer than seven new heads of houses were drawn from that Puritan stronghold, Emmanuel. By the time Parliament had completed its purge more than 200 fellows had gone, half the entire total.

Purging the ungodly meant not only persons but also premises. Usually the 'purification' of places of worship of 'Popish' practices, by removing altar rails and images, was done by churchwardens, or more destructively, by soldier zealots; but in Cambridge, uniquely, this was the work of a specific appointee, who, also uniquely, carefully recorded his activities relating to 'the utter demolishing, removing and taking away of all Monuments of Superstition and Idolatry'. A Suffolk farmer's son, William Dowsing (1596–1668), appointed Provost Marshal of the Eastern Association in August 1643, in December was ordered to 'cleanse' Suffolk and Cambridgeshire. Dowsing was at Cambridge from 20 December to 2 January, visiting 16 college chapels and 14 parish churches. St Mary the Less lost 60 images. St John's, Jesus and Christ's all lost statues of their sacred patrons which adorned their gatehouses. Dowsing's notes reveal that he believed his 'work' contributed directly to the victories of Parliament's armies. His elation evaporated after the war when, deeply disillusioned by divisions between the victors and the abuses perpetrated by the self-styled 'godly', Dowsing returned to rural obscurity.

Securely under Parliamentary control, Cambridge was spared the horrors of combat, although a Royalist incursion in August 1645, reaching nearby Huntingdon, provoked temporary panic and flight. Mostly, however, Cambridge suffered only the inevitable unpleasantness of a military occupation. The city's fortifications were dismantled by the winter of 1645 and the quartering of soldiers in colleges was finally discontinued in 1652.

There were even some positive developments. The completion in 1651 of the Denver Sluice was a landmark in the drainage of the Fens, opening up new areas for cultivation. For Cambridge, however, the downside was a lowering of the level of the Cam, necessitating the use of smaller boats, thus diminishing the town's role as an inland port. In 1653 the first public coach service to London was inaugurated from the Devil's Tavern, then on the present site of the Senate House. The journey usually took around seven hours in good weather.

John Evelyn, visiting Cambridge in 1654, was distinctly unimpressed – 'the whole town is situate in a low, dirty, unpleasant place, the streets ill-paved, the air thick and infected by the fens, nor are its churches (of which St Mary's is the best) anything considerable in compare to Oxford.' The library at King's was 'too narrow', St Catharine's 'a mean structure', its chapel 'meanly erected, as is the library'. The Schools were 'very despicable'. Evelyn's only praise was grudging – 'The Mercat place of Chambridg is very ample and remarkable for old Hobson's the pleasant Carrier's beneficence of a fountain' – or backhanded – 'Trinity College is said by some to be the fairest quadrangle of any university in Europe, but in truth is far inferior to that of Christ Church, in Oxford.'

Restoration

At Cambridge the Restoration of the *status quo ante* brought changes in both personnel and the appearance of the city. Bridges over the Cam were rebuilt and the landscaping of 'the Backs' was begun. In college chapels altar rails and organs were restored. St John's paid £11 for the statue of St John the Evangelist that still adorns its main entrance. Samuel Pepys, attending Sunday service at King's in July 1661, was greatly struck by the contrast with a decade before – 'the schollers in their surplices at the service with the organs – which is a strange sight to what it used in my time to be here'. The Restoration and its ideological reverberations brought some academic careers to an abrupt end and revived others. It did not, however, revive the appeal of the university as a whole. The average annual number of students matriculating in the early 1660s was 280; by 1700 it had fallen to 190. By 1750 it would be down to 150.

The last of the plague

The 'Great Plague' of 1665–6, famously the last to devastate London, eventually reached out as far as Cambridge. Between July 1665 and March 1666, 366 died in the city, 171 recorded as plague victims. A second outbreak (June 1666 – January 1667) was even worse, at least for the townsfolk – 'All the Colledges (God be praised) are and have continued without any Infection of the Plague'. Most of their residents, like the young Isaac Newton, fled their homes and took refuge in the countryside. The town, however, was devastated, with almost 600 dying at home and another 155 in the pesthouse. Mass graves on Midsummer Common received the corpses.

Casualty of conscience

The civil wars wrecked many academic careers; others were destroyed by the Restoration. John Ray (1627–1705) is now honoured for establishing 'the species' as the fundamental category for classifying nature. Posthumously hailed as a founding father of British botany and for establishing zoology as a systematic discipline, Ray enjoyed little security or reputation in his lifetime. The son of a village blacksmith and a herbalist, at Trinity Ray taught Greek and mathematics, mastered Hebrew and became an effective preacher. But his personal passion was for plants, which he collected and categorised on summer expeditions when released from his duties as junior dean and college steward. In 1660 Ray published his *Catalogus plantarum circa Cantabrigiam nascentium*, the first-ever comprehensive catalogue of the plants of an English locality, identifying 626 varieties found around Cambridge. Shortly afterwards, he, and a dozen other fellows, refused on grounds of conscience to take the oath of submission to the Restoration's religious settlement. Resigning his college position, Ray wrote ruefully 'I shall now cast myself upon Providence and good friends. Liberty is a sweet thing.' Freed from regular teaching, he undertook a three-year botanic odyssey from the Netherlands to Malta. For him this was the equivalent of Darwin's voyage round the world aboard HMS *Beagle*, an opportunity to collect data which would take years to digest. Cut off from Cambridge, Ray was at least recognised by election as a fellow of the newly-established Royal Society. In 1680 he settled in his Essex birthplace, Black Notley. Less than a day's ride from Cambridge, it was still, he felt, 'barren of wits.' He nevertheless produced a three-volume history of plants, plus major works on birds, fishes and insects and collected data on fossils, mining, proverbs and dialects.

Ray's bust, by L F Roubiliac (1705–62), is in the Wren Library at Trinity College. In 1942 a masterly appreciation, *John Ray: Naturalist,* was published by Charles Raven (1885–1964), Master of Christ's and Regius Professor of Divinity, himself a pioneer in the art of photographing birds in flight. Doubtless Raven felt a sympathy for Ray's career, wrecked on the rocks of principle; his own pacifism during World War Two and his pioneering support for the ordination of women cost him high office in the Church of England.

Not until 1724, more than 60 years after Ray's ejection, did Cambridge finally appoint its first Professor of Botany. Richard Bradley (1688–1732) was a prolific and popular horticultural writer, but knew neither Latin nor Greek, and failed to lecture or to create the botanic garden he had promised to get his professorship. He died before the creaky university administration could sack him. His successor, the polymath John Martyn (1699–1768), a devoted disciple of Ray, met so little encouragement that he gave up lecturing in 1735 – but hung onto the chair for his son, Thomas (1735–1825), who held it for 63 years, despite leaving Cambridge for good in 1798. It was just as bad in other disciplines. No Regius Professor of History between 1725 and 1773 ever gave a single lecture, and the learned preacher Dr Samuel Ogden (1716–78), Professor of Geology from 1764 to 1778, freely admitted his complete ignorance of the subject.

'Whose heart and soul were one'

Such place-bound time-servers contrast strikingly with the careers of alumni who remained devoted to learning and hazarded their lives in service to others. On the north wall of Christ's College Chapel, a monument dating to 1684 marks the joint grave of Sir John Finch (1626–82) and Sir Thomas Baines (1622–80). They met in 1649 and were inseparable thereafter, both qualifying as doctors at Padua and Cambridge and becoming Fellows Extraordinary of the College of Physicians. Finch became an early Fellow of the Royal Society, and Baines Professor of Music at Gresham College in London. Together they served as diplomats in Tuscany and at the court of the Ottoman Sultan, where Finch, after seven dogged years, won confirmation of English merchants' trading rights and where Baines died. Finch brought Baines's body back for burial, gave the funeral oration and himself died soon after. A long Latin inscription tells their story.

Self-made man

The archetypal Restoration professional, Samuel Pepys (1633–1703), son of a London tailor, became head of the biggest-spending government department, responsible for the nation's navy, which, under his energetic administration, more than doubled in size. If Britain was protected by 'wooden walls' for two centuries, it was Samuel Pepys who built them. He also became an MP, Master of Trinity House and, as President of the Royal Society, authorised the publication of Isaac Newton's *Principia*. Pepys was, in the words of fellow diarist, John Evelyn, a friend of 40 years, 'a very great cherisher of learned men', including Christopher Wren and John Dryden; but he is still best known for the most famous diary in English history, a racy romp through a turbulent decade, during which he survived London's last great plague and personally brought news of the Great Fire to King Charles II himself.

As an undergraduate at Magdalene, Pepys was once 'solemnly admonished' for being 'scandalously overserved with drink' but he also found time to learn shorthand from Shelton's *Tachygraphy*, published by Cambridge University Press. This later proved invaluable, not only for his famous *Diary* but for his role as a busy bureaucrat. Indeed, shorthand became an obsession, leading him to collect 32 textbooks and pamphlets on the subject. Pepys retained a lifelong affection for Magdalene, often passing through Cambridge en route to family property at Brampton in Huntingdonshire. In 1667, returning to show the sights to his wife, he was cheered to see 'at our College of Magdalene the posts new-painted'; but, on another visit, in May 1668, was greatly irritated when he 'lay very ill by reason of drunken scholars making a noise all night', although he cheered up after visiting the buttery where he 'drank my bellyful of their beer, which pleased me as the best I ever drank'.

Raised to eminence by industry and integrity, Pepys fell through the malice of enemies, even enduring a spell in the Tower; but his last 14 years were spent in tranquil retirement, meticulously ordering his superb collection of books, maps, papers and pamphlets. This numbered 2,903 volumes, housed in 12 bookcases, built by the Admiralty's own master carpenter. Dying childless, Pepys left his fortune and library to his nephew, upon whose death in 1726 it passed to Magdalene, where it remains intact. In 1677 Pepys had partly funded the new buildings, which, fittingly, now house the Pepys Library, an unforeseeable outcome which would doubtless have given him much satisfaction.

The celebrated diary, running to 1,250,000 words, in six bound volumes, was carefully preserved but not intended for publication, not least because it was written in coded shorthand with more confessional passages rendered into French, Latin, Greek or Spanish. Not until the successful publication of Evelyn's diary in 1818 were four years spent deciphering and transcribing Pepys's. Since its publication in 1825 Pepys's diary has established itself as 'the best bedside book in the English language', according to Sir Arthur Bryant. A portrait of Pepys, by Sir Peter Lely, is in the Pepysian library; another, by the prolific Sir Godfrey Kneller (1646–1723) (another friend!) is in Magdalene's dining hall.

Cantabrigia Illustrata

Born in Danzig and trained in Holland, the artist David Loggan (1634–92) arrived in England as a teenager. In 1669 he was appointed official engraver to the University of Oxford and in 1674 issued a work, with 12 plates, illustrating various academic costumes, followed in 1675 by a work with 40 plates, showing the architecture of the colleges. Loggan's treatment of Cambridge began in 1676 with his publication of Wren's designs for the new library at Trinity College. *Cantabrigia Illustrata*, a companion volume to the Oxford project, also took more than a decade and was probably published in 1690, the year in which Loggan was appointed engraver to the University of Cambridge and awarded £50 for his efforts.

Cantabrigia Illustrata contains a portrait of the Chancellor, Charles, Duke of Somerset; a plan of the city; two general views of Cambridge; a view of Eton (the feeder school to King's College) and 26 views of the colleges and public buildings. Packed with lively detail the volume indeed constitutes, in the words of a Victorian enthusiast, 'not merely a record of the architecture but of the life of the period.' Plate IX, for example, shows a grave being dug in the churchyard of Great St Mary's, the skull and bones of a previous occupant casually strewn nearby. Plate XXV gives a bird's-eye view over Christ's College, revealing collegiate self-sufficiency in the form of beehives, a dove-cote and an extensive orchard and herb garden. Plate XXIX, showing Trinity College, features the celebrated garden and apartments of Isaac Newton. More distant prospects feature hunters and harvesters, a reminder of the rustic rim which still defined the perimeters of the academic world.

Genius

> Nature, and Nature's Laws lay hid in night,
> God said, Let Newton be! And all was light.

Alexander Pope

Britain's £1 banknote, circulated from 1978 to 1988, bore a portrait of Sir Isaac Newton (1642–1727). Dressed with uncharacteristic formality in coat and wig, he sits, unsmiling, beneath a blossoming tree, on his knees an open book, with a diagram. Beside him, on a table, are a telescope and prism – tributes to his work in astronomy and optics. The banknote is dominated by an enlargement of the diagram, depicting the planets' orbits around the sun. Nowadays the £2 coin bears an enigmatic inscription around its edge, 'Standing on the Shoulders of Giants', an incomplete quotation from Newton – 'If I have seen further is it by standing on the shoulders of giants' – a valedictory reference to such illustrious predecessors as Copernicus, Galileo and Descartes. Tributes on the nation's currency are peculiarly appropriate because Newton was, in later life, Master of the Mint, and as such was responsible for introducing coins with milled edges to make counterfeiting and debasement much harder.

Born on Christmas Day, the posthumous son of a Lincolnshire farmer, Newton in youth showed versatility as a carpenter, bricklayer, metalworker and maker of ingenious models. Entering Trinity College as a good Latinist, he was as yet entirely ignorant of 'natural philosophy'. Despite his mother's splendid annual income of £700, Newton had to scrape by on £10 a year, working his way through college as a sizar, while devouring books on science. Within 10 years the first Lucasian Professor of Mathematics, Isaac Barrow (1630–77), gave up his seat in Newton's favour. The inscription on Barrow's statue (1853) in Trinity's ante-chapel, however, claims that he had 'a better title to that position because of his outstanding mathematical discoveries'. Charles II regarded Barrow, astronomer, preacher, wit and former Professor of Greek, as the outstanding scholar of the age and appointed him Master of Trinity.

Newton's early Cambridge career was interrupted by prolonged absence when plague emptied the university. Returning home, Newton formulated his basic notions of the differential and integral calculus and began experiments revealing that white light was in reality composed of the fusion of many colours. He also famously sat under an apple tree whose fruit, dropping – the tale varies – onto his head, hand or book, gave him his fundamental insight into the nature of gravity. In physics a 'newton' is the amount of force needed to move an object of one kilogram so that it accelerates at one metre per second. As a unit of weight a newton is equal to 100 grams – roughly a medium-sized apple. Newton spent 35 years at Trinity in rooms on E staircase, overlooking the Great Court and, on the street side, a small, walled garden set aside for his own exclusive use. The garden, to the right of the main college entrance, now features an apple tree, planted some half century ago, from a cutting taken from the original at Newton's Lincolnshire home. The variety, pleasingly named 'Flower of Kent', is not, apparently, very nice to eat.

In 1687 Newton published his magnum opus, the *Philosophiae Naturalis Principia Mathematica*. Newton's theories of gravitation and inertia and 'three laws of motion' appeared to contemporaries to provide an elegant and comprehensive explanation of the workings of the physical universe, from the movements of the heavens to the principles governing the physics of everyday life. The *Principia* immediately established Newton's reputation as a scholar of European standing and coincidentally made him a figure of consequence within the university at a crucial moment.

A fierce Protestant, Newton was one of the leaders of the Cambridge resistance to James II's efforts to interfere in university affairs. He was, in fact, on thin ice as a defender of orthodoxy, being a closet socinian – a denier of the doctrine of the Trinity – which was ironic for a professor at Trinity College. Elected MP for Cambridge, Newton spoke only once in Parliament, to ask for a window to be opened.

Newton was eventually persuaded to leave Cambridge for London. As Warden, then Master, of the Mint, Newton received a massive £2,000 a year. The appointment was supposed to be a sinecure in recognition of his scientific eminence but Newton threw himself into the work, masterminding a major recoinage and becoming the terror of London counterfeiters, many of whom he gleefully sent to the gallows. The most celebrated mathematician of the age, however, was so hopeless at simple arithmetic he had to have his accounts done for him. In 1705 Newton was knighted, the first scientist to receive this honour.

Absent-minded, antisocial and a vegetarian, Newton was fonder of pets than of people. (He is credited with inventing the cat-flap.) As President of the Royal Society he presided over its meetings like an unpredictable volcano, often dozing but sometimes tyrannising over lesser mortals. Famously quarrelsome, Newton fell out with his former collaborator Robert Hooke (1635–1703), with John Flamsteed (1646–1719), the Astronomer Royal, and even with Samuel Pepys. His most famous quarrel was a sustained vendetta with Leibniz (1646–1716) over which of them had invented calculus. Modern scholarship has established that Newton did first – but also that Leibniz did so, if later, quite independently.

Academically Newton's later life was, from the perspective of modern science, relatively barren. He spent some time elaborating editions of his earlier works, but even more on perfecting a chronology of the ancient world, dabbling with alchemy and obsessively pursuing the hidden meanings of the *Book of Daniel* – hence J M Keynes's summary of Newton as 'the last of the magicians'. Like Keynes, Newton dabbled in investments and lost £11,000 in the South Sea Bubble debacle of 1720. Like Keynes, however, he still died rich, indeed, very rich, leaving a fortune of more than £60,000.

Newton was buried in Westminster Abbey; his flamboyant monument, designed by William Kent (1685–1748) and executed by the Flemish master Peter Scheemakers (1691–1781), features terrestrial and celestial globes for his work as an astronomer and coins in reference to his role as Master of the Mint. It also has the dubious honour of featuring in Dan Brown's *The Da Vinci Code*. Voltaire (1694–1778), then in exile in London, attended Newton's funeral in person and subsequently popularised his work in French, making it accessible to a general European readership and establishing Newton as virtually the Father of the Enlightenment.

In an uncharacteristic outburst of modesty Newton referred to his career as that of 'a boy playing on the sea-shore ... while the great ocean of truth lay all undiscovered before me.'

Succeeding generations remained in awe of Newton's achievements. Trinity's tribute, in its ante-chapel, is a superb statue of 1755 by the French master Roubiliac, commissioned by Robert Smith (1689–1768), Master of Trinity (1742–68), as part of his campaign to assert the intellectual pre-eminence of the college. Referring to his work on optics, Newton is shown holding the prism he bought at Stourbridge Fair. The Latin inscription on the plinth is Lucretius's tribute to the philosopher Epicurus – *'Qui genus humanum ingenio superavit'* ('who surpassed the human race with his genius'). There is also a bust by Roubiliac in the Library and a stained-glass window by Giovanni Battista Cipriani (1727–85) which, with masterly disregard for chronology, shows Francis Bacon (1561–1626), dead before Newton was born, presenting Newton to George III (1738–1820), not born until after Newton died. A generation later it was Roubiliac's depiction that inspired Wordsworth's tribute, in *The Prelude*, to

Newton with his prism and silent face,
The marble index of a mind for ever
Voyaging through strange seas of thought, alone.

The Library at Trinity also possesses Newton's walking-stick, while his death mask is at King's. The computerised catalogue of the University Library is named after Newton, as is a pub at the top of Castle Hill. The Isaac Newton Institute for Mathematical Sciences was opened in purpose-built premises in 1992. Appropriately this also has its own offshoot of the apple tree at Woolsthorpe and the original maquette of the statue of Newton which stands outside the British Library in London.

Self-made man

While Newton was revolutionising the understanding of physics

throughout Europe, a foreign-born contemporary laid the foundations of chemistry in Cambridge. Born in Verona, Giovanni Vigani
(1650–1712) travelled widely from Spain to the Netherlands, studying mining, metallurgy and pharmacy, but never acquired any formal
qualifications. Settling in Cambridge around 1683, Vigani began
teaching on a purely private basis, attracting pupils by his growing
reputation and eventually developing links with Queens' and Trinity.
In 1703 the Senate recognised Vigani as the university's first Professor
of Chemistry, explicitly acknowledging his track record of 20 years'
teaching. Vigani's preference for systematic experimentation rather
than abstract theorising may be partly explained by the fact that he
never mastered English competently, despite having an English wife.
This did not, apparently, prevent him from telling 'a loose story about
a nun', which cost him the friendship of the ultra-prim Newton.

Self-help in science

Vagani was certainly known to William Stukeley (1687–1765), who
entered Corpus to study 'Physick' (medicine) and whose experience
shows how a scientific education might be haphazardly acquired at
that time. Armed with Ray's 'catalogus', Stukeley forayed into the
Cambridgeshire countryside 'simpling' (collecting medicinal herbs
to make 'simples' or home remedies), collecting fossils, butterflies and
frogs and stealing dogs and other animals for dissection. Stukeley also
benefited from the teaching of Dr Stephen Hales, FRS (1677–1761) a
Corpus don and distinguished botanist and physiologist, who introduced him to 'the doctrine of Optics & Telescopes & Microscopes
and some Chymical Experiments'. He also knew Dr Addenbrooke and
John Waller, later parson of Grantchester (d.1718), who performed
'Philosophical Experiments in Pneumatic Hydrostatis Engines and
instruments'. In 1706 Stukeley's tutor assigned him a college room as
a laboratory 'which had a very strange appearance ... the wall ... hung
round with Guts ... & all sorts of Chymical Implements'. By his own
admission Stukeley 'sometimes surprised the whole College with a

sudden explosion,' and claimed 'I cur'd a lad once of an ague with it by fright'. He also distilled his own hooch which 'I used to distribute ... with a plentiful hand to my Tutors'. Stukeley himself became a Fellow of the Royal Society, an early Freemason, a vicar and, as a founder of the Society of Antiquaries, put forward the entirely erroneous idea that Stonehenge was the work of Druids.

Wren

The late 17th century saw great advances in the arts as well as the sciences. The first project completed by England's greatest – and entirely self-taught – architect was the chapel of Pembroke College (1663–5), the gift of his uncle, Matthew Wren, Bishop of Ely. Though modest in scale, this was an architectural milestone as it was the first chapel at either university to be entirely without Gothic features – its design was derived from Sebastiano Serlio's *L'Architettura* (1537–51), an Italian treatise already more than a century old.

The son of the Dean of Windsor, Christopher Wren (1632–1723) was hailed by Evelyn as 'this miracle of youth' while still an undergraduate at Wadham College, Oxford, where he was a member of the scientific circle which became the Royal Society. Until he became Savilian Professor of Astronomy at Oxford at 29, Wren's interests ranged from medicine, mathematics and meteorology to hydraulics, ship-design and etching. From then onwards, architecture dominated Wren's life.

Wren's second major Cambridge project was a new chapel for Emmanuel College (1668–74), sponsored by a former Master and future Archbishop of Canterbury, William Sancroft (1617–93). The basic conception echoes the chapel at Peterhouse, where Wren's uncle, Bishop Matthew, had once been Master. Its most dominant feature is the central pedestal with a clock breaking through the pediment to support a jaunty cupola.

Wren's Cambridge masterpiece is the 150-foot-long library he built between 1676–90, without a fee, for Trinity College, establishing an entirely new standard for collegiate architecture in Cambridge and beyond. Derived from an unrealised plan for a combined Senate House and University Library, its upper, Ionic storey contains the actual library; the lower, Doric level being an arcade or stoa. To the onlooker the two seem of equal height, but to accommodate tall bookcases and long, light-giving windows, the upper floor is much higher, the difference cunningly but simply concealed by the solid upper sections of the cloister arches. Supplying a fourth side to complete Nevile's Court, the main façade of Wren's library is surmounted by four statues representing the academic disciplines of Divinity, Law, Physic and Mathematics, carved by the Danish sculptor, Caius Gabriel Cibber (1630–1700), for £80. The interior boasts exquisite limewood carvings (1691–3) of fruit, flowers and heraldic devices by the Anglo-Dutch master, Grinling Gibbons (1648–1721). Wren himself designed the library fittings, observing that 'the disposition of the shelves along the walls and breaking out from the walls must needs prove very convenient and graceful and the best way for the students will be to have a little square table in each cell, with two chairs', which he also designed. Trinity was thus the first library to have bookcases standing along the walls as well as at right angles to them. The rear façade of the library, greatly admired by visitors approaching the college from the Backs, is much plainer, because it was built when the Cam was a working waterway, not a landscape feature.

The treasures of Trinity Library now include a Gutenberg Bible, a Shakespeare First Folio, letters by Michael Faraday, David Livingstone, Anthony Trollope, George Eliot and Robert Louis Stevenson, Wittgenstein's notebooks and the original manuscript of A A Milne's *Winnie-the-Pooh*, not to mention Newton's own personal library.

Critical visitors

Between 1685 and 1703 the indefatigable Celia Fiennes, riding side saddle and often alone, visited every county in England, keeping a journal of her travels, eccentric in spelling but lively and opinionated.

Cambridge got the Fiennes treatment in 1697. Like Evelyn, she was less than bowled over – 'the Buildings are old and indifferent, the Streets mostly narrow'. Like Evelyn she compared Trinity unfavourably with Christ Church but she liked the river – 'they have fine stone bridges over it and gates that lead to fine walks' – and was very taken with Wren's Library and King's College Chapel.

Street-wise Ned Ward (1667–1731), who ran a London pub, poured on a full blast of metropolitan scorn:

> The Buildings in many parts of the Town were so little and so low, that they look'd more like Huts for Pigmies, than Houses for Men; and their very Shop-keepers seem'd to me to be so well-siz'd to their Habitations, that they appeared like so many Monkeys in their Diminutive Shops mimicking the Trade of London ... the Town .... in plain Terms is a Corporation of Ignorance, hem'd round with Arts and Sciences, a Nest of Fools, that dwell on the Superfluities of the Learned...

The German bibliophile Zacharias Conrad von Uffenbach (1683–1734) came to Cambridge in 1710 specifically to visit the libraries. His guide was the Italian Domenico Ferrari (1685–1744), who spoke to him in French, and 'told us of the state of this university, which is certainly very bad.' Scholarly but supercilious, Uffenbach thought much the same of most of the libraries. The University Library he found in 'utter confusion' and Emmanuel's the same, while at Magdalene 'all the books, with hardly one single exception, are entirely overgrown with mould'. At Peterhouse the library was housed in 'a poor room of moderate size ... The manuscripts ... were so buried in dust, that the librarian was forced to send for a towel, for me to wear as a pinafore, that I might not dirty myself too much.' Corpus Christi 'one of the ugliest colleges ... lying entirely among the houses' did, he conceded, have 'the choicest manuscripts of all' and the librarian of St John's was 'friendly and learned'. The high point was Wren's library at Trinity, which he praised as exceedingly handsome ... It could not be handsomer or more convenient ... very light, long and well lighted and also highly decorated ... no only is the floor inlaid with white and black marble, but also the cases are all of oak, with excellent and very artistic carvings. It is very neat, made like little closets – an excellent device because ... you can stow away many more books ... and it is good for those who study there as they are not put out by seeing others facing them ...

Cambridge itself the disgruntled German dismissed as 'no better than a village ... were it not for the many fine colleges it would be one of the sorriest places in the world.' He had come to England with the thought of settling, but disliked it so much, Oxford and Cambridge in particular, that he simply went back to Frankfurt.

Daniel Defoe (1660–1731) came through Cambridge in the course of gathering material for his *Tour through the Whole Island of Great Britain* (1724–6). A man of many incarnations – journalist, merchant, manufacturer, government spy – Defoe's take on Cambridge was that of a businessman and moralising Dissenter. Immediately grasping that 'the trade of the town very much depends' on the colleges and their residents, he saw that

this is the surest hold the university may be said to have of the townsmen and by which they secure the dependence of the town upon them, and consequently their submission ... 'tis to the honour of the university to say that the governors so well understand their office, and the governed their duty, that here is very little encouragement given to ... dancing, gaming, intriguing ...

A forceful fellow

Richard Bentley (1662–1742) would exhibit all the steely stubbornness expected from a Yorkshire yeoman. Arriving at Cambridge at just 14, Bentley became a classicist of distinction, bringing a new level of rigour to textual criticism and making determined efforts to reform the university's disordered press. In 1696 the press, traditionally run as a licensed commercial venture, came under the charge of university-appointed 'Curators', who supervised both the business and editorial aspects of its activities, even sharing personally in its financial risks. The press would later secure the services of the famed typographer John Baskerville (1706–75), whose majestic Folio Bible of 1763 proved a triumph of the printer's art – if also something of a commercial disaster.

As a preacher, Bentley dazzled congregations by invoking Newtonian thought in defence of orthodox Christian belief. A Fellow of the Royal Society at 30, Bentley became Royal Librarian and chaplain in Ordinary to William III (r.1689–1702) before becoming Master of Trinity and Vice-Chancellor in 1700. As Master he conducted a vendetta with the fellows of his college which, in the words of a contemporary, 'lasted a year longer than the Peloponnesian War'. Tyrannical in disposition, abusive in manner and high-handed in methods, Bentley nevertheless had a worthy aim in view, to make Trinity 'not only a great college but a miniature university in itself'. He did manage to establish a chemical laboratory and an astronomical observatory, and pioneered the introduction of written college examinations, but these were limited victories in a campaign against inertia and spite stretching over 38 years, and showed just how much effort over how long a period would be needed to rescue Cambridge from self-indulgent somnolence. A statue of Bentley can be seen on the outside of the chapel of St John's College, where he had been an undergraduate. Appropriately he stares across St John's Street at the Divinity School.

Sightless star

In 1710 William Whiston (1667–1752), Newton's successor, was sacked from the Lucasian Professorship of Mathematics for publishing a denial of the Trinity. His successor, Nicholas Saunderson

(1682–1739), had lost both eyes from smallpox as a baby but had nevertheless mastered Latin, Greek and French and was an accomplished flautist. Whiston brought him to Christ's to teach an informal class on Newtonian science. Appointed to Newton's chair on the express intervention of Queen Anne, Saunderson spent eight hours a day teaching and was elected a Fellow of the Royal Society in 1719. Saunderson was also acutely perceptive in dealing with individual students and dismissed the young Horace Walpole within a fortnight – 'Young man, it is cheating you to take your money: believe me, you can never learn these things: you have no capacity for them.' A two-volume edition of Saunderson's *Algebra* was published posthumously in 1740 by the University Press.

Stourbridge Fair

Stourbridge Fair was a commercial institution of national importance long after comparable gatherings had withered away and was almost certainly the inspiration for 'Vanity Fair' as depicted by John Bunyan (1628–88) in *The Pilgrim's Progress*. Daniel Defoe gave an enthusiastic account of it in the 1720s, especially impressed by its orderly arrangement as a half-mile square, divided into regular streets, with 'Rows' for sellers of books, brushes, trunks, cheeses, joinery and lathe-turned woodwork, and 'Hills' for the sale of fish, soap and tallow. He was even more impressed by what was on offer:

> ... scarce any trades are omitted, goldsmiths, toyshops, braziers, turners, milliners, haberdashers, hatters, mercers, drapers, pewterers, china-warehouses ... all trades that can be named in London, with coffee-houses, taverns, brandy-shops and eating houses innumerable.

Apart from London luxuries, like the celebrated prism Newton bought, there were also the specialities of particular cities, brassware from Birmingham, steelwares from Sheffield and stockings from

Leicester. At the heart of the fair was 'the Duddery', a square, a hundred yards along each side, for the sale of woollens, cottons, rugs, quilts, sacking, ticking, blankets and garments. The second most important trade was in hops – 'there is scarce any price fixed for hops in England, till they know how they sell at Sturbridge Fair' – the major dealers converging from Chelmsford in neighbouring Essex, from Canterbury and Maidstone in Kent and from Farnham in Surrey.

Defoe held Stourbridge to be 'not only the greatest in the whole nation but in the world', far outstripping the celebrated fairs at Leipzig, Frankfurt, Nuremburg and Augsburg. This claim he made, not on account of its size but its importance for face-to-face dealing:

… wholesale men from London and all parts of England …
transact their business wholly in their pocket-books … make up
their accounts, receive money chiefly in bills, and take orders:
These they say exceed by far the sales of goods actually brought to
the fair, and delivered in kind; it being frequent for the London
wholesale men to carry back orders from their dealers for £10,000
worth of goods a man … This especially respects those people who
deal in heavy goods, as wholesale grocers, salters, brasiers, iron-
merchants, wine-merchants …

The great exception was the trade in hops, moved in bulk. Scarcely any hops were cultivated north of the River Trent, so 'vast quantities' were taken back into Derbyshire, Yorkshire and Lancashire as a return freight on shipping used to bring down wool and textiles from those sheep-rearing and manufacturing counties. All because the Cam was still navigable – 'all heavy goods are brought even to the fair-field, by water carriage from London and other parts; first to the port of (King's) Lynn and then in barges up the Ouse, from the Ouse into the Cam, and so … to the very edge of the fair.'

The fairgoers' spending was a huge cash injection into the local economy. Cambridge, emptied by the university vacation, naturally welcomed lodgers but was quite inadequate to cope with the number of transients so that, as Defoe observed, 'all the towns around are full; nay, the very barns and stables are turned into inns ... to lodge the meaner sort of people'. And all had to be fed, so every morning countryfolk converged on the incomers with eggs, chickens, cheeses, butter and bread. And 'when the great hurry of wholesale businesses begins to be over, the gentry come in, from all parts of the county round ... for their diversion', spending freely at the booths of the goldsmiths and milliners and strewing loose change for the benefit of the 'puppet-shows, drolls, rope-dancers and the like'.

Defoe also saw, with surprise, that 'there are sometimes no less than fifty hackney coaches, which come from London, and ply night and morning to carry the people to and from Cambridge'. Defoe's sharp-eyed contemporary, Ned Ward, noted that the well-sprung hackney carriages also served another purpose. Observing of the fair's patrons that 'their pretence is coming down to meet their customers, though it's plain by their Loitering, they have little else to do but to Drink, Smoke and Whore and to help support the fair in its Ancient Custom of Debauchery', Ward recorded that the going rate for a strumpet and her client to hire a hackney for their transaction was one shilling and sixpence – hence the pointed title of his account of Stourbridge as *A Step to Stir-Bitch Fair*. The last event of all, following the closure of a horse fair, was a series of 'horse and foot-races, to divert the meaner sort of people only, for nothing considerable is offered ... Thus ends the whole fair and in less than a week there is scarce any sign left that there has been such a thing there'.

A century after Defoe saw it, Stourbridge Fair remained a major occasion for the sale of cheese, leatherwares, earthenwares, ironmongery, groceries, woollens and hops, only finally dying in the 1930s.

An embarrassment of riches

In 1709, when Cambridge was recognised as a copyright library with the right to receive a free copy of any book newly published in the kingdom, the university collection ran to some 15,693 books and 658 manuscripts. Shortly afterwards, in recognition of the University's conspicuous loyalty to the newly-established Hanoverian dynasty during the attempted Jacobite rising of 1715 (on behalf of the exiled Stuart 'Old Pretender'), 'James III', George I (r.1714–27) presented the library with 30,000 books, including the fabulous collection recently bequeathed to the Crown by Dr John Moore (1646–1714), Bishop of Ely. The collection included first editions of Palladio, Shakespeare and Newton and more than 40 volumes produced by the first English printer, William Caxton (c.1422–91). Ironically, Moore was no scholar but an Episcopal bully who plundered the libraries of his clergy to bolster his personal standing as a patron of learning. Oxford, by contrast, suspected of Jacobite sympathies, had its garrison reinforced.

George I's actions prompted a famous exchange of versified insults between the two ancient universities. Joseph Trapp (1679–1747), Oxford's first Professor of Poetry, fired the opening salvo:

> The King, observing with judicious eyes,
> The state of both his universities,
> To Oxford sent a troop of horse; and why?
> That learned body wanted loyalty;
> To Cambridge books he sent, as well discerning
> How much that loyal body wanted learning.

Sir William Browne (1692–1774), an eccentric but wealthy Society doctor, riposted on behalf of Cambridge:

> The King to Oxford sent a troop of horse,
> For Tories own no argument but force;
> With equal skill to Cambridge books he sent
> For Whigs admit no force but argument.

Not really as good, is it?

The royal windfall provoked discussion of an ambitious building plan, which was entrusted to James Gibbs (1682–1754). Best known for St Martin-in-the-Fields in London, Gibbs was the first British architect to have received professional training in Italy, under the eminent Carlo Fontana. For Cambridge, Gibbs proposed a major complex of library, printing press, senate house and other buildings to constitute a state-of-the-art administrative and ceremonial centre. In the end, only the Senate House was built (1722–30), the first university, as opposed to collegiate, building since the 15th century. Inside is a statue by John Michael Rysbrack (1694–1770) of Charles Seymour, sixth Duke of Somerset (1662–1748), Chancellor of the University for almost 60 years, memorably described as 'a well-meaning man of slender understanding'.

Apart from Gibbs's work, little of architectural note was accomplished in the half century after Wren. At Emmanuel the south range of First Court was rebuilt between 1719 and 1722, renamed Westmoreland Building and refaced with ashlar, as the Old Court at Pembroke had been in 1712 and Trinity Hall would be in 1728–42. Pevsner took this as evidence of a complete lack of appreciation for medieval architecture during this period, and of a preference for face-lifts over innovation or expansion.

The Fellows' Building at Peterhouse (1736) by gifted amateur architect Sir James Burrough, FSA (1691–1764), Master of Caius, is a notable exception to this generalisation. His Peterhouse project, for which he received £50 and a piece of plate, is praised by Pevsner as 'a building in the Palladian style purer than any other in Cambridge.' At Sidney Sussex Burrough was responsible for the bijou classical arch (1762) which now stands in the north-east corner of the garden but was once the main entrance to the college. He also designed the chapel (1763–9) at Clare College, which was completed by his protégé, James Essex.

Addenbrooke's

Dying in 1719, not yet 40, John Addenbrooke, MD, a Fellow of Catharine Hall, with a reputation for dabbling in necromancy, left

£4,500 'to erect and maintain a small physical hospital' for the benefit of Cambridge. Addenbrooke's Hospital, however, only finally came into being in 1766. Barring the infectious and the incurable, in its first year it treated 106 in-patients and 157 out-patients. Half the subscriptions for its maintenance came from college fellows, who thereby acquired the right to treatment. Local Cambridge stationer and bookbinder John Bowtell (1753–1813) bequeathed a further £7,000 to enlarge the hospital. An enthusiastic and expert bell-ringer, Bowtell also compiled a mammoth history of the town of Cambridge but failed to publish it.

Addenbrooke's hospital was rebuilt in 1864–5 by Sir Matthew Digby Wyatt (1820–77). By then it was being transformed from a merely local facility to a centre of excellence, thanks to two men, both eminent in their profession, the university and the town. Sir George Paget, FRS (1809–92), a physician at Addenbrooke's for 45 years, was responsible in 1842 for instituting bedside examinations as part of the medical degree, thereby establishing the UK's first regular clinical examinations. In the same year Sir George Humphrey, FRS (1820–96) became the youngest hospital surgeon in Britain. Humphrey was also the first surgeon successfully to remove a tumour from the male bladder and in 1866 established the *Journal of Anatomy and Physiology*. At 60 he also wrote an excellent guidebook to Cambridge.

LAND OF LOST CONTENT: A POETIC INTERLUDE

> The Cambridge poet of today is generally the Oxford Standard Author of tomorrow.
>
> Advertisement, Deighton Bell's bookshop, 1951

This boast is not without substance – consider Sir Thomas Wyatt (1503–42, St John's); Edmund Spenser (c.1552–99, Pembroke); Robert Herrick (1591–1674, St John's/Trinity Hall); Andrew Marvell (1621–78, Trinity Hall); John Dryden (1631–1700, Trinity); Matthew Prior (1664–1721, St John's); Christopher Smart (Pembroke); Christopher

Anstey (Trinity); Edward Fitzgerald (1809–83, Trinity); Siegfried Sassoon (Clare), Rupert Brooke (King's) and Ted Hughes (1930–98, Pembroke). Christopher Isherwood (1904–86, Corpus Christi) is not chiefly remembered as a poet but was sent down for answering Tripos questions in limericks and blank verse. And then there were these chaps ...

'Something understood'

Unrestrained in his flattery of royalty, would-be courtier George Herbert (1593–1633) of Trinity craved the post of University Orator, attained it and was hailed by James I as 'the jewel of the university'. Disillusioned by experience, however, Herbert resigned in 1627 to restore a decayed church in Huntingdonshire, become an exemplary country parson in Wiltshire and die of tuberculosis at 40. Herbert's poetry was all published posthumously, some in the form of typographical conceits, forerunners of 'concrete poetry', where the arrangement of the words conveys meaning. 'Easter-Wings', for instance, is laid out on the page as a butterfly – sideways on. Herbert's recurrent theme, the soul's attempt to engage with God as 'something understood', has given the title to a long-running BBC radio programme of reflective verse, music and prose. Lines composed by Herbert are engraved on the glass doors through which visitors enter Little St Mary's:

> A man that looks on glass, on it may stay his eye,
> Or if he pleaseth through it pass, and then the heaven espy.

'Fame is the spur'

Entering Cambridge at 16, shy, slightly built John Milton (1608–74) was soon nicknamed 'the Lady of Christ's' in compliment to his delicate looks and a fastidiousness which he regarded as 'a certain niceness of nature, an honest haughtiness' – not entirely unjustified for an accomplished organist and a better-than-average fencer, already competent in Latin, Greek, French and Italian and knowing some Hebrew. Milton studied diligently but was openly scornful of the surviving medieval tradition of scholastic disputation in which his personal tutor excelled – which may explain why, in 1626, Milton was briefly rusticated, and may even have been beaten. He returned to take his BA in 1629, the year in which he gave a foretaste of his talent with 'On the Morning of Christ's Nativity', a talent confirmed in 1631 with 'l'Allegro' and 'Il Penseroso'. By the time of his MA in 1632 Milton had renounced plans to enter the Church in favour of a literary career. He would become nationally notorious for writing a pamphlet advocating divorce and producing the classic defence of free speech, *Areopagitica*. He then became a man of great consequence under Cromwell as Secretary for Foreign Tongues, before blindness and obscurity provided the discomforting context for his masterpiece, *Paradise Lost*.

Gray's anonymity

'Far from the madding crowd', 'destiny obscure', 'useful toil' – originally neither book nor film titles but all phrases first turned by Thomas Gray (1716–71) in his best-known work, *Elegy Written in a Country Churchyard,* one of the most anthologised of English poems. The *Elegy* speaks also of 'the short and simple annals of the poor' and 'some mute inglorious Milton' and warns that:

> Full many a flower is born to blush unseen,
> And waste its sweetness on the desert air.

Son of a City of London scrivener (violently abusive) and a milliner (long suffering), Gray was the only survivor of 12 children. Despite a humble background, he went to Eton and Cambridge, where he had family connections. Enrolled at Peterhouse, Gray pursued his own intellectual interests, rather than the prescribed ones, leaving, without a degree, to accompany Horace Walpole (1717–97), son of Prime Minister Sir Robert Walpole (1676–1745), on a European Grand

Tour. Gray proved an unusually conscientious 'Tourist', making careful, detailed notes on churches, antiquities and works of art. While Gray's mother retired, doubtless gratefully, to rural seclusion in Buckinghamshire, Gray returned to Peterhouse. Ostensibly studying to follow his father into the legal profession, he actually devoted himself to Greek literature. Professing to dislike the university, Gray was reconciled to Cambridge by its libraries, its cheapness and its indifference – 'I have a sort of reluctance to leave Cambridge, unamiable as it may seem; 'tis true Cambridge is very ugly, she is very dirty & very dull; but I'm like a cabbage, where I'm stuck I love to grow.'

Gray's celebrated *Elegy* was crafted over eight years. Finally published in 1751, it went through four editions in two months. Gray let the publisher take all the profits, receiving not a penny for the poem that made him instantly famous.

Reclusive and melancholic, Gray harboured a morbid fear of fire. When he had a rope ladder installed in his room, however, the temptation to practical jokers proved irresistible and he was startled awake by mischievous cries of 'Fire!' The college dismissed the incident as trivial but Gray left Peterhouse for good and crossed the road to Pembroke.

A year later Gray declined the post of Poet Laureate, despite assurances that he would never have to compose anything. In the same year, 1756, Gray's *The Progress of Poesy* and *The Bard* became the first works from the private printing press set up by Horace Walpole at his neo-Gothic *palazzo* at Strawberry Hill, Twickenham. The first was an essay towards a never completed history of English literature. The second was inspired by the Cambridge concerts given in 1755 by a blind Welsh harpist.

In 1759, just before his daring night cliff climb to assault the French stronghold of Quebec, General James Wolfe (1727–59) read a sixpenny copy of the *Elegy*, a parting gift from his fiancée, and told his (doubtless startled) comrades that he would rather have composed the poem than take the city. Fate having decreed otherwise, Wolfe took Quebec the next day – ensuring that henceforth Canada would be British, not French – and was killed in the hour of victory. In his copy of the *Elegy*, now in the archives of the University of Toronto, Wolfe had underlined Gray's admonition that 'The paths of glory lead but to the grave'.

Sparse in his poetic output, Gray devoted himself to self-indulgent pastimes, ranging from botany and heraldry to the harpsichord and the mastery of Italian, Icelandic and Welsh. He travelled widely throughout Britain, writing appreciatively of its natural beauties and lauding the Lake District a full generation before Wordsworth, inadvertently staking a claim to be the first of 'the Romantics'.

In 1768 the Professor of History and Modern Languages broke his neck falling from his horse while coming home from a dinner drunk. Three days later Gray was appointed to replace him. As the duties were non-existent, sightseers were advised to seek him out, not in the lecture hall, but at the Rainbow coffee-house. Gray died three years later and was buried in the same vault as his mother at Stoke Poges, the country churchyard which probably inspired his most famous literary legacy, although it may have been St Lawrence's, Upton, which has now been swallowed up by Slough. A full century after Gray's death the fund launched in his memory by friends financed a major rebuilding programme at Pembroke.

Romantic reactions

The Lake District, with which he is indelibly associated, provided the true education of William Wordsworth (1770–1850), but the poet's Cambridge years were still remembered with fondness in his autobiographical masterpiece *The Prelude*. In Book III he described the transformation which overcame him in the whirlwind days after his arrival:

Questions, directions, counsel and advice
Flow'd in upon me from all sides, fresh day
Of pride and pleasure! To myself I seem'd
A man of business and expense, and went

From shop to shop about my own affairs,
To Tutors or to Tailors, as befell,
From street to street with loose and careless heart.

I was the Dreamer, they the Dream; I roam'd
Delighted, through the motley spectacle:
Gowns grave or gaudy, Doctors, Students, Streets,
Lamps, Gateways, Flocks of Churches, Courts and Towers:
Strange transformation for a mountain Youth,
A northern Villager. As if by word
Of magic or some Fairy's power, at once
Behold me rich in monies, and attir'd
In splendid clothes ...

Arriving at St John's in 1787, Wordsworth occupied rooms ('a nook obscure') above the college kitchens and thrived on pedagogic neglect, learning Italian, French and Spanish, filling his idle hours with riding and sailing and making a sentimental pilgrimage to Milton's rooms at Christ's, where he got drunk toasting to the poet's memory but still made it back in time for chapel. He also took half of his final year off to tour revolutionary France and dip into Switzerland and Italy, but managed to bag a BA without honours.

The poet's scholarly youngest brother Christopher Wordsworth (1774–1846), by contrast, was appointed Master of Trinity in 1820 and served twice as Vice-Chancellor. As Master he arranged for New Court to be built as extra undergraduate accommodation and tried to raise academic standards by founding new college prizes, but his pettifogging enforcement of college regulations, especially chapel attendance, roused opposition which blocked further efforts at reform.

Coming up to Jesus in 1791, Samuel Taylor Coleridge (1772–1834) was depressed by 'the quiet ugliness of Cambridge' and the 'sixteen colleges that look like workhouses' and disgusted by having to attend chapel twice daily on pain of a two-pence fine. This led him to become, as he confessed, 'remarkably religious upon an economical plan.' A promising career in Classics foundered as Coleridge became diverted by French revolutionary politics, a failed love affair, debts and heavy drinking. He dropped out to enlist in the 15th Light Dragoons under the alias of Silas Tomkyn Comberbache. His brothers used an insanity clause in King's Regulations to buy him out, but despite returning to college, he left without a degree. Realising later that the college had treated him very leniently, Coleridge retained a lifelong affection for Cambridge.

As an aristocrat, Lord Byron (1788–1824) was under no pressure to study when he came up to Trinity in 1805, which was fortunate as he had absolutely no intention of doing so. He informed his mother that 'the mode of going on does not suit my constitution, improvement at an English University to a Man of Rank is you know impossible, and the very Idea ridiculous.' Byron later informed his tutor in writing that 'I certainly do not feel that predilection for Mathematics, which may pervade the Inclinations of men destined for a clerical or collegiate Life … To bewilder myself in the mazes of Metaphysics, is not my object'. As for his recurrent disappearances back to London – 'I have other Reasons for not residing at Cambridge, I dislike it', and, to clinch the matter, 'I was originally intended for Oxford'.

Lame since birth, Byron asserted his manliness by reckless riding and ferocious boxing. Above all he excelled at swimming, where his powerful upper physique offset his disability. Almost a century after the poet's death, another poet, Rupert Brooke, paid tribute to his prowess and the name of Byron's Pool at Grantchester:

> Still in the dawnlit waters cool
> His ghostly Lordship swims his pool,
> And tries the strokes, essays the tricks,
> Long learnt on Hellespont, or Styx.

Learning that college statutes forbade keeping dogs, Byron exploited their silence on other species and kept a bear. As might be expected, he accumulated massive debts to tradesmen. His *initial* order of drink on arrival consisted of '4 Dozen of Wine, Port – Sherry – Claret &

Madeira, one Dozen of Each.' In his first four months he also ran up college bills of £231 – about the annual stipend of a country vicar.

In the summer of 1807 Byron explained to a friend that he was delaying his end of term departure to fit in '3 Oratorios, 2 concerts, a fair, a boxing match & a Ball.' Appropriately, his first collection of verse, published that year, appeared under the title *Hours of Idleness.* 'Thoughts Suggested by a College Examination' gave the dons a well-aimed kicking:

> Where on Cam's sedgy banks supine they lie,
> Unknown, unhonour'd live, unwept for die:
> Dull as the pictures which adorn their halls,
> They think all learning fix'd within their walls:
> In manners rude, in foolish forms precise,
> All modern arts affecting to despise;
> Yet prizing Bentley's, Brunck's or Porson's note,
> More than the verse on which the critic wrote:
> Vain as their honours, heavy as their ale,
> Sad as their wit, and tedious as their tale.

Byron determined to return, however, for another year on the grounds that his College rooms were 'finished in great Style'. In 'Hints from Horace' (1810) he later sketched the undergraduate life with indulgent cynicism:

> Fines, tutors, tasks, conventions threat in vain,
> Before hounds, hunters and Newmarket plain.
> Rough with his elders, with his equals rash,
> Civil to sharpers, prodigal of cash;
> Folled, pillaged, dunned, he wastes his term away,
> And unexpelled, perhaps retires MA

After Byron's death fighting for Greek independence, his admirers commissioned a statue from the Danish sculptor Bertel Thorvaldsen

(1770–1844). Carved in Rome in 1831, it was rejected by its intended recipient, Westminster Abbey, on account of the poet's scandalous personal life. Trinity College finally accepted it for the Wren Library in 1845. The poet is shown holding a copy of *Childe Harold*, following the publication of which he 'awoke and found myself famous'.

In memoriam

Alfred Tennyson (1809–92) initially found Trinity a bore – 'the country is so disgustingly level, the revelry of the place so monotonous, the studies of the University so uninteresting'. Already a published poet, he nevertheless found Cambridge a liberation from Lincolnshire, and in Arthur Hallam (1811–33), the son of an eminent historian, found a friend who was 'as near perfection as mortal man could be'. Recognising Tennyson's gifts, Hallam introduced him to the 'Apostles', toured the Pyrenees and Rhine with him and became engaged to his sister, Emily. Tennyson meanwhile won the Chancellor's Prize for Heroic Verse by recycling a poem about Armageddon to fit the set subject of *Timbuctoo*. Left responsible for a large family following the death of his father, the poet was then devastated by the sudden death of Hallam, who forever remained a haunting presence in his mental life.

Tennyson then endured a decade blighted by financial catastrophe and a thwarted engagement to emerge as the nation's greatest living poet, his living secured by the grant of a Civil List pension. In 1850, *In Memoriam*, a long, complex, elegiac tribute to Hallam, crafted over the course of 17 years, appeared anonymously; but no one doubted its authorship. Within the year Tennyson was at last married and created Poet Laureate. The poem, greatly admired by Prince Albert, became Victoria's greatest consolation following her husband's early death. In 1869 Trinity made Tennyson an Honorary Fellow. The 1909 statue of Tennyson in the ante-chapel at Trinity is the work of the eminent Hamo Thornycroft, RA (1850–1925); his name is near the carved laurel wreaths, which also contain Tennyson's clay pipe – a supposed reference to the then Master, Henry Montagu Butler, who hated smoking. As the plinth proclaims (in Latin), the statue was the gift of a Trinity Man, Harry Yates Thompson (1838–1928), sometime editor of *The Pall Mall Gazette*, a pre-eminent collector of medieval manuscripts, whose many other gifts included a library for Newnham College and, in the Fitzwilliam Museum, the illuminated masterpiece known as the 'Metz Pontifical'.

More than a Shropshire lad

A star student at Oxford who failed his degree, A E Housman (1859–1936) worked as a clerk in the Patent Office until in 1892 he was offered the Professorship of Latin at University College, London. In 1896 Housman published, at his own expense, his best-known work, an evocation of an English Arcadia in language of sublime simplicity, which has never been out of print since.

Into my heart an air that kills,
   From yon far country blows
What are those blue remembered hills
   What spires, what farms are those?

That is the land of lost content
   I see it shining plain
The happy highway where I went
   And cannot come again.

A slim volume of 63 poems, easily carried in a pocket or knapsack, *A Shropshire Lad*, after an indifferent reception, sold steadily, attaining its peak of popularity during World War One, when many soldiers found it variously a refuge, a solace and an inspiration.

Housman came to Cambridge in 1911 as Professor of Latin and a Fellow of Trinity, and stayed until his death. Fundamentally uninterested in teaching, he yet quivered with emotion when reading Latin poetry aloud. An exacting textual scholar, he devoted his *magnum opus* to a five-volume definitive edition (1902–30) of the *Astronomia* of the obscure Manilius, a verse rendering of the mathematics of Roman astronomical knowledge.

Housman regarded his own poetry as a product of instinct rather than intellect, once famously describing a poem as 'a morbid secretion, like the pearl in an oyster', provoking F R Leavis to complain that this pronouncement had set back literary criticism by a decade. 'Shropshire' to Housman was an idea, not a place, and criticisms of topographical 'errors' in his poems simply proved that the reader had missed their point. The poet was, in any case, not a Shropshire village boy, having been brought up in the industrial town of Bromsgrove in Worcestershire.

Homosexual, reclusive and acerbic, Housman once told his publisher to reject a proposed interview on the grounds that 'the wish to include a glimpse of my personality in a literary article is low, unworthy and American ... some men are more interesting than their book ... my book is more interesting than its man.' Housman nevertheless found compensation in gardens and in the sybaritic side of life at Trinity, once pronouncing playfully that 'Malt does more than Milton can, To justify God's ways to man.'

5

Unwillingly to School

In 1748, Thomas Pelham-Holles, Duke of Newcastle (1693–1768) became Chancellor of the University. At Clare Hall he had 'acquired a certain tincture of the classics' but not bothered to graduate. A career politician, he was pompous and dithering, but also devout, genial and, by the standards of the day, honest, ending half a century of public life £300,000 the poorer. He was also astute enough to impose new disciplinary regulations in 1750 to fend off the threat of outside intervention which hung over Oxford, still tainted by Jacobitism. Cambridge undergraduates were accordingly banned from coffee-houses, tennis courts and cricket grounds in the mornings, subjected to an 11pm curfew in the evenings and prohibited from leaving town without permission. Newcastle also founded medals for distinction in the Classical Tripos and even visited the university regularly.

Having a powerful politician as Chancellor was good news for dons angling for appointments in the state-controlled Church of England. As university historian Elizabeth Leedham-Green observes, ambitious dons needed to declare their allegiance, Whig or Tory, early and often; politicking 'absorbed a vast amount of time and energy and often displayed organisational skills rarely exhibited within the university.' 'University politics' had nothing to do with what the university was *for*, much less effecting – God forbid! – change; it was all about place and position – from country curacies and college fellowships to university offices, college headships and the university's seats in Parliament. Administering college properties was the next priority, learning coming a very poor third. Some fellows served on the university 'syndicates' (committees) which controlled the Press, the Library and the Botanic Gardens, or busied themselves organising ceremonial occasions, supervising building works or raising funds for new projects.

Teaching was something lesser mortals did, Cambridge being awash with private tutors who gave intensive coaching to undergraduates aiming to excel in the university examinations, which consisted almost entirely of mathematics, with a dash of moral philosophy. Classics tutors catered for students aiming at prestigious university or college prizes for compositions in Latin or Greek. Still others taught polite accomplishments, such as French or Italian, music, watercolour painting, fencing, or more abstruse specialisms, like Hebrew. The remarkable William Hopkins (1793–1866), a failed farmer who didn't even enter Peterhouse as an undergraduate until he was 30, still produced some 200 top-rank mathematicians, including half a dozen professors, notably James Clerk Maxwell. Hopkins also had a parallel career as a geologist, applying mathematical techniques to the discipline and becoming President of the Geological Society.

The university broadened the scope of its instruction haphazardly as new chairs were established in Geometry (1749), Divinity (1777) 'Natural Experimental Philosophy' (1783, with special reference to gout!) and Mineralogy (1808). An undergraduate who genuinely wanted a well-rounded education could, by combining the resources of his personal tutor, college library, university lectures and private cramming, get a good grounding in classics, philosophy (moral and political), natural history, medicine and theology, as well as dabbling with a little science. For anyone wanting a *really* first-class education there was always Edinburgh and, for cultural polishing, the Grand Tour, until the war with revolutionary France in 1793 stopped that for a generation.

Undergraduate stars aspired to election as fellows of colleges or to well-paid livings as country vicars, hoping to ascend the Church hierarchy to the glory of a bishopric. Either way, most hoped to trade youthful days of strenuous labour for a life of gentlemanly ease. Unfortunately many fellowships were insufficiently paid for their holders to enjoy the lifestyle of their often wealthy students. Some dons supplemented their incomes by teaching. Those with a legal qualification could find profitable work in London's courts. Fellows of Trinity Hall effectively controlled the peculiar institution known as Doctors' Commons, which administered canon and civil law, rather than English common law, in respect of ecclesiastical and Admiralty cases and disputes involving international arbitration. Medical doctors could profit from private practice while also holding a chair. Charles Collignon (1725–85), himself 'a walking skeleton', was Professor of Anatomy at just 28, holding the post until his death. Like most medics, he bought corpses for dissection without enquiring too closely where they came from. In 1768, while friends watched him at work – 'one of them uncovered the face of the dead man and recognised it as that of Laurence Sterne, whom he had known'. The celebrated author of *Tristram Shandy*, buried in London two days previously, had been immediately disinterred by 'resurrectionists'. Undeterred, Collignon simply carried on.

Richard Watson (1737–1816) pursued a spectacular career of dazzling opportunism. A Trinity sizar, he performed brilliantly in examinations to become a fellow. In 1764 he was 'unanimously elected by the Senate, assembled in full congregation, Professor of Chemistry ... I knew nothing of Chemistry, had never read a syllable on the subject; nor seen a single experiment in it; but I was tired with mathematics ... I buried myself as it were in my laboratory' – which he blew up – and 14 months later gave his first course of lectures 'to a very full audience'. In 1771 the Regius Professor of Divinity died – 'This Professorship ... had long been the secret object of my ambition ... I immediately applied myself with great eagerness to the study of divinity.' Watson got the chair and became a noted Biblical scholar. In 1781, as an afterthought, he published his *Chemical Essays*, which went through seven editions by 1800. In 1787 Watson advised the government on a new way to make gunpowder, which saved it £100,000 a year. In that same year he was promoted from Bishop of Llandaff to Bishop of Carlisle.

'The ingenious Mr Essex'

Born in Cambridge, James Essex (1722–84) was the son of the master joiner who made the windows in the Senate House. Essex trained under Sir James Burrough and, like him, was much employed in altering existing buildings, notably covering brick facades in stone to give them a more 'classical' look, as at Christ's First Court (1758–69) and on the south side of St John's First Court. Essex's major works include the Ramsden Building on the east side of St Catharine's Principal Court, the north and south ranges of Nevile's Court at Trinity (1758), the west range at Queens' (1760), the stone bridge at Trinity (1764–5), the imposing west front at Emmanuel (1769–75) and the New Chapel at Sidney Sussex (1776–82). Essex also built (1749–50) the much-photographed 'Mathematical Bridge' at Queens'. Constructed with wooden pegs, rather than nails, it was designed by an undergraduate, William Etheridge (1709–76), who had visited China, which may have been its inspiration. Etheridge got £21 for his design. Essex's fee was £160. The bridge was rebuilt in 1867 and again in 1902.

Essex's civic projects include the rebuilding in stone of Magdalene Bridge (1754) and the rebuilding of the Guildhall (1784). He also undertook the skilful preservation of the fine early-Tudor roof of Great St Mary's and made extensive alterations at Ely and Lincoln cathedrals. Elected a Fellow of the Society of Antiquaries, Essex was an early enthusiast for the then despised Gothic style of architecture. He planned a history of King's College Chapel and worked for many years on a history of ecclesiastical architecture. Although neither was published, Essex has been hailed as 'the earliest architectural historian in the modern sense of the word.' He lies at St Botolph's, with a memorial tablet in the north aisle of the church.

The competence and energy of a James Essex could, however, still be trumped by the power of a personal connection, and the commission for a new library block (1754–8) to match Gibbs's Senate House went to an outsider, Stephen Wright (d.1780), thanks to the intervention of the Duke of Newcastle as Chancellor of the university. A pupil of the versatile William Kent, Wright owed his entire career to Newcastle's patronage, the Library being his crowning achievement, praised by Pevsner for its 'unusual daintiness and delicacy'.

A Cambridge character

In 1752 John Nicholson married Anne, the only child of Robert Watts, proprietor of a local circulating library. When Watts died the same year Nicholson took over and proved himself 'indefatigable in the pursuit of business', doing the rounds of each college, room by room. Known as 'Maps' by the sales cry with which he announced himself, in practice he got most of his income from loaning out textbooks. Nicholson was held in special affection by poor students who had to cope with financial pressures and the humiliations these often involved. The business he built up was carried on by two more generations of John Nicholsons until 1822. A celebrated portrait of 'Maps' Nicholson, laden with hefty volumes, was painted by Philip Reinagle (1749–1833) and hangs in the University Library. The likeness was so well regarded in Cambridge that engraved prints of the portrait were sold to raise money for Addenbrooke's Hospital. Nicholson is buried at St Edmund's.

Industry and idleness

For 18th-century undergraduates, studying was optional. Tutors habitually classified their charges as 'hard-reading', 'reading' and 'non-reading'. Some worked and subsequently made good. Many did not, and subsequently made good.

Too delicate for school, William Pitt the Younger (1759–1806) entered Pembroke at 14 with a 'strong desire ... to acquire useful knowledge.' A contemporary noted that 'he never seemed to learn, but merely to recollect'. Diligent and secluded, Pitt occupied the rooms at the Hall end of the first floor of Hitcham Building, formerly belonging to Thomas Gray. As the son of an aristocrat he became Master of Arts without the indignity of an examination, although he later claimed to have read Adam Smith's *The Wealth of Nations* from cover to cover when it was published in 1776.

Pitt stayed on in Cambridge to come last in the election for the university seat in 1780. Shortly afterwards the future scourge of corruption was nominated for a corruptly controlled seat, entered the Commons at 21, and made a stunning first speech. Pitt became Chancellor of the Exchequer at 23 and Prime Minister at 24, the youngest in the history of Britain, before or since. He also served as University Member for Cambridge.

Unfortunately Pitt's Pembroke years gave him a taste for port, medically prescribed to strengthen his constitution. He drove and drank himself to death in the service of his country, providing unyielding leadership in the titanic struggle against Napoleon. Allegedly killed by the news of Napoleon's smashing victory at Austerlitz, Pitt's dying words are variously reported as 'Oh! How I leave/love my country!' or 'I think I could eat one of Bellamy's pork pies.'

Three days after Pitt's death a Cambridge meeting resolved to collect funds for a statue. Committees set up in London and Cambridge raised £17,400. The handsome marble statue by Joseph Nollekens (1737–1823), installed in the Senate House in 1812 for £3,000, was modelled on a death mask taken by the sculptor, which doubtless accounts for its lack of animation. In 1813 £1,000 from the Cambridge fund established Pitt Scholarships in Classical Learning.

The bronze statue of Pitt (costing £3,500) by Sir Richard Westmacott (1775–1856), clad in a Roman toga to symbolise his eloquence and patriotism, was originally erected in 1819 in the National Debt Office in London as a tribute to the statesman's wizardry in managing the nation's finances, and not as an ironic comment on his own personal affairs, as he died £40,000 in debt. Bombed out in the Blitz, the statue finally found a resting-place in 1969 outside the library of Pembroke College.

A surplus from the London fund was put towards the erection in 1821–33 of the Pitt Building on Trumpington Street for the University Press. Coupled with the early adoption of the stereotype printing process, these purpose-built premises enabled the Press to cash in on the massive demand for Bibles stimulated by the Evangelical Revival of the early 19th century, the growth in attendance at church-based schools and the consequent growth in literacy and the global spread of Christian missionary efforts. J W Parker, Printer from 1836–54, installed steam-powered presses, facilitating the mass production of standard educational texts by Cambridge authors.

Prodigies

Thomas Young (1773–1829) could read at two, had tackled 10 languages by 16 and at 21 was elected Fellow of the Royal Society for a paper on astigmatism and colour blindness. Having studied at 'Bart's', Edinburgh and Gottingen and qualified as a doctor, 'Phenomenon Young' entered Emmanuel at 24 and stayed on even after inheriting £10,000 and a London mansion. Subsequently an expert on gas lighting, shipbuilding, tides, weights and measures and life insurance, Young also made the decisive breakthrough in deciphering the hieroglyphics of the Rosetta Stone by demonstrating that they stood for sounds, not concepts. None of which had much to do with Cambridge, but Young's time at the university wasn't entirely wasted – ripples on the Emmanuel College duck-pond are supposed to have inspired him to formulate his wave theory of light.

A child prodigy whose parents skilfully kept him from knowing it, Thomas Babington Macaulay (1800–59) began writing history at seven and claimed he could recite *Paradise Lost* entirely from memory. At Trinity he won prizes for Latin declamation and an original poem in English (twice). Mathematics, however, was sheer torture – 'Oh for words to express my abomination of that science', which required him to 'get a headache daily without acquiring one practical truth or beautiful image in return.' (He was also troubled by arithmetic, claiming to be cheated by his tutor, tailor and wine-dealer). Failing at mathematics, Macaulay was denied an honours degree and entry to the most prestigious university prizes; but at the third attempt he became a fellow, later declaring that 'of all the titles which I have a right to add to my name that of late Fellow of Trinity is the one of which I am proudest'. An MP at 30, twice a Cabinet Minister, and the author of position papers which framed the educational and legal systems of India for decades, Macaulay won fame with a *History of England,* which trumpeted that it was 'emphatically the history of progress'. The *History* rivalled Dickens and Scott as an international bestseller, was translated into every major European language plus Czech, Polish, Russian and Farsi and gained Macaulay a peerage. It has never been out of print. The third volume brought Macaulay a royalty cheque for £20,000; the publisher kept a copy as an historical curiosity.

Offered the Professorship of Modern History at Cambridge, Macaulay sensibly declined it because it would interfere with his historical writing. His last honour was to be made High Steward of Cambridge. The inscription on Thomas Woolner's 1868 statue of Macaulay in the ante-chapel of Trinity hails him as 'the first to write history in such a way that truth might be read with more pleasure than fiction.' Lord Acton regarded much of Macaulay's cocksure triumphalism as little better than fiction, but could not withhold admiration. Condemning Macaulay as 'base, contemptible and odious', Acton paradoxically hailed him as 'the greatest of all writers and masters'.

Slackers

Flunking medicine at Edinburgh, Charles Darwin (1809–82) came to Christ's in 1827 to become an Anglican clergyman, but indulged a boyish mania for collecting beetles while accompanying Henslow, the

Professor of Botany, on his field excursions. Henslow helped Darwin overcome his distaste for geology and was directly responsible for his selection to accompany the voyage of HMS *Beagle*, thus changing the course of Darwin's life and the history of the world. A modest blue plaque, fixed above the entrance to Boots the Chemist on Sidney Street, marks the site of Darwin's former lodgings. A postgraduate college commemorates his name. A groundbreaking work by Professor Gillian Beer, *Darwin's Plots* (1983), reveals how his theory of evolution profoundly affected Victorian literature as well as science.

As an undergraduate, William Makepeace Thackeray (1811–63) formed lifelong friendships with the poets Tennyson and Edward Fitzgerald. As a dilatory pupil of the great William Whewell, Thackeray began the slide into debt and gambling which cost him his fortune before he made it back as a novelist with *Vanity Fair* in 1847. He also contributed to a short-lived undergraduate magazine, *The Snob*. Leaving without a degree, Thackeray later wrote *The Snobs of England by One of Themselves* and in his novel *Pendennis* invented the term 'Oxbridge' – so not an entirely wasted time at Trinity, then.

Born again: Simeon and the 'Sims'

18th-century Cambridge was solidly Anglican and deeply contemptuous of the 'enthusiasm' associated with Methodism. Enthusiasm, however, proved a prelude to a new seriousness pervading religious life in both universities in the 19th century. In Cambridge, the pioneer of Evangelicalism was Isaac Milner (1750–1820). A self-educated weaver who walked from Hull to enter Cambridge as a sizar, Milner was marked *Incomparabilis* in his Mathematics examinations and became a Fellow of the Royal Society at 26. He later switched to Chemistry and then again to Divinity. As President of Queens' from 1788 he was obdurate in blocking the advancement of fellows suspected of radicalism or irreligion and energetic in recruiting men sharing his views.

What Milner effected in a single college, Charles Simeon (1759–1836) attempted first for a single parish church and then for Cambridge as a whole. Simeon's undergraduate experience was one of the few clear examples of the potential impact of compulsory chapel. Alarmed to learn, three days after coming up, that he would be obliged to take Communion three weeks later – 'the thought rushed into my mind that Satan himself was as fit to attend as I: and that, if I must attend, I must prepare for my attendance there.' Devouring *The Whole Duty of Man* – 'the only religious book that I ever heard of' – he became inspired. His graduation coinciding with a vacancy at Holy Trinity, Cambridge, Simeon, aged 23, was imposed on the congregation by the Bishop of Ely against their strongly expressed wishes. He stayed for the rest of his life, grinding down opposition by his integrity and industriousness. Some undergraduates were initially attracted to him as a skilful and fearless horseman, with a well-developed taste for the fashionable clothes and fine wines they also aspired to enjoy. Others attended the 'conversation parties' attracting 60 or more to his rooms in the Gibbs' Building at King's as the nearest Cambridge offered to a training in what one might call 'applied divinity'.

Clusters of 'Simeonites' became established at Caius and St John's and especially at Magdalene, where the college boat was called The Tea Kettle in acknowledgment of the commitment among 'Sims' to drink nothing stronger. Many 'Sims' devoted their Sabbath to working as Sunday School teachers in the town. Eschewing sports as well as drink, with a reputation for being down-at-heel and out of pocket, they were largely despised, and certainly ignored, by the bulk of undergraduates. Simeon himself eventually won grudging respect for his imperviousness to hostility and ridicule and was widely admired outside Cambridge as a founder of the Church Missionary Society, into whose ranks he directed many candidates for overseas evangelism. His commitment to the pulpit was complemented with his pen. Simeon's *Collected Works* eventually ran to 21 volumes, including 11 sketching outline sermons based on every single book in the Old and New Testament. Simeon was buried with great ceremony in King's College Chapel where there is a memorial to him. His chair is still in the vestry at Holy Trinity, where his umbrella is kept in a glass case like an *ersatz* crozier.

Classical great

> I can never recollect him except as drunk or brutal ... He used to recite, or rather vomit pages of all languages, and could hiccup Greek like a helot.
>
> Byron to John Murray, 1818

Scruffy, unpunctual, cursed by insomnia and asthma, saddened by his only wife's death after a mere six months of marriage, embittered by professional slights and the unscrupulousness of publishers, and prey to habits 'which were wholly incompatible with steady labour' (nightly drinking to insensibility), Richard Porson (1759–1808), the Regius Professor of Greek, was in his last years, in Byron's recollection 'tolerated in this state ... for his talents, as the Turks think a Madman inspired and bear with him.' Porson once called on a friend, reading Thucydides, who asked him the meaning of a word. Porson not only told him but recited the precise passage from which it came. How did he know this? the friend asked in wonderment. 'Because the word only occurs twice in Thucydides, once on the right hand, and once on the left. I observed on which side you looked, and therefore knew the passage'.

On another occasion Porson was discussing the doctrine of the Trinity with a friend when a buggy drove by with three men in it. 'There is an illustration of the Trinity,' said Porson's friend. 'No,' said Porson, 'you must show me one man in *three* buggies ... if you can.' The son of a Norfolk parish clerk, intended for a weaver, as a child Porson showed such prodigious powers of memory and calculation that wealthy sponsors sent him to Eton. A brilliant career at Trinity was then stymied by Porson's conscientious refusal to take Holy Orders, leaving him as 'a gentleman in London with sixpence in his pockets'. As if by heavenly intervention, the Regius Professorship unexpectedly became vacant in 1792 and Porson was elected. Declining to lecture on the grounds he had nothing new to say, he continued to live in London, working painstakingly on manuscripts in bouts of ferocious industriousness alternating with days of indolence. Indifferent to money or reputation alike, writing minutely in a hand so perfect it was used as the basis of a typeface, Porson knew absolutely what he was about – 'I doubt if I could produce any original work which would command the attention of posterity. I can be known only by my notes; and I am quite satisfied if, three hundred years hence, it shall be said that one Porson lived towards the close of the eighteenth century, who did a good deal for the text of Euripides.'

While the former undergraduate Byron recalled only the wreckage of a man, his contemporary Coleridge acknowledged Porson as 'a giant in literature, a prodigy in intellect, a critic whose mighty achievements leave imitation panting ... and whose stupendous Powers, strike down all ... suggestions of rivalry into silent admiration and passive awe.' Porson's grave lies at the foot of Newton's statue in the ante-chapel at Trinity; the wall monument is by Sir Francis Chantrey (1781–1841). A portrait, by John Hoppner (1758–1810) no less, was painted for the University Library.

Renewal

In the half-century between 1750 and 1800 the number of undergraduates matriculating annually remained stagnant at around 150. This was followed by a period of significant and sustained expansion – to 235 by 1810, 410 by 1820 and 440 by 1830. In response to the increased demands made upon it, the University Library increased its staff to five, and a 'library tax' of a shilling and sixpence a quarter was imposed on all members of the university except sizars. From 1829 BAs were actually allowed to borrow books. In the 1820s the tradition of answering questions called out by examiners in the Senate House in freezing January was finally abandoned in favour of printed question papers. Disputations in Latin were finally dropped from the examination process in 1839 – although not formally abolished.

Several colleges undertook building programmes to accommodate the increase in undergraduate numbers. At Sidney Sussex a New Court was built in 1821–4 by royal architect Sir Jeffry Wyatville (1766–1840), who had been knighted for Gothicising Windsor Castle. Regrettably, he also decided to refurbish the existing Tudor buildings by adding crow-stepped gables, battlements and corbelled 'Elizabethan' chimneys, and smearing over the brickwork with Roman cement. Hence Pevsner's unforgiving verdict that 'Sidney Sussex is architecturally the least attractive of the old colleges (at either Cambridge or Oxford!) ... This has nothing to do with its small size ... What it has to do with is chiefly Sir Jeffry Wyattville.' He does, however, win praise for the Lodge facing onto the street, which unites the college's two main courts into a single composition. The college gardens are also commended as 'amongst the finest at Cambridge'.

St John's College made the daring decision to cross the river to build Fourth/New Court in 1825–31. It was the largest court any college had ever put up, almost big enough to be a college in itself, costing the fabulous sum of £77,878. Rising out of the meadows like a stage set, its style has been called 'fairy-tale perpendicular'. It is the greatest work of Thomas Rickman (1776–1841), an entirely self-taught architect, who invented the terms 'Early English', 'Decorated' and 'Perpendicular' to describe the main phases of English Gothic style. New Court is linked to the existing complex by the 'Bridge of Sighs', one of the university's most photographed architectural icons, designed by Rickman's young pupil, Henry Hutchinson (1800–31), who died the year it was completed.

William Wilkins (1778–1839), a former Fellow of Caius, was employed to design the Second Court at Corpus Christi (1823–7), which reorientated the college towards Trumpington Street, as well as its chapel, where he is buried. He also designed the New Court at Trinity (1823–5), and the Screen and Hall ranges at King's, as well as its Provost's Lodge, the fanciful gateway onto King's Parade (1823–8), and its re-sited bridge over the Cam. All these were exercises in the Gothic. Wilkins was also simultaneously working on two of London's most prominent landmarks – University College and the National Gallery. But elsewhere in Cambridge, Wilkins had already been long engaged on a completely different and far more ambitious project

– the building of the first entirely new college at Cambridge for more than 200 years.

Downing College

Downing College is, very indirectly, derived from the fortune accumulated by Sir George Downing. His son, also Sir George, being 'of weak intellect', was judged unfit to bring up his son, ditto Sir George (c.1684–1749), who at 15 was married to a girl of 13. After a three year tour of Europe he returned and repudiated (but never divorced) her. As MP for the rotten borough of Dunwich, Suffolk (which was almost entirely under the sea) Sir George voted obediently for his patron, Sir Robert Walpole (1676–1745) and was accordingly made a Knight of the Bath, meanwhile living a 'most miserable, covetous and sordid existence' at his Cambridgeshire mansion. Downing's will assigned his considerable estates to a cousin, who died without issue, as did every other relative specified in the will, which left the money to found a Cambridge college. Judgment was given for the university in 1769, but Lady Downing and her heirs, in actual possession of the relevant properties, fought a rearguard legal action which meant that it was not until 1800 that George III was able to confer a charter on the new institution.

There had, meanwhile, been a number of architectural false starts, with early enquiries from James Essex in 1771 and the submission – and rejection – in 1784 of draft plans by the fashionable James Wyatt (1746–1813). Before relapsing into complete derangement, George III had thrown in his own command that 'it may not be a Gothic building'. The commission was finally given in 1804 to Wilkins, recently returned from a four-year architectural study tour of Italy, Greece and the Near East. Despite being his first-ever commission, Wilkins opted for a design radically new in two respects. Downing College was to be the first Cambridge example of what became known, in opposition to the previous Palladian consensus, as the 'Greek Revival' style. Even more innovatively, it was to be the first college to be built as a 'campus' (literally 'field'), with separate pavilions ranged around a central lawn, rather than the traditional format of interlinked courts. The first stone was laid in 1807, preceding by a decade the most famous exemplar of this layout, Thomas Jefferson's University of Virginia at Charlotteville.

Wilkins managed to get through £50,000 by 1811 with only a fragment of his ambitious original plan executed, most notably the Ionic Hall and Master's Lodge at the south-west and south-east corners of the site. The daring central Doric Propylaeum was never built and, as Professor Michael Grant has noted, it took a century and a half 'to fill in three sides of the extensive greensward with buildings of various degrees of mild classicality'. The novelist Maria Edgeworth was distinctly underwhelmed by what she saw in 1813, having been told to expect something 'like the Parthenon – Got at last ... within view of Downing College, and was sadly disappointed'. The first undergraduates were not admitted until 1819, and in the early years fellows outnumbered students comfortably, in every sense. Attached to the new foundation were new Professorships of Medicine and the Laws of England, intended to challenge mathematics' monopoly over the official mind of the university.

The first Downing Professor of Medicine was Sir Busick Harwood, FSA, FRS (c.1745–1814), who had made a fortune in India from doctoring maharajahs and was already Professor of Anatomy. On one occasion Harwood astonished Cambridge by saving the life of a badly wounded dog by giving it a blood transfusion from a sheep; on another by challenging the Professor of Physic to a duel. (He declined to respond). Demonstrations of a blood transfusion became a regular feature of Harwood's course on Comparative Anatomy. A witty bon-vivant, 'very licentious in his conversation', Harwood habitually invited to lunch people he met on his morning walk, often serving up whatever he had dissected in the lecture-room the previous day. Harwood's successor as Professor of Anatomy, John Haviland (1785–1851), was the first to lecture on the actual practice of medicine and to establish a proper curriculum and rigorous examinations (1829).

'... *ad astra*'

At his death, clergyman Thomas Plume (1630–1704) left funds for a chair in 'astronomy and experimental philosophy' with an associated observatory, which was established in the gatehouse on Trinity Great Gate. The funds, however, proved inadequate, and an enquiry in 1792 found that 'the professor had neither occupied the said rooms ... for at least fifty years; the observatory and instruments belonging to it were, through disuse, neglect and want of repairs, so much dilapidated as to be entirely unfit'. Although this was dismantled in 1797, not until 1820 was it agreed that £10,000 should be spent on a replacement on land off the Madingley Road bought from St John's. Completed in 1823, the new facility went wildly over budget, coming in at £19,241. At least the young Plumian Professor, George Biddell Airy (1801–92), could assure the university that it had the best observatory in Europe.

Corruption and progress

Spared the impact of industrialisation, Cambridge as a town modernised by fits and starts. The Guildhall was rebuilt in 1782 and the historic Market Cross removed in 1786. The expansion in undergraduate numbers was matched by an expansion in the town's population. The first national census, conducted in 1801, reckoned the population of Cambridge at 9,000; by 1841 it was 24,453. In the parish of St Andrew, on the Newmarket Road, the population rose over the same period from 252 to 9,486.

Acts of Enclosure were finally passed to break up the vast open fields which had long confined the town's physical expansion. 'West or Cambridge Field' of 1,284 acres between the Huntingdon Road and Barton Road was enclosed in 1802. 'East or Barnwell Field' of 1,150 acres, embracing Jesus Green, Midsummer Common, Stourbridge Common and Coe Fen, in 1807. From the 1820s a 'New Town' of terraced housing was built up between Hills Road and Trumpington Road. It was at first jokingly referred to as 'New Zealand' to denote its supposed remoteness.

Newspapers were founded as commercial ventures but also articulated community concerns as well as university affairs. Publication of the *Cambridge Journal and Weekly Flying Post* began in 1744 and was complemented from 1762 onwards by *The Cambridge Chronicle*. Closer contact with the capital was achieved in 1792 with the inauguration of a direct Cambridge–London stagecoach service.

Town and gown joined forces to upgrade the streets of Cambridge. A Paving Act of 1788 placed responsibility for paving and lighting in the hands of 70 commissioners, almost 30 of whom were drawn from the university, which also provided two-fifths of the funding and an interest-free loan of £1,500. The first street to be paved, in the year of the Act's passage, was Petty Cury, and the first lamps were lit in that same year. The work was completed by 1797. Gas lighting was installed from 1823 onwards, only six years after it had appeared in London. Improved lighting was welcomed not merely as an amenity but as a measure against street crime. An Act for the Better Preservation of Peace and Good Order in the Universities of England was passed in 1825, empowering the vice-chancellor to appoint constables to keep a general watch over the streets of the town. In 1827 a new Town Gaol was built on Gonville Place. In 1836 a modern professional police force was at last established.

For decades local administration was in the unscrupulous hands of John Mortlock (1755–1816), founder of Cambridge's first bank (1780) and fixer *extraordinaire,* elected Mayor in 1784 and re-elected 12 times more by 1809. Mortlock ran Cambridge as a private fiefdom. When not actually Mayor himself, he filled the post with his clerk Samuel Francis (four times Mayor between 1788 and 1794) or his son, the appropriately named John Cheetham Mortlock (nine times Mayor between 1802 and 1820), or his grandson Frederick Cheetham Mortlock (four times Mayor between 1810 and 1816). A crowd-pleaser who supported parliamentary reform, when John Mortlock was himself elected an MP he was censured by the unreformed Parliament for his shady dealings. Coleridge claimed that Mortlock drank three bottles of claret a day to cover the blushes that would otherwise have revealed his skulduggery every five minutes. Other Mortlock family honours included a knighthood, the post of High Sheriff of Cambridge, a Fellowship at Christ's and transportation to Australia. A blue plaque on the wall of Barclay's Bank in Bene't Street marks the site of the senior Mortlock's original premises.

With reference to the Mortlock legacy in Cambridge, *The Times*, commenting on the Report of the Municipal Corporations Commission, in 1833 declared that:

> Probably no judicial investigation into a public trust ever brought to life more shameless profligacy or more inveterate dishonesty, more bare-faced venality in politics, a more heartless disregard of the claims of the poor in the perversion of funds left for their benefit ... or a more entire neglect of their duties and functions as magistrates ...

But things were about to get better.

ALL IN HARMONY? A MUSICAL INTERLUDE

As befits the city which gave birth to the King's Singers and Syd Barrett, founder of Pink Floyd, music in Cambridge now takes many forms, with over 50 clubs, groups and associations whose interests range from the brass band and Gilbert and Sullivan, to steel pans, hip-hop, jazz, opera and Chinese music. A number of concert societies are known to have existed in the city from the late 17th century. Some were based in colleges and some in inns, most notably the Red Lion and the Black Bear. The Cambridge Philharmonic Society was founded in 1833 and the Cambridge University Music Society a decade later.

Cambridge claims to have awarded the oldest recorded degree in music – but it took another five centuries for it to establish a fully-fledged faculty devoted to the subject. In 1464 the degree of Bachelor of Music was conferred on Henry Abyngdon (1418–97), Master of the Children of the Chapel Royal under Edward IV – so the link between Cambridge music and boys' voices can claim an unarguable antiquity.

As one of the four subjects of the *quadrivium*, music has been part of a Cambridge education since the formalisation of a curriculum. Conceived as a mathematical discipline, music was variously defined as harmonics and the study of ratios, or the understanding of number in time, as opposed to geometry – number in space. Music thus represented the continuous in motion, geometry the continuous at rest. However defined, music constituted a compulsory field of study for all students and continued to remain an essential skill even after the Reformation. The statutes of Corpus Christi of 1580 declared that 'schollers shall and must at the time of their election be so entred into the skill of song as that they shall at the first sight ... singe plainsong.'

Music by degrees

Early degrees awarded for music, as in the case of Robert Fayrfax (1464–1521; Bachelor 1501, Doctor 1504), constituted *de facto* recognition of accomplishment. Subsequently candidates were expected to submit a composition. Christopher Tye (c.1505–72), a former King's College boy chorister, was awarded a doctorate in 1536 for a Commencement mass. As there were no academic robes officially sanctioned for music he was permitted to wear those of a doctor of medicine. Tye became choirmaster at Ely Cathedral, music tutor to Edward VI and quite possibly also to the musically gifted Elizabeth I. He was referred to as 'an authority' a quarter of a century after his death in Morley's *Introduction to Practicall Musicke* (1597) and featured as a character in plays by Thomas Nashe and William Rowley.

Other early Cambridge music graduates achieved more lasting fame than Tye. The celebrated lutenist John Dowland (1563–1626) received bachelor's degrees from both Oxford and Cambridge but lived a wandering life and must be counted a bird of passage. Orlando Gibbons (1583–1625), by contrast, was brought up in Cambridge and sang in King's College choir as a boy (1596–9), under his elder brother Edward, then choirmaster. Organist of the Chapel Royal at just 21, Gibbons received his bachelor's degree in music from Cambridge in 1606. One of the earliest musicians to compose for instruments, rather than voices, he was an outstanding keyboard player, recognised by contemporaries as 'the best hand in England'. Responding to the new possibilities of his day, Gibbons yet adhered to the medieval ideal, enshrined in the *quadrivium*, that 'it is proportion that beautifies every thing, this whole Universe consists of it, and Musicke is measured by it.' Gibbons's prolific output includes 20 madrigals, almost 40 anthems, almost 50 fantasies for strings or keyboard and a work for voices and strings based on London street cries. He is buried in Canterbury, where he was to play music specially composed to welcome King Charles I's new French bride, Princess Henrietta Maria, but died of a seizure.

Under the repressive rule of the Puritans, choral services were abolished throughout Cambridge. Any temptation towards backsliding was frustrated by the removal of organs from college chapels. (One does wonder where they all went.) Oliver Cromwell himself, however, was not opposed to music as such – just not in church. In 1658 he insisted that Cambridge confer a degree on his protégé, the organist Benjamin Rogers (1614–98). Rogers went on to become organist at Eton and Magdalen College, Oxford, where one of his compositions still figures as part of the traditional college May Day morning repertoire.

Musical chairs

In 1684 Charles II proved as dictatorial as Cromwell in requiring Cambridge to honour one of his protégés, not with a degree, which had already been granted at royal request in 1682, but with an appointment as the university's first Professor of Music. The favoured candidate, Nicholas Staggins (c.1650–1700), was 'Master of the King's Band', whom the *Dictionary of National Biography* would two centuries later dismiss as the author of some 'very slight compositions'. The notion of a professorship for such a courtly lightweight sounds just like the sort of wheeze the King was likely to come up with when he was drunk and remain determined to carry through when he was sober. Cambridge responded dutifully by electing Staggins a professor – but omitting to establish any salary for the post. Not requiring that the appointee give any lectures, the university may have hoped that the post would lapse when the holder either lost the fickle favour of the court or eventually died. As it turned out, Staggins may not have been much of a musician, but he was adept enough as a courtier to survive the transition to the Catholic rule of James II and then to the anti-Catholic regime of William III.

Little more than a decade seems to have been required for the idea of a Professorship of Music to become accepted at Cambridge for, when Staggins died, the post was not allowed to lapse but perpetuated. Its duties, however, were entirely limited to the examination of exercises submitted for the conferment of a degree. Lectures were still not required and, even more pointedly, nor was residence. As it happens, however, Staggins's successor, Thomas Tudway (d. 1726), was very much a Cambridge man. Already organist of King's, Pembroke and Great St Mary's, he proved an assiduous collector of historical manuscripts, though never managed to write the history of music they were intended to illustrate. Tudway also set a precedent for professorial compositions for university occasions, his own examination exercise, 'Thou, O God, hast heard our desire', becoming the anthem performed to welcome Queen Anne on the occasion of her visit to the university in 1705. Tudway's successor, Maurice Greene (1696–1755) provided a setting of Alexander Pope's *Ode on St Cecilia's Day*, for the opening of the Senate House in 1733, Pope himself obliging with a specially composed extra verse. In 1768 Greene's successor, John Randall (1715–99), professor for 44 years, did the same for Thomas Gray's *Ode for the Installation of the Duke of Grafton as Chancellor of the University*.

Randall's successor, Charles Hague (1769–1821) completed the trio with a similar effort for HRH the Duke of Gloucester. A celebrated violinist, Hague also organised seasons of subscription concerts. John Clarke-Whitfield (1770–1836) passed most of his tenure (1821–36) out at Chesterton, industriously setting the compositions of Sir Walter Scott and Lord Byron to music, or over on the other side of the country, at Hereford, where he was cathedral organist and the linchpin of its famed festival. Appropriately, that is where his memorial stands.

Foreign visitors to Cambridge were struck by what they took to be characteristically English tastes in music-making. The German Conrad von Uffenbach, visiting in 1710, was impressed by the organ playing at Trinity – 'The English excel specially herein, whereas on all other instruments they are mean performers'; but he was less than enchanted by the local penchant for campanology – 'they also make much ado of their chimes, and aim at an artistic and agreeable style of ringing; but we could not fancy the clatter, rather were much annoyed, to hear it so often; for the scholars ... mount the towers and ring when they please, often for hours together.' There is a touch of *schadenfreude* in his observation that 'accidents often happen in bell-ringing, some students being struck, or falling down and breaking leg and arm.' In 1724 the Society of Cambridge Youth was established at Great St Mary's to set bell-ringing on a regular basis. The distinctive chimes of the new clock installed there in 1793, known as the Cambridge Quarters, would eventually become recognisable around the world when they were adopted by Parliament as the chimes for Big Ben.

English eccentricity

It was Thomas Atwood Walmisley (1814–56), appointed organist to Trinity and St John's at just 19, who first established a formal programme of university music lectures, in one of which he astounded listeners by predicting the eventual triumph of the music of Bach, then virtually unknown in England.

William Sterndale Bennett (1816–75) was the first professor to establish rigorous requirements for a university music degree. A King's chorister, Bennett had studied in London and Leipzig, been befriended by Mendelssohn and Schumann and in 1854 had conducted the first English performance of Bach's *St Matthew Passion*. Appointed professor in 1856, in 1867 his efforts were belatedly acknowledged by the Senate with the award of an annual salary of £100.

Conducting matters seriously

The remarkable career of George Alexander Macfarren (1813–87) was cursed by defective eyesight from childhood, but he nevertheless became the founder of the Handel Society and a conductor at Covent Garden. Forced to dictate to an amanuensis from 1860 onwards, in 1876 Macfarren, although by then totally blind, was appointed both Principal of the Royal Academy of Music and professor at Cambridge and knighted in 1883.

In Irish-born Charles Villiers Stanford (1852–1924) the university acquired another musician of national repute and a composer of indefatigable industriousness, whose immense output would eventually include a dozen operas, seven symphonies, eight concertos and dozens of chamber works and liturgical compositions. A choral scholar at Queens' and organist of Trinity at 21, Stanford combined his Cambridge duties with the role of conductor at London's Bach Choir and Professor of Composition at the Royal College of Music. Stanford also took the Cambridge Music Society under his comprehensive wing. Founded in 1843 as the Peterhouse Music Society, it had changed its name to reflect a wider membership but had remained an undergraduate institution until Stanford's advent. Stanford used his prestige to introduce women into the chorus and to promote the performance of new works. In 1877 the virtuoso Hungarian violinist Joseph Joachim (1831–1907) conducted the first performance of Brahms's *First Symphony*, which, according to Stanford 'attracted almost every musician of importance in England'. He also noted that 'much interest was excited among Cambridge men by the curious coincidence that the horn theme in the introduction to the last movement was nearly note for note a quotation of the famous hour-chimes of St Mary's bells.'

In 1893, to mark the jubilee of CUMS's foundation, Stanford organised a celebration which involved the conferment of honorary degrees on Saint-Saens and Tchaikovsky. At the Guildhall, Tchaikovsky, 'with wildly energetic baton', conducted the first-ever performance of *Francesca de Rimini*. A member of the audience surmised that 'to most of us present, it was our first introduction to the music of this master', which he thought memorable for its 'awful fury and madness'. Saint-Saens noted approvingly of college chapel services that they were 'very short and consist mainly of good music very well sung, for the English tend to make admirable choristers.' Unfortunately Stanford later fell out with the university, to the extent that he gave his classes at the station hotel to limit his time in Cambridge to the absolute minimum.

Extending the musical range

Edward Dent (1876–1957), professor from 1926 to 1941 and founder of the Music School, was a pupil of Stanford but far more wide-ranging in his interests. Drawing on his own experience as a teacher at King's, he broadened the curriculum extensively, especially with regard to earlier music, being himself an expert on Domenico Scarlatti and Wolfgang Amadeus Mozart, then much neglected.

In terms of composition and performing talent, a 20th-century renaissance was inaugurated by Ralph Vaughan Williams (1872–1958), who read history at Trinity (1892–4) and composed music for a college production of Aristophanes' *The Wasps* in 1909. The future Sir Arthur Bliss, KCVO, CH (1891–1975), Master of the Queen's Music, secured degrees in both classics and music at Pembroke before distinguished service in World War One. His 150 works included music for six films and four ballets, two operas and 30 fanfares. As wartime

Music Director of the BBC, Bliss drafted the policy statement which led to the creation of the Third Programme. His *Golden Cantata* was composed to celebrate the quincentenary of the awarding of the first Cambridge music degree in 1464.

At King's, organist Bernhard 'Boris' Ord, CBE (1897–1961) built the international reputation of its chapel choir and, as founder of the Cambridge University Madrigal Society in 1920, he inaugurated a unique annual May Week concert performed from massed punts moored on the Cam. In (Robert) Thurston Dart (1921–71) Cambridge acquired (1947–64) an outstanding harpsichordist who was also an expert on early musical instruments, Byrd, Bach and the history of music printing. Other significant Cambridge names have included John Rutter, sometime Director of Music at Clare; Christopher Hogwood and Sir John Eliot Gardiner in the field of 'early music'; and conductor Sir Andrew Davis.

A BA Honours course in Music was finally established at Cambridge in 1947 during the professorship of Patrick Hadley (1899–1973), an expert on folk song, who also quadrupled the faculty and, in an oddly appropriate way, was a co-founder of the Noise Abatement Society.

The University Music School on West Road was inaugurated in 1977 and completed in the 1980s. It includes a concert hall for 500, the Pendlebury Music Library and a collection of historical musical instruments. Ethnomusicology was established as a regular focus of study in 1983 and a Centre for Music and Science was founded in 2003. Other major areas of study, teaching and research include musical composition and historical musicology.

Cambridge University Press publishes learned journals devoted to such specific musical genres as *Plainsong and Medieval Music, Popular Music* and *Eighteenth Century Music*, as well as *Early Music History, the Journal of the Society for American Music* and the *British Journal of Music Education*, plus such no-nonsense, if somewhat intimidating, titles as *Tempo* and *Organized Sound* – which arguably is what music actually is.

6

An Age of 'Improvement'

Reform one: Town

The Municipal Corporations Act of 1835 removed corrupt, self-recruiting oligarchies throughout the country and enlarged the electorate for the selection of their replacements. In Cambridge this strengthened Town against Gown, but even more important in this respect was the Cambridge Award Act of 1856, containing many concessions from a university increasingly preoccupied with its own need for internal reform. Oaths requiring the Town Council to uphold the privileges of the university were abolished; the Chancellor's Court lost its power to judge university members guilty of misbehaviour; the Vice-Chancellor's powers to license ale houses, regulate markets and fairs and inspect weights and measures were transferred to Justices of the Peace. Most university and college properties became liable for rates, the main source of local government revenue.

In 1850 the *Cambridge Chronicle* revealed that Falcon Yard, off Petty Cury, was home to 300 people, sharing just two privies; but while the town was still disfigured by poverty, pollution and prostitution, there is evidence of rising living standards in the opening of two stores which became Cambridge institutions – Robert Sayle's in 1840 and Joshua Taylor's in 1861. In 1842 new Assize Courts were built on Castle Hill. In 1849 a major fire destroyed many properties in the market area, necessitating much rebuilding; not until 1875, however, was a regular, professional fire brigade established. Cambridge also became one of the earliest towns in England to open a public library; the dome-lit premises in Wheeler Street served as the Tourist Information Centre until recently and are now occupied by a smart restaurant. The beginnings of a modern public water supply were finally laid on in 1853–5. In 1858 the Cambridge College of Art was opened by the art historian and social critic John Ruskin (1819–1900); it would eventually evolve into Anglia Ruskin University. In 1869 a group of cobblers banded together to establish the first Cambridge Co-operative Society to sell cheap, unadulterated provisions to the humbler members of the community.

Thwarted ambition

My father will probably have informed you how little I was at first captivated by the external appearance of Cambridge ... a dull and shabby town ... The river Cam both in colour and width strongly resembles a ditch.

Thus, the unprepossessing first impressions of Alexander Chisholm Gooden (1817–40), son of a wealthy and cultured London businessman, upon arriving at Trinity in 1836. Lodged in Jesus Lane, five minutes from his college, which he immediately pronounced most inconvenient, Gooden soon fell thrall to accepted routine – chapel at 7:00am and lectures at 9:00, with dinner at 4:00 as a brief break, if not a decorous occasion – 'a savage piece of business; every man mangles the joints for himself ... this meal takes not more than twenty minutes.' Apart from that, as Gooden confided to a former school friend, 'Hall, chapel, walk in alternate monotony ... are the literature, philosophy and science of a Cambridge *continuation*, I do not call it *life*'.

Gooden found the town 'enlivened by very few amusements', a visit by Wombwell's celebrated menagerie being one rare high spot and the lodging of circuit judges with their colourful attendants another. The laying of the foundation stone of the Fitzwilliam Museum was a 'very dull affair', accompanied by a Latin speech 'not of Augustan purity'. When Gooden later moved into college rooms his 'continuation' would be 'enlivened' by the ravings of a neighbouring don drinking himself into dementia.

The freshman's dutiful letters home reveal a constant preoccupation with colds and constipation. The famously penetrating frosts of Cambridge meant that one night 'every liquid whatever in my bedroom was turned to ice'. Winter examinations were taken in the unheated Senate House with participants shivering in greatcoats. Gooden's letters to his mother are replete with euphemistic references to the laxative properties of rhubarb, morbid fears of damp bedding and effusive gratitude for parcels of warm underwear, referred to coyly as 'unmentionable articles'. Anxieties about the lower social orders – his landlord, landlady and bedder – inhibited Gooden from accepting further home comforts: 'Mother's offer of a ham is tempting but I have no keeping place under my own hands and though my people are decently honest, it would not be fair to tempt their virtue by placing unlimited confidence in them.' In fact they were entirely upright and caring.

Gooden's overriding aim was a Trinity Fellowship. This involved much tactical thinking, undertaken with agonised advice from his tutors and father, about which prize and scholarship examinations he should contest. These opportunities for academic virtuosity provoked rivalries both collegiate and personal. St John's and King's figure frequently on Gooden's horizon of academic combat, other colleges meriting scarcely a mention. Competitors were judged by character as well as scholarly competence, Gooden dismissing one as 'a Sim' (follower of the evangelical Rev Simeon) and 'a sloven' (to many the two were inextricably associated), and expressing the fervent wish that 'a gentleman in creed and cleanliness may beat him'.

Like many good classicists, Gooden laboured over compulsory mathematics, which embraced astronomy and aspects of physics treated mathematically rather than experimentally, such as optics and dynamics. This involved extensive revision in vacations, lest he forget material painstakingly acquired from paid tutors during term-time. Overshadowing all, however, was the university test that labelled a man for life – 'a man can take his degree but once and there is nothing afterwards to make up for failure in *that* examination.'

In the end Gooden achieved the foothills of academic eminence, winning the prestigious Chancellor's Medal in 1840, gaining a creditable degree, attracting pupils and looking forward to election to a junior fellowship. During a vacation in Germany, however, he so over-exerted himself rowing that he died within days, just 23. Apparently his hypochondria wasn't so misplaced after all.

Railway revolution

In 1845 the Eastern Counties Railway at last reached Cambridge – just about. As anyone with heavy baggage who has missed the last taxi will know, it's a long mile from the station to the city centre. The university deplored a form of communication by which undergraduates could reach London, and its limitless temptations, in just over an hour. Just as bad, the railway would also enable 'day-trippers' to descend on Cambridge, ruining its accustomed serenity. In 1851 the Vice-Chancellor protested that it would 'convey foreigners and others to inflict their presence on the university and its day of rest' and that therefore Sunday excursions were 'as distasteful to the University Authorities as they must be offensive to Almighty God'. The university therefore extracted extraordinary powers from Parliament regarding railway business. University officers were empowered to quiz railway employees about any person on the station 'who shall be a member of the University or suspected of being such'. On Sundays the railway was forbidden to pick up or set down passengers at Cambridge or within three miles of it between 10:00am and 5:00pm. This ban remained in force until 1908.

For an altogether more positive approach to this new marvel of human ingenuity one must turn to Ely Cathedral, where a fatal accident on the Norwich line in 1845 prompted the inscription of a 24-line verse – *The Spiritual Railway* – on the grave of the two victims. The following extract conveys an appealingly up-beat message:

The Line to Heaven by Christ was made
With heavenly truth the Rails are laid,
From Earth to Heaven the Line extends,
To Life Eternal where it ends.

Repentance is the Station then
Where Passengers are taken in ....

In First, and Second, and Third Class
Repentance, Faith and Holiness,
You must the way to Glory gain
Or you with Christ will not remain.

Come then, poor Sinners, now's the time
At any Station on the Line,
If you'll repent and turn from sin,
The Train will stop and take you in.

In 1863 Cambridge station was rebuilt in its present form with the longest platform in Europe, stretching for almost a quarter of a mile. In 1866 a second London route was opened, terminating at King's Cross. By 1871 the number of day-trippers had grown large enough to stimulate the publication of a forerunner of this book – *A Railway Traveller's Walk Through Cambridge*.

Some limited industrial development took place alongside the railway, notably the premises of James Sendall & Co, Horticultural Builders, Heating Engineers and Iron Founders, whose speciality was glasshouses. In the 1880s and 1890s Romsey Town developed as a working-class suburb of brick terraces, many inhabited by railway workers. In 1894 Fosters opened their giant flourmill by the station. Another minor industrial nucleus developed along the Newmarket

Road with quarries, half a dozen brick and tile works, an iron foundry, a gas works and coal yards. The concentration of men doing heavy industrial work created a corresponding demand for places where they could 'put the sweat back in'. At one time there were no fewer than 22 pubs between Wellington Street and Hutchinson's Court, one every 22 yards.

Speaking volumes

A significant commercial development occurred in the town centre in 1843 when the corner shop at 1 Trinity Street was taken over by Daniel Macmillan (1813–57) and his brother Alexander (1818–96), who soon branched out from bookselling into publishing. Thackeray and Tennyson both gave readings on the premises. In April 1857 the firm published that enduring classic *Tom Brown's Schooldays,* which ran through five editions before the end of the year. Other key Macmillan titles would include Francis Turner Palgrave's *Golden Treasury of English Songs and Lyrics* (1861) and Charles Kingsley's *The Water Babies* (1863). When the firm moved to London in 1863, the former premises passed to a nephew, Robert Bowes (1835–1919), and the business traded as Macmillan and Bowes until 1907 and then as Bowes and Bowes. Robert Bowes became a civic stalwart, a town councillor and a major in the local Volunteers, governor of the Perse School, promoter of Cambridge Working Men's College and Newnham College and an expert on John Siberch and the history of printing in Cambridge. He was also responsible for publishing the *Concise Guide to Cambridge* (1898) by John Willis Clarke and a facsimile edition of *Cantabrigia Illustrata.*

Polymath

You'll find, though you traverse the bounds of infinity,
That God's greatest work is – the Master of Trinity.

Sir Francis Doyle, 1866

William Whewell (1794–1866) – pronounced Hyou-well – was the scientist who invented the word 'scientist', and 'physicist' as well. He was also a priest, poet, philosopher and translator and wrote authoritatively on subjects ranging from tides to German Gothic churches. Born a carpenter's son, he died the immensely rich Master of Trinity. A gangling youth, Whewell matured into a prizefighter's physique and, even in middle age, could jump the entire flight of steps up to Trinity's Dining Hall in a single bound, a feat generations of undergraduates have tried – and often failed – to emulate. Winner of a university prize for English poetry, Second Wrangler, President of the Union Society, a founder of the Cambridge Philosophical Society and FRS at 26, Whewell spoke German so well he was turned away from meeting Humboldt (1769–1859) because a porter was told to admit only an Englishman. Successively Professor of Mineralogy and Professor of 'Moral Theology and Casuistical Divinity', Whewell also served as President of the Geological Society and of the British Association for the Advancement of Science. His *magnum opus* was a comprehensive account of the history and philosophy of all science. Whewell *described* science; he was not interested in experiment.

Whewell was contemplating quiet retirement when in 1841 his life was totally transformed by his belated marriage and unexpected election as Master of Trinity. Whewell used this powerful position to secure the election of Prince Albert, husband of the young Queen Victoria, as Chancellor of the University in 1847, aiming, with Albert's enthusiastic support, to broaden the curriculum by promoting the teaching of philosophy and science. Whewell's views on what science should be taught to undergraduates were, however, decidedly cautious, not to say reactionary. Mathematics offered certainties, science rather too much speculation. Nothing, therefore, should be allowed on the curriculum which had not been generally accepted among the scientific community for at least a century. Standing outside academia, Prime Minister Sir Robert Peel (1788–1850), who had personally chosen Whewell as Master of Trinity, wondered wryly whether the young gentlemen of Cambridge were to be exposed to such apparently contentious matters as electricity. Reformist, but no radical, Whewell believed that if Cambridge needed reforming, it should be left to reform itself, ferociously defending such traditions as college autonomy and the exclusion of Dissenters.

Outside Cambridge Whewell was known for a tract arguing that Earth was not unique in the universe as the only populated planet. This view was readily endorsed by that perennial punster the Reverend Sydney Smith (1771–1845) who, being told that Whewell's strong point was science, riposted that his weak point was 'omniscience'. Whewell also took as a proof of the existence of God as Designer of the Universe that the daily rotation of the earth provided exactly the time humans needed to sleep.

Whewell made two happy marriages, which, with the incomes from his various offices, made him wealthy enough to pay for the building of two student hostels as well as endowing a chair of international law, to promote perpetual peace between nations. A notoriously poor horseman, Whewell died after a fall, accompanying his nieces in the Gog and Magog hills. He is buried in the ante-chapel at Trinity, where there is a statue (1872) by Thomas Woolner (1825–92). Opposite him is a statue (1845) of one of Whewell's own heroes, Francis Bacon, which Whewell had himself set up. The fourth line on the front describes Bacon as *Scientiarum Lumen Facundiae Lex* (Light of Knowledge and the Law of Eloquence) while the fifth refers to his slumped posture *Sic Sedebat* (he used to sit like this) when cogitating deeply. On the side of his chair is an extract from a letter Bacon wrote to Trinity, urging the study of science as evidence of God's Creation. Whewell can also be seen in effigy on the outside of Whewell's Court, looking down on the former All Saints churchyard.

In contrast to the flamboyant Whewell, Isaac Todhunter (1820–84) was the archetypal ascetic recluse. Asked how long a 'hard-reading man' could take off, he advised that 'the forenoon of Christmas Day would be in order'. Despite having been 'unusually backward' at school, he became a teacher himself through evening classes at University College, London. Entering St John's at an elderly 24, he devoted

15 years to monastic frugality and highly profitable industriousness. Using his college lodging as an austere classroom, he inhabited two closets, one as his bedroom, the other his study, lined with books; 'each in a brown paper cover inscribed in exquisite handwriting with the title'. Apart from an hour walking college footpaths for exercise and an hour for dinner, Todhunter devoted every waking moment to teaching or compiling mathematical textbooks which became runaway bestsellers. According to his former pupil Leslie Stephen, editor of the *Dictionary of National Biography*, by 1864 he 'had saved enough money to give up the drudgery of teaching, married and wrote books for the learned upon the history of mathematics'. Todhunter also mastered nine languages.

Reform two: Gown

The reforms initiated by the Duke of Newcastle in 1750 fended off further change at Cambridge for a century. He was succeeded in 1768 by the Duke of Grafton (1735–1811), who made no official visit after 1774 – i.e. for almost 40 years. On his election his successor, William Frederick, Duke of Gloucester (1776–1834) – one of several royal personages to be thought the original 'Silly Billy' – gave a celebratory dinner so lavish that guests were seated in Trinity's cloisters. After that he visited just twice. At 75, his successor, the Marquis of Camden (1759–1840) was an unlikely candidate for firebrand reform and fended off threats of external interference with promises that the colleges were diligently beavering away at their own proposals for improvement. His successor, the Duke of Northumberland (1785–1847), maintained this semi-fiction and probably felt he'd done his bit by donating in 1842 the immense Warwick Vase that stands on the Senate House lawn.

The election of Prince Albert in 1847 therefore marked something of a break with a tradition of torpor and obfuscation. Not yet 30, Albert was itching to be useful and, as a German and a fully paid-up intellectual, was painfully aware how far the ancient English universities languished behind their continental counterparts – or even their newer rivals in London and Durham.

Some of the colleges had begun tentative reforms. Trinity had introduced an entrance examination. Peterhouse had no longer limited fellowships to men from particular counties. Theologian Dr John Graham (1794–1865), Master of Christ's and a close ally of Prince Albert, even suggested fellows might marry and the university be opened to non-Anglicans.

In the event the ancient universities were unable to fend off the appointment in 1852 of a Royal Commission, whose brief was 'to enquire into the state, discipline and revenues' of the university and its colleges. They interpreted this very broadly to recommend the establishment of courses in engineering, modern languages, history and theology, to suggest the establishment of Boards of Studies to ensure what was taught matched what was examined and to establish new professorships and lectureships open to married men, plus the creation of new laboratories and museums. The commissioners did not, however, propose anything as radical as a general entrance examination and made only anodyne proposals in relation to the colleges. In the end Caius took the lead in abolishing celibacy, though other colleges followed only hesitantly over the following 20 years.

The university predictably tried to pre-empt external reform by making its own proposals but, equally predictably, failed to finalise them in time. Accordingly, in 1856 the Bill for Cambridge was passed by Parliament to revise the complex structure of governance of the university, abolish obsolete offices, redirect ancient endowments to fund new professorships, lengthen terms and tighten up residence requirements. Henceforth a declaration of faith was only required of those taking degrees in divinity, although fellowships and membership of the senate were still limited to Anglicans. Religious restrictions were finally lifted from 1871 onwards, although it was decreed that Morning and Evening Prayer should still be observed in college chapels. Subsequent Royal Commissions recommended raising standards in Scientific Instruction (1873) and decreed that college contributions be *required* to support university teaching (1877), a move which was denounced as an assault on the autonomy of colleges – which it was.

Revival: Gothic

While Downing College and the Fitzwilliam Museum were large-scale exercises in the neo-Classical mode, interest in the newly-fashionable Gothic mode of architecture was quickened by the drastic but highly praised restoration of Holy Sepulchre church undertaken by Anthony Salvin (1799–1881) as a consolation prize for not getting the commission for the Fitzwilliam. A protégé of John Nash, Salvin was Britain's leading authority on medieval castles. At Cambridge his first college project in 1852 was to remodel the east range of the Principal Court at Trinity Hall in a restrained Italianate manner. In 1853 he undertook a complex remodelling of the hall and library on the west side of Caius. Salvin had by then found favour with Whewell of Trinity, for whom he had restored the façade of the Master's Lodge (1843) and then built Whewell's Court (1859–60, 1866–8), commended by Pevsner as

> amongst the most satisfying of nineteenth-century Cambridge buildings ... The best thing ... is the sensitive scaling of the three parts ... The first court ... small, irregular in shape and paved ... the second no more than a strip of turf ... Yet ... visually ... an extremely pleasant interlude. The other main court ... much larger and squarer, with a turfed centre and two big square towers as its main accents ...

Salvin was also responsible for the east window at St Mary the Great in 1857. All Saints, Jesus Lane (1864), the work of G F Bodley (1827–1907), brother-in-law and first pupil of Sir George Gilbert Scott (1811–78), replaced the demolished All Saints in St John Street, traditionally known as All Saints in the Jewry or All Saints by the Hospital.

Its former churchyard now features a memorial cross designed by Basil Champneys. Bodley's All Saints (now closed) features decorative work, notably the famed east window, by William Morris and his usual collaborators Ford Madox Brown and Edward Burne-Jones. Their collaboration began in 1861 with restoration work on the hall at Queens', one of the very earliest of Morris's projects, and there was a similar collaboration on the 1864–7 restoration of the chapel at Jesus College and the installation there in 1873–7 of new stained-glass windows. Bodley's work at Cambridge continued over more than 40 years, beginning in 1858–61 with the redecoration of the chapel at Queens'. In 1885 he redecorated Holy Trinity, Market Street, the former stronghold of Charles Simeon. Bodley's Buildings (1893) at King's is a bold, L-shaped neo-Tudor block, while Christ's library (1895–7) is a discreetly tactful addition.

Sir George Gilbert Scott built up the largest architectural practice in Victorian England and is credited with some 700 projects. Pevsner scathingly characterises Scott's Chapel of 1863–9 at St John's College as 'eminently High Victorian in that it is oversized, correct in its details and utterly unaware of what the unity of a court demands'. 193 feet long, with a tower 163 feet high, its late-13th-century Gothic is supposed to represent what Scott thought the original college chapel would have looked like, modified by nods towards the chapel of Merton College, Oxford and the Saint-Chapelle in Paris. Scott also (1862–5) enlarged the Hall at St John's. His other Cambridge work included the rebuilding (1862–7) of most of the West Court of the Old Schools, the 1867 restoration of medieval St Mary Magdalene and the design of the Chetwynd Building (1873) at King's College. He also made *major* alterations at Ely Cathedral – moving the choir stalls, inserting a choir screen and reconstructing the famous lantern.

Scott's successor as doyen of the profession was Alfred Waterhouse, RA (1830–1905), best known as the architect of the Natural History Museum in London. Having established a solid reputation in Manchester and Liverpool, Waterhouse approached Cambridge with even more self-confidence than Scott. The Union building of 1866 was at least tucked away, but his 1868–70 rebuilding of Tree Court at the south-east corner of Caius could scarcely have been more prominent. Pevsner is incandescent about its external frontage:

> at the corner the building blossoms out into a tall tower ... a spire, big chimneystacks, a monumental gateway ... statuary in niches, in fact everything the architect could think of ... The tower ... dwarfs the Senate House ... competes with St Mary and ... is pretentious and ... utterly unconscious of the character of the architecture into which it should fit ...

The work was, however, hailed as an outstanding success when completed and in 1883 the architect returned to Caius to build a set of Lecture Rooms.

In the meantime, Waterhouse had made a Tudor undergraduate block at Jesus, a new Master's Lodge, Hall, Library and accommodation block at Pembroke (1871–5) and the east range of New Court at Trinity Hall (1872). Noting that Waterhouse was 'the last architect to be guided by respect for the character of old work', Pevsner observes of his efforts at Pembroke that 'in every case where he added ... he spoiled something that was there and replaced it by something out of keeping'. Pevsner does, however, warmly commend the eclectic New Building (1878) added by Gilbert George Scott Junior (1839–97), with its mixture of Gibbsian window-surrounds, Arts & Crafts angels and Dutch gables.

Waterhouse rounded off his Cambridge collegiate *oeuvre* at Girton, employing his favourite materials of red brick and red terra cotta. The first building, for the Mistress, one lecturer and 21 students was completed in 1873 and now forms part of Emily Davies Court. Far more important, however, was Waterhouse's major innovation in student accommodation, substituting corridors for staircases to link student rooms. This not only introduced much more light and air but also minimised social isolation and maximised social interaction and rapidly became the norm. Waterhouse continued to make additions in the same style at Girton before handing work over to his son, Paul (1861–1924), followed by his son, Michael (1888–1968).

Alfred and Paul Waterhouse were jointly responsible for Fosters' (now Lloyd's) Bank (1891) on Sidney Street. Striped bands of lime-stone and brick emphatically mark the building off from nearby colleges as being unmistakably 'town' not 'gown'. The bank's Dutch-style gables and tower assert a brash, bourgeois self-confidence, which implied that any cash left in the care of the Fosters – local millers-turned-bankers, who also supplied four Cambridge Mayors – could not be more secure. Exuberance, however, was reserved for the stunning tiled interior. Do pop in for an exhilarating glance.

No 10 Trinity Street was built in the 1880s for a firm of solicitors, which included two members of the Foster family, one of them a Cambridge Town Clerk. The Gothic pediment above the doorway is an hourglass (a warning to clients not to waste time?) surrounded by finger-wagging advice – *Praeteritum Corrige* (Correct the Past) *Praesens Rege* (Control the Present) *Futurum Cerne* (Perceive the future). Decades of 20th-century undergraduates knew this building as The Whim, which, when Clive James was a postgraduate in the 1960s, served the self-defined 'artistic world ... as a headquarters, clearing house, comfort station, watering hole and gossip exchange. The Whim worked on the French café system: you could sit for a long time over a single cup of coffee as long as you didn't mind paying too much for it in the first place. I enjoyed writing there because there was a good chance of being interrupted.'

'This very unrevolutionary woman'

Girton College was essentially the creation of (Sarah) Emily Davies (1830–1921). Denied education by her clergyman father, following his death at 30 she threw herself into campaigning for women's rights to employment, education, medical training and the vote. Small and plain, Miss Davies proved a first-rate organiser and public speaker. In 1867 she began to plan the establishment of a woman's college offering education at university level. It opened in 1869 with five students in temporary accommodation at Benslow House, Hitchin, Hertfordshire, 30 miles from Cambridge. In 1873, the college, by now with 15 students, relocated to an extensive 46-acre site near Girton, two miles from the male-dominated centre of Cambridge. Emily Davies had enlisted capable and influential supporters to her cause, not least the eminent novelist George Eliot (1819–80), but Girton nevertheless represented the triumph of her own unspectacular combination of tact and tenacity. (Her tact was, however, sometimes selective – 'Girton is for ladies, while Newnham is for governesses'.) The university's official history is unusually fulsome in its praise – 'one of the heroic figures in Cambridge history; firm as a rock, endlessly fertile in plans and schemes, ruthlessly persuasive, all at once friendly and formidable' but also admits that 'she had little conception of scholarship; she never knew much of Cambridge – she escaped to London whenever she could.'

Eschewing any form of pedagogic apartheid, the first Mistress of Girton aimed to have her students perform at the same level as the men and, as far as possible, under the same conditions. She was triumphantly vindicated in 1887 when Agnata Ramsay (1867–1931) was awarded higher marks than the officially-recognised Senior Classic. Henry Montagu Butler (1833–1918), Master of Trinity, promptly married Miss Ramsay (34 years his junior) – certainly some sort of recognition; but it would be another 60 years before Cambridge women were actually entitled to a degree for their examination performance. Agnata's marriage proved happy and fruitful. The eldest of her three sons, James Ramsay Montagu Butler (1889–1975) became Regius Professor of History.

Miss Davies' other main aim was to build accommodation and teaching facilities for *hundreds* of future students. A chapel, library and garden could wait. In fact they were realised long before her demise, which was nice but not, in her view, the point. As the university's official history notes 'she left Girton loaded with debt, but very amply provided with buildings'.

On the Cam

Harvard graduate William Everett (1839–1910) read classics at Trinity between 1859 and 1863 before returning home to an unspectacular academic career. He did, however, produce what the distinguished American historian Henry Steele Commager hailed as the best American account of Cambridge life, *On the Cam* (1866). Everett argued that both England's ancient universities were essentially aristocratic institutions – 'not means for diffusing education among the people, but ... the great training schools for the governing classes.' But he drew a fundamental distinction between the two. Whereas Oxford was chiefly patronised by the 'old aristocracy' of hereditary landed wealth, Cambridge attracted the offspring of the 'new aristocracy' of business and the professions – 'the wing devoted to progress and the new world of thought is devoted to Cambridge'. Certainly in the promotion of science Cambridge would increasingly set the pace.

THE INNER MAN: A GASTRONOMIC INTERLUDE

The first guidebook to Cambridge, *Cantabrigia Depicta* (1763), rhapsodised over the excellence of the 'Flesh, Fish, Wild-Fowl, Poultry, Butter, Cheese and all Manner of Provisions from the adjacent country'. Butter, in particular, was singled out for its abundance and the peculiar way it was sold, which fascinated the novelist Maria Edgeworth (1767–1849) in 1813 – 'All the butter in Cambridge must be stretched into rolls a yard in length and an inch in diameter, and these are sold by inches, and measured out by compasses, in a truly mathematical manner, worthy of a university'. 'Yard Butter' survived until the rationing regulations of the Great War killed it off. The other local speciality was 'the best Saffron in Europe'.

Short commons

These observations were written after the draining of the Fens had opened up an immense new region of highly productive soil and when

East Anglia was at the forefront of an 'agricultural revolution' which was transforming breeds, crops and techniques of cultivation. Two centuries previously a future Master of St John's, preaching at Paul's Cross in London, had envisaged the average Cambridge scholar living a life of extreme frugality. Rising between 4:00 and 5:00, he should dine at 10:00am, sharing 'a penny piece of beef amongst four, having a ... porridge made of the broth of the same beef, with salt and oatmeal, and nothing else'. Supper, at 5:00pm, was to be 'not much better than their dinner'. The austere Bishop Fisher commended keeping students half-starved, a 'low diet' being 'necessary to concentration.' The confessional diary of undergraduate Samuel Ward in 1595–6 shows him failing to live in Puritanical self-denial – bingeing variously on cheese, pears, walnuts, raisins and damsons and 'going to drink wine and that in the Tavern'. Writing in March 1625, Lady Paston kept her son William, at Corpus Christi, supplied with home-made treats, which she repeatedly urged him to share: 'I have sent thee, as thou desirest, some edible Commodity for this Lent to eat in your chamber, your good tutor and you together: a Cake and Cheese, a few puddings and links [sausages]: a turkey pie pasty: a pot of Quinces and some marmalade.'

Outbreaks of plague could disrupt local food supplies so badly that colleges would be reduced to a state of nutritional siege. In 1625 college steward Joseph Mede recorded distractedly that 'all our market today could not supply us commons for night', so he had to serve 'eggs, apple-pies and custards, for want of other fare'. The plague of 1630 caused most of his colleagues and students to flee while the rest remained gated inside, relying on their regular 'Butcher, Baker and Chandler' to 'bring the provisions to the college gates, where the Steward and Cook receive them'. Communal dining was not to everyone's taste, anyway. The high-handed Master of Pembroke, Samuel Harsnett (1561–1631), thought his status as a bishop entitled him 'to keep state at his meals in his lodgings' and to make 'both the Cooks at once his men ... so that sometimes the kitchen was without a cook the whole day together ... leaving the College but one poor sole boy to dress commons.'

Writing in 1662, John Strype (1643–1737), a Jesus freshman, reassured his mother that his college was better than most in the matter of 'Commons', the daily fare consumed communally in hall, but, even so, it sounded rather dreary:

> we have ... such meat as you know I do not use to care for; and that is Veal, but now I have learnt to eat it. Sometimes ... we have boiled meat, with pottage; and beef and mutton, which I am glad of: except Fridays and Saturdays, and sometimes Wednesdays; which days we have Fish at dinner, and tansy or puddings for supper.

The custom of 'fish days', a hangover from Catholic practice, was regarded as patriotic; maintaining a large fishing fleet created a 'nursery of seamen' as a reserve for war. If a meal left one hungry one could buy extra snacks of basics such as bread, butter, cheese or beer, or more self-indulgently, slices of tongue or cake. Veal remained in favour at Jesus for centuries as Coleridge remembered a waiter presenting cuts from a large, coarse animal, 'tottering on the edge of beef!'

Thomas Gray, newly-arrived in 1737, wrote, in much the same terms as Strype:

> if any body don't like their Commons, they send down into the Kitchen to know, what's for Sizing: the Cook sends up a Catalogue of what there is; and they choose what they please: they are obliged to pay for Commons, whether they eat it or no: there is always Plenty enough: the Sizers feast upon the leavings of the rest.

In some colleges sizars ate leavings from the fellows' table – a far more delectable perquisite.

The fastidious Conrad von Uffenbach, visiting in 1710, was less impressed by Trinity's dining hall than repelled by its ambience

– 'Very large, but ugly, smoky and smelling so strongly of bread and meat that it would be impossible for me to eat a morsel in it.' He also thought Cambridge inns 'very ill-appointed and expensive' and complained that 'one must dine every day pretty near alike, as on mutton etc.' Culinary relief came from the celebrated Dr Bentley of Trinity, where Uffenbach was 'very sumptuously entertained', though 'as his wife dined with us, we did not converse upon serious matters.' Coffee-houses supplied another welcome refuge, offering refreshments, the solace of tobacco and the opportunity to read the – then very expensive – newspapers. The Greek's Coffee House was run by a genuine Greek, whose nationality was thought sufficient to guarantee a mastery of preparing the mysterious brew.

A century later, as a nervous Trinity freshman, future novelist Edward Bulwer-Lytton (1803–73) learnt the hard way that dining in common had a Darwinian edge to it:

When the dishes were all placed on the table, there was ... a murmur and a sudden rush ... I dropped into place by an enormous sirloin of beef. This was abruptly seized and a fork stuck in it. A pile then suddenly rose on the plate of my opposite neighbour. Scarcely had he relinquished the sirloin than it was pounced upon by another ... A third succeeded and I began to cast a disconsolate glance at a hacked and maimed shoulder of mutton ... when I found the beef before me ... and was just going to make up for lost time ... it vanished in a trice.

Something to celebrate

Major events in the life of colleges – the anniversary of its foundation, the inauguration of a new Master, the completion of a major building project – have for centuries been marked by feasts of splendour, not to say excess. University, as well as college, occasions were traditionally marked by consumption on a heroic scale. As late as the 1820s the formal proclamation of Stourbridge Fair involved rituals of eating and drinking spread over most of a day. At 11:00am the Vice-Chancellor, attended by an entourage of university officers, went to the Senate House 'where a plentiful supply of mulled wine and sherry ... with a great variety of cakes, awaited their arrival'. Having despatched these, the official party proceeded by carriage to the Fair itself, where, after making the formal proclamation, they were 'joined by numbers of Masters of Arts, who had formed no part of the procession, but who had come for the express purpose of eating oysters. This was a *very serious part* of the day's proceedings and occupied a long time.' After a brief interval, during which waiters reordered the dining area, a dinner was served for some 30 to 40 persons, consisting of an unvarying annual menu of herrings, roast neck of pork, 'an enormous plum pudding', legs of pork boiled, pease-pudding, goose, apple pies and 'a round of beef in the centre'. The wine, apparently, was 'execrable' but a great deal was drunk before the party broke up at 6:30pm.

To mark Queen Victoria's coronation in June 1838, the people of Cambridge had a huge picnic on Parker's Piece, attended by 3,000 Sunday school pupils and 'charity children' and 12,000 of 'the poor'. £1,758 collected from the city's affluent residents paid for 7,029 joints of meat, 4,500 loaves of bread, 1,650 plum puddings and 99 barrels of beer.

The more affluent mid-Victorian undergraduates entertained each other to substantial breakfasts between 9:00 and 10:00. Coffee, tea and muffins were bought in from 'town' while the college kitchen supplied hot dishes such as soles, cutlets, steaks, chops or 'spread eagle' – a fowl split and stewed with mushrooms. This was followed by the smoking of pipes and the consumption of ale or cider before the party dispersed to aid their digestion by sitting through a lecture or two before lunch.

As the cult of sport came to dominate the late Victorian university the proliferation of sporting clubs provided occasions for lavish formal dinners – at least formal when the evening began. The menu for the University Drag and Beagle Hunt in 1892 consisted of solid stuff to fill solid young men – mock-turtle or clear spring soup, salmon with cardinal sauce or smelts with hollandaise sauce, sirloin of beef or saddle of mutton, followed by braised fowl a la Milanaise or York ham and topped off with Winchester puddings, rhubarb tarts and jellies. The Bump Supper served at Caius a couple of years later was even more pretentious, the Frenchified menu studded with in-jokes based on the local landscape – 'Potage a la get-out-at-the-Pike-and-Eel' and 'Canard Sauvage a la Ditton Fen' etc.

Victorian dons indulged in domestic dinner parties, gargantuan by modern standards, throwing a huge burden on their servants. Lady Caroline Jebb (1840–1930), an American by birth, knew she had a gem in her Mrs Bird who, with only the help of a girl hired for the day, single-handedly prepared for a dozen guests fresh-baked rolls, 'white soup', sole fillets with lobster sauce, roast leg of mutton, turkey with oyster sauce and roast duck with its sauce. Two entrées – foie gras and 'sweetbreads stewed with mushrooms and truffles' – were sent over from the college kitchen to give Mrs Bird breathing-space between courses. College also supplied a plum pudding and a *Charlotte russe*, followed by cheese and 'desserts'.

Gwen Raverat (1885–1957), the celebrated wood engraver, remembered the social perils of such occasions:

> The guests were seated according to the Protocol, the Heads of Houses ranking by the dates of the foundations of their colleges, except that the Vice-Chancellor would come first of all. After the Masters came the Regius Professors in the order of their subjects, Divinity first; and then the other Professors according to the date of the foundations of their chairs ... It was better not to invite too many important people at the same time or the complications became insoluble to hosts of only ordinary culture. How could they tell if Hebrew or Greek took precedence, of two professorships founded in the same year?

In April 1885 Raverat's parents gave a small dinner party, with only two male guests, but the menu still ran to tomato soup, fried smelts and

butter sauce, mushrooms on toast, roast beef, cauliflower and potatoes, apple charlotte, toasted cheese and a dessert selection of candied
peel, oranges, peanuts, raisins and ginger. In October of the same
year the guest of honour was eminent scientist Sir William Thomson
(1824–1907), so the menu was even grander – clear soup, brill and
lobster sauce, chicken cutlets and rice balls, oyster patties, mutton
with potatoes, artichokes and beets, partridges and salad and then
a choice of caramel pudding or pears and whipped cream, followed
by cheese ramequins or cheese straws, followed by an ice, concluded
with grapes, walnuts, chocolates and pears – the whole extravaganza
prepared and served by three household servants, Gwen's mother
eschewing College staff as an extravagance.

Bachelor dons in the wealthier colleges needed no outside invita-
tions to indulge themselves. Larger-than-life historian, Oscar Browning, a Fellow of King's for 50 years, began daily with bread and butter
and tea in bed, followed by a full breakfast in hall, had lunch, with
claret, then afternoon tea and for dinner soup, fish, a joint, hot dessert,
cold dessert and savoury, with champagne. He then set his alarm clock
for 3:00am to drink a bottle of strong ale. 'Hard daily tennis and a
Turkish bath' and vacation exertions, like crossing the Alps on a tricy-
cle, helped him live to 86.

After the Great War large-scale domestic dinner parties were cur-
tailed by the rising cost of servants and the falling value of academic
salaries. But collegiate bachelors were largely cushioned from these.
Mansfield Forbes (1889–1936) of Clare 'entertained with erratic
munificence', characteristically Sunday breakfast parties for a dozen
guests which started at 9:00 and 'were apt to go on indefinitely.' For
the host the guests mattered more than the food. On one occasion
he 'scoured the country to collect seven red-haired curates as a sort of
centrepiece ... and on another ... a large number ... all of whose names
ended in -bottom or -botham, and left them to mutual introductions.'

In 1929 A E Housman hosted a dinner for 'the Family', an exclusive donnish dining club originating as a semi-secret Jacobite clique.
Members included the Masters of Clare, Magdalene and Downing,

the Regius Professor of Physic, the Professor of Astrophysics and the University Librarian. Their meal began with Whitstable oysters, with a 1918 Meursault; then came a pastry appetiser with Oloroso sherry, sole fillets with a 1921 Auslese, mutton cutlets, noisette potatoes and buttered green beans, with a 1921 Pommery, followed by a savoury, four desserts, two more wines, port (1878!) and cognac (1869!).

Virginia Woolf, lunching at King's in the 1920s, ate sole and partridge – 'many and various ... with all their retinues of sauces and salads ... potatoes, thin as coins ... sprouts, foliated as rosebuds' and then, 'wreathed in napkins, a confection which rose all sugar from the waves.' This was in the most blatant contrast to the austerity described in her depiction of fictional 'Fernham' (i.e. Newnham) College where dinner consisted of 'plain gravy soup ... beef with its attendant greens and potatoes ... prunes and custard ... biscuits and cheese', with tap water to drink. Noting fair-mindedly that 'the supply was sufficient and coal-miners doubtless were sitting down to less', she yet cannot have imagined the gastronomic privations that a second World War would inflict on a future generation of female students, when the young ladies of Girton would consume the college swans, first as roasts, then as rissoles and finally as soup.

7

Empires of the Mind

Cambridge around 1870 had a high reputation for Mathematics, Geology, Botany and, of course, the Classics, but the teaching of Medicine and Law were still limited and the teaching of the Sciences was generally rudimentary. Serious History had scarcely begun, let alone medieval, modern and non-European languages, Engineering or Economics, all of which would become established before 1914. The university remained essentially a federation of colleges, fundamentally Anglican and misogynist in its forms and assumptions.

Over the next half-century Cambridge would acquire new departments, laboratories, museums, playing fields, pavilions and boathouses, even new colleges and new suburbs, while becoming increasingly secular, and accustomed, if reluctantly, to a female presence. Ironically in a university which had originated as a cluster of religious foundations, had been dominated by clergymen and had become in large part a factory for producing more of them, it was only after the abolition of religious tests that it became an eminent centre for theology and formal clergy training – even as agnosticism became accepted among both staff and students. Compulsory chapel – usually at 7:00am – remained normative for undergraduates, however, not least because it ensured that they got out of bed. As dons ceased to be a species of clergy in this period, they married and became more professional, though they remained as eccentric and instinctively conservative as their predecessors, still more noteworthy as great 'characters' than as great teachers.

Between 1870 and 1900 the undergraduate population rose by almost half, from 2,019 to 2,985. At the collegiate level the picture was more complex, depending largely on the extent to which change was embraced or resisted. Trinity increased its undergraduate number by more than 100 to 676, while St John's fell by 124 to 237. In 1880 Pembroke and Corpus each had 122 undergraduates; by 1900 Pembroke had 226, Corpus just 59. A major depression in agriculture hit college rent-rolls hard, providing reactionaries with a readymade excuse for doing nothing, but the more enterprising colleges compensated by developing urban properties. Caius, for example, commemorated such college worthies as Harvey and Willis in the names of streets it built in south-east Cambridge.

Powerhouse

The Cavendish Laboratory was established in 1870 thanks to an extraordinarily generous endowment from William Cavendish (1809–91), seventh Duke of Devonshire, Chancellor of the University from 1861 and a very entrepreneurial aristocrat with interests in agriculture, iron and railways. For the first time Cambridge would have a purpose-built facility for experimental science, albeit in the Tudor Gothic design of a Jesus graduate, local architect W M Fawcett.

The first Cavendish Professor (1871–9) James Clerk Maxwell (1831–79), was a Scot, Apostle, protégé of Whewell and professor at King's, London before he was 30. Clerk Maxwell's *Treatise on Electricity and Magnetism* (1873) brought a new mathematical rigour to Faraday's pioneering work in those fields, preparing the way for the invention of radio and the telephone. The leading theoretical physicist of his day, Clerk Maxwell also contributed major advances to the understanding of gases, heat, colour and radiation.

Next (1879–84) came the third Baron Rayleigh, John Strutt, (1842–1919), whose interests included vibratory motion, the theory of sound and the wave theory of light. As the co-discoverer in 1894 of a new element, the inert gas argon (used in lighting and lasers), Rayleigh was awarded the recently-established Nobel Prize for Physics in 1904, the first of 85 awarded to Cambridge scientists since then. Although his tenure at the Cavendish was brief, Rayleigh's own stature as a scientist and later eminence as President of the Royal Society and Chancellor of the University added lustre to its reputation. A section of the Whipple Museum is devoted to Rayleigh's career.

The international standing of the Cavendish as a major research institution was achieved under the direction (1884–1919) of J J Thomson (1856–1940) – commemorated by a handsome plaque in Free School Lane as the discoverer of the electron. Without an understanding of the electron there would be no electronics – no radio, CDs, TV, computers, robots, satellites, microwave ovens or mobile phones – none of the inventions which have revolutionised life since 1897 when Thomson announced his discovery of a subatomic particle he called a 'corpuscle'. Realising cathode rays consisted of rapidly moving particles, he measured their speed and specific charge to deduce that 'corpuscles' must be nearly 2,000 times less in mass than the lightest known atomic particle, the hydrogen ion. Thomson's breakthrough was, in the words of another Nobel Laureate, Owen Richardson (1879–1959), less a discovery than a revolution, giving birth to a 'new physics'. For his discovery Thomson received the Nobel Prize for Physics and was knighted in 1908.

A teenage engineering prodigy, like Clerk Maxwell, Thomson had entered Owens College, Manchester at just 14. He came to Trinity College and stayed there for the rest of his life, becoming Master in 1918, the first scientist to hold that august office. Elected FRS at 28 in 1884, Thomson, scruffy and sociable, attracted to his team disciples who would garner seven Nobel Prizes, an achievement still unequalled. Others would serve as professors in 55 different universities. Thomson himself became President of the Royal Society, a holder of the Order of Merit and the recipient of 23 honorary degrees. A devout Anglican, keen walker and amateur botanist, he was also interested in psychic research, telepathy and dowsing – but made an exception of philosophy, which he likened to looking for a shadow in a room without any light.

Other Cambridge contributions to science in this period included work on adrenalin by John Newport Lanley (1852–1925), the pioneering study of vitamins by Frederick Gowland Hopkins (1861–1947) and investigations of X-rays and crystallography by Sir William Bragg (1862–1942).

Henry Sidgwick's 'little garden of flowers'

Cambridge's second women's college, Newnham, was largely the brainchild of Henry Sidgwick (1838–1900), an 'Apostle' and classicist turned philosopher. At 26 Sidgwick had confided to his mother from Trinity: 'I find that I have saved £1,700 and hope to save £400 a year as long as I stay here: in spite of all my travelling, books and the extremely luxurious life that I can hardly help leading.' Soon after, however, he confessed to having opposed the proposal for a college ball as 'an unseemly proceeding on the part of a charitable foundation ... of which the majority are clergymen' and also because it would be 'a great expense', in conflict with his own 'miserly tendencies', which led him to become a self-trained expert on academic financing. As Professor of Philosophy he would set aside enough of his salary to fund a second Chair in his discipline.

Sidgwick, as well as championing female education, became what might be called a devout agnostic. (Keynes later remarked acidly that Sidgwick 'never did anything but wonder whether Christianity was true and prove it wasn't and hope that it was'.) Sidgwick was additionally a pioneer of psychic research and also promoted and helped pay for the foundation of the university's Museum of Physiology. Sidgwick's wife, Eleanor 'Nora' Balfour (1845–1936), sister of the future Prime Minister, Arthur Balfour (1848–1930), would serve as Treasurer, Vice-Principal and Principal of Newnham. The venture began in 1871–2 with five females in a house at 74 Regent Street, then moved to

Merton House in the grounds of St John's. When the first of its purpose-built premises, Newnham Hall (now Old Hall), opened in 1875, it was still 'in the midst of open country with hedgerows all about.'

Newnham College was designed by Basil Champneys (1842–1935), who remained responsible for all the additional buildings put up until 1910. Himself a Trinity classicist, Champneys took to architecture as an art rather than a profession, devoting his talents largely to educational projects. Champney's choice for Newnham was a 'Queen Anne' style with Dutch detailing and neat white woodwork, which set it apart from the Gothic and Tudor still favoured by men's colleges and has been praised for its welcoming domesticity. Dividing student accommodation into separate houses linked by corridors enabled undergraduates to identify with both the larger community of the college and a smaller unit within it. Whitstead, where Sylvia Plath would live on the third floor, became a house for foreign students.

The first Principal of Newnham was Miss Anne Jemima Clough (1820–92), a self-educated schoolmistress, beloved of her students but, by her own admission, lacking in organisational skills. After her death, the headship passed to Mrs Sidgwick, whose husband came to live in college with her. The main road running beside the college is Sidgwick Avenue, which is only fair, because he paid for it to be made. Mrs Sidgwick wisely suggested the handsome avenue of plane trees to complement it. (Though she, doubtless, never had to sweep up the leaves each autumn.)

Unlike Girton, Newnham did not aim to match male students on terms of exact equality. Newnham students were permitted to proceed at their own pace and, in the early years, were not even required to enter for the university examinations. This did not inhibit a striving after excellence. In 1890 Philippa Fawcett of Newnham was ranked above the Senior Wrangler. Another early student was Florence Ada Keynes (1861–1958), the future mother of J M Keynes. Florence went on to serve as Mayor of Cambridge (1932–3) and to write *By-ways of Cambridge History*.

Newnham's most charismatic and colourful 'character' was the archaeologist Jane Harrison (1850–1928), whose work on Greek myth had a profound influence on Francis Cornford. She lectured on Greek art in the galleries of the British Museum and, even more daringly, in boys' public schools. She wrote a guide to the myths and monuments of Athens and was remarkably uncondescending towards students. In her celebrated essay *A Room of One's Own*, Virginia Woolf imagines the recently deceased Harrison's spirit on the terrace, glancing over the garden, a 'bent figure, formidable yet humble, with her great forehead and her long shabby dress.' Augustus John, no less, was commissioned to paint her portrait. Mary Beard's *The Invention of Jane Harrison* (2000) attempts to penetrate the personality behind the legend.

Hughes Hall was established in 1885, initially at Newnham as the Cambridge Women's Training College to produce teachers for girls' secondary schools. Its creator, Miss Elizabeth Phillips Hughes (1851–1925) was a Welsh schoolmistress who had belatedly entered Newnham College at 30. The college which would eventually bear her name was essentially her creation. When it opened with 14 students she not only ran it but did all the teaching. By the time she left, it had its own purpose-built premises on Wollaston Road, facing Fenner's cricket ground. Designed in a neo-Dutch style reminiscent of Newnham College, it was also the work of W M Fawcett. Fawcett, 'not a man of much talent' in Pevsner's view, was also employed on projects by Caius, Queens', St Catharine's, King's College School, the University Press, the Cavendish Laboratory, the Local Examinations Syndicate and the Botanic Gardens.

The missionary impulse

If mid-Victorian Britain had an undisputed hero it was the missionary-explorer David Livingstone (1813–1873). On 4 December 1857 he electrified a packed Senate House recounting his endeavours to bring Christianity and commerce to Africa to undermine the abomination of the trade in slaves, closing his remarks with a climactic, accusatory challenge – 'The sort of men who are wanted for missionaries are such as I see before me. I beg to direct your attention to Africa ... do you carry out the work which I have begun. I LEAVE IT WITH YOU!'

George Augustus Selwyn (1809–78) had heard the call to mission long before. Forsaking the comforts of a fellowship at St John's, he was ordained as first Bishop of New Zealand at 32, after the Treaty of Waitangi (1840) formalised British annexation, clearing the way for systematic white settlement. On the long voyage out to his new home Selwyn proved the value of a classical education by mastering the Maori language so well he could preach in it as soon as he arrived. He also learnt as much seamanship as enabled him to become his own sailing-master when he discovered that – by a clerical error (in both senses) – a vast slew of Pacific islands had been included in his diocese. Outstanding as an administrator, Selwyn created an organisational template for the subsequent development of colonial churches throughout the British empire. A key principle was the officeholder's signed pledge to resign when required, emphasising that Church office was a path to service, not a species of property like the Anglican country livings traditionally taken by Cambridge ex-fellows on marriage. Selwyn's legacy also included another template, drawn from his grounding in the classical tongues – *A Verbal Analysis of the Holy Bible intended to facilitate the translation of the Holy Scriptures into Foreign Languages.*

An Anglican establishment, opened in 1882 in conscious imitation of Keble College, Oxford, 'Selwyn Hostel' took its name and inspiration from Selwyn's example and career. (The Selwyn Divinity School, built in 1879, commemorates and was paid for by his older brother, the considerably less adventurous Lady Margaret Professor of Divinity, William Selwyn (1806–75).) The new foundation aimed to cater for men aspiring to the ministry, especially those whose vocation would otherwise be frustrated by poverty. A shoestring enterprise itself, the college was built in stages over several decades. It was also required that the Master should be in holy orders. To those elements in the university who had recently achieved victory in their long campaign to abolish religious tests, this 'strictly sectarian seminary' looked very retrograde, though they were probably mollified by the fact that Selwyn wasn't quite a college in the traditional sense. Although it had a resident body of students, it had no fellows (until 1913), was technically a 'public hostel', not a college, and its principal, denied the standing of a 'head of house', was ineligible to serve as Vice-Chancellor. The tone of the establishment was austere. The same food was served at high table as to undergraduates. A limit of £5 per term was set on 'such luxuries as are eaten, drunk or smoked.' Known from 1923 as Selwyn College, in 1926 Selwyn's status was revised to that of an 'Approved Foundation', the last way-station on the route to full collegiate status and incorporation within the formal university structure of governance. Thanks to the efforts of its eminent Anglican master, Prof Owen Chadwick, revised statutes in 1956 relieved students of the obligation to be Anglicans. Selwyn achieved full collegiate status in 1958, expanding across Grange Road into Cripps Court in 1967. Since 1989 the Master – or Mistress – has been required to do no more than 'respect the Anglican traditions of the College'.

George Selwyn's own son, John Richardson Selwyn (1844–98) served as Master from 1890 until his death. As an undergraduate J R Selwyn had been a keen oarsman, but unlike his remarkable father, an indifferent scholar. Originally aiming for the law, when he paid a filial visit to New Zealand he was so inspired by his father's work that he became a missionary himself, until as the second Bishop of Melanesia, he wrecked his own powerful constitution and was forced to retire to England. As Master of Selwyn he founded 'Cambridge House' to undertake missionary work in the slums of London.

Selwyn's original buildings (1882–9) were built in red brick in a Tudor style to the designs of the appropriately budget-conscious Sir Arthur Blomfield (1829–99), himself the son and brother of Anglican bishops. The 'loosely Jacobean' hall (1907–9) features an outside staircase, commended by Pevsner as 'bold' and by Casson as 'larky'. The panelling, of c.1700, was presented by A C Benson and may be by Wren. In the chapel the side windows feature saints and church leaders. Some of the stalls feature heads of contemporary (1895) statesmen. The pectoral cross of Bishop J C Patteson (1827–71), a disciple of G A Selwyn's, is set into the altar. Patteson had abandoned a brilliant Oxford career to become first Bishop of Melanesia, where he mastered 23 local tongues and was eventually killed by the islanders of Nukapu in revenge for the murder of five of their people by white slavers.

Fieldwork feedback

As the careers of the Selwyns, father and son, showed, for Cambridge the tides of empire flowed to and from even the most remote frontiers of cultural contact. In 1888–9 Cambridge scholars journeyed to the Torres Strait, north of Australia, and returned there a decade later, some then going on to New Guinea and beyond, to Sarawak. On the basis of fieldwork thus accomplished, the men who made these strenuous expeditions were to pioneer entirely new fields of study in the university and beyond.

A C Haddon (1855–1940), the youthful director of the Museum of Zoology, became a convert to ethnography after a fieldtrip to Ireland. Going out to Torres Strait as a marine biologist he returned to become part-time Lecturer in Physical Anthropology. He then led the second expedition and was elected an FRS as University Lecturer in Ethnology and Curator of the university's Museum of Archaeology and Anthropology. Haddon's extraordinary expertise was deployed in some 600 articles and books on subjects ranging from textile design to the construction of canoes. After taking a First in Natural Sciences at St John's, William McDougall (1871–1938) qualified as a doctor at St Thomas's Hospital in London. His Torres straits fieldwork on the psychology of vision and attention led to ground-breaking work in social psychology at Oxford, Harvard and Duke University. Charles Samuel Myers (1873–1946) likewise forsook medicine for psychology, opening England's first laboratory for experimental psychology at Cambridge in 1912. During World War One he worked on 'shell shock' cases and then devoted the rest of his career to the emerging field of industrial psychology. Charles Gabriel Seligman (1873–1940), another product of St Thomas's, went out as an expert on tropical diseases but turned to ethnography to produce definitive monographs on peoples of New Guinea, Sri Lanka and the Nilotic Sudan. In 1925 he became the second recipient of the medal established by the Royal Anthropological Institute in memory of his former Torres Strait colleague W H Rivers.

Monumental scholarship

In 1886 Cambridge University Press published a four-volume survey of *The Architectural History of the University and Colleges of Cambridge*, which had been begun by Robert Willis, FRS (1800–75) and was completed after his death by his nephew John Willis Clark, FSA (1833–1910). The expertise of the extraordinary Robert Willis embraced practical talents as a carpenter, draughtsman and musician and, as a scholar, ranged from explaining the workings of the larynx to the cutting of cogwheels, the decipherment of medieval handwriting, the use of iron in railway construction and the history of the Great Seals of England. From 1837 until his death Willis was Jacksonian Professor of Applied Mechanics. A spellbinding lecturer who never used notes, he wrote a standard text on the classification of machines but devoted most of his spare time to the history of architecture. Analysing buildings with the eye of an engineer, he unerringly distinguished the structural from the decorative, the original elements from the imitative. Willis compiled detailed accounts of the architectural history of 15 English cathedrals, plus an authoritative study of the Church of the Holy Sepulchre in Jerusalem, despite never having visited it. Clark, son of the Professor of Anatomy, became a masterly university administrator and produced dozens of publications about every aspect of Cambridge life, including an edition of Loggan's *Cantabrigia Illustrata*. Writing in 1954, Pevsner hailed Willis as 'that giant amongst scholars on matters of building history' and his great work as still 'fresh ... amazingly correct ... beautifully clear and well-ordered', noting wistfully 'The likes of him could never exist in our century of specialisation.' A modern facsimile edition of Willis & Clark's *Architectural History* is available today. Visitors to Little St Mary's can see two monuments to John Willis Clark, a modest bronze plaque to the right of the altar, beneath the organ loft, and the east window, which includes his coat of arms (third from the left at the base).

The history boys

'Cambridge History' was founded by practitioners who were all, from the point of view of their professional successors, untrained amateurs. Frederic William Maitland (1850–1906) had the posthumous honour, almost a century after his death, of being the first academic historian to be recognised with a memorial in Westminster Abbey. A star pupil of Henry Sidgwick and later a practising lawyer, Maitland was recalled to Cambridge in 1884, and resolved to write the history of England's legal heritage with all its ramifications – constitutional, religious, economic and social. Having set himself this monumental task, Maitland recognised the desirability of research-based collective effort. He was therefore responsible, in 1887, for founding the Selden Society. Named after the lawyer, antiquary and manuscript collector John Selden (1584–1654), this aimed to preserve and publish legal records to benefit scholars internationally. When the Society's treasurer shot himself after embezzling funds Maitland bailed it out. Maitland himself read widely in several languages, mastered the intricacies of medieval court and parliamentary procedures, taught himself palaeography and wrote a grammar of Norman French.

Maitland was the first historian to recognise that the Public Records Office represented not a mere mountain of dead documents but a window into medieval England. His major publications, *The History of English Law before the time of Edward I* (1895) and *Roman Canon Law in the Church of England* (1898) were formidable tomes, immediately hailed as indisputably authoritative. A course of polished lectures given in 1886–7 was published posthumously as *The Constitutional History of England* (1908). He reached a wider audience with a volume of essays, *Domesday Book and Beyond* (1897), in which he demonstrated how the known facts of the Domesday Book could reveal previously unknown aspects of Anglo-Saxon society. Maitland showed that the task of the historian was not merely to describe the past but to explain it. He understood that our medieval ancestors thought differently from us and used words and legal terms in a different sense from us. We must therefore aim to understand not just what a document means in the present day but what it meant to the people who wrote it and by whom it was intended to be read.

The founding father of History as a subject of undergraduate study at Cambridge was Sir John Seeley (1834–95), a classicist who had written no substantial work of history before being appointed Regius Professor at 35. A pompous, henpecked insomniac, Seeley was also a superb lecturer, who attracted many students not studying the historical Tripos, which he helped to establish in 1873. Seeley believed that history should be a school of statesmanship. Politics, and particularly the inter-state rivalries of the 18th and 19th centuries were his central interests; a history of British imperialism his lasting legacy. *The Expansion of England* chronicled the global rivalry of Britain and France between 1688 and 1815, emphasising the growth of an empire acquired, in Seeley's most memorable phrase, 'in a fit of absence of mind'. Implicit in its account of a haphazard and improvised process was the call to make coherent a 'Greater Britain' of English-speaking settler societies from Newfoundland to New Zealand. The publication in 1883 of Seeley's extended essay coincided fruitfully with the rapid extension of railway, steamship and telegraph services, binding the empire ever closer through trade, emigration and investment. *The Expansion of England* thus provided a timely historical rationale for the zenith of the imperial project. Seeley's *Expansion* sold more than 80,000 copies in two years and remained in print until 1956.

Born in Naples of a German mother and educated in Paris, Edinburgh and Munich, Sir John Emerich Edward Dahlberg, first Baron

Acton of Aldenham, FSA (1834–1902) was therefore 'never more than half an Englishman'. By 25 he had attended constitutional debates in Philadelphia and the coronation of a Tsar and been elected an MP. At 35 he became a peer at the behest of Gladstone, who treated him as a one-man Brains Trust. Said to have read a book a day, Acton accumulated some 59,000 volumes, divided by category, the largest sections being ecclesiastical history and political history. A consistently anti-Papal Roman Catholic, Acton deployed massive erudition to champion liberty of conscience and scientific objectivity against Vatican authority and traditionalist obscurantism, but somehow managed to escape excommunication. In 1886 he helped to establish the *English Historical Review* as the premier learned journal of professional historians. In 1895 Lord Rosebery nominated him Regius Professor. Throwing himself into his work, Acton attracted packed audiences to his finely-crafted lectures on the French Revolution. But his major legacy was the multi-volume *Cambridge Modern History*, the detailed planning of which broke his health and whose publication he never lived to see. Purchased for the reference sections of thousands of libraries worldwide, it set a pattern for similar projects in ancient, medieval, economic, Islamic, urban and other histories which became a mainstay of the University Press. Lord Acton is chiefly remembered for his dictum that 'all power corrupts and absolute power corrupts absolutely'; in fact he said, 'all power *tends* to corrupt and absolute power *tends* to corrupt absolutely'. When Acton died the Scottish–American millionaire philanthropist Andrew Carnegie bought his great library and presented it to the Liberal statesman John, Viscount Morley, who immediately donated it to Cambridge University Library.

Magdalene man

The son of Edward White Benson, Archbishop of Canterbury, Arthur Christopher Benson (1862–1925) took a First in Classics at King's, taught brilliantly at Eton for almost 20 years, then resigned to write 100 books of biography, criticism and essays, including a three-volume edition of the letters of Queen Victoria, the words for *Land of Hope and Glory* and an affectionate account of Cambridge life, *From a College Window*. Writing gave Benson the financial independence to accept an unpaid Fellowship at Magdalene in 1904, expressing his affection for 'the poor little College – so beautiful and stately and venerable and yet so out at elbows and out of heart. I made a prayer that I might perhaps be allowed to raise her up.' Which is exactly what he did, becoming Master of Magdalene and effecting a domestic and academic revolution by installing electricity and a bath house, improving the food and establishing its May Ball. Cultured, rather than scholarly, Benson was renowned as a delightful conversationalist thanks to childhood training, the Archbishop's offspring 'being criticised and schooled by their father after every party.' Benson was also, apparently, trained not to let the mask of urbanity slip, keeping a surprisingly acerbic diary of 5,000,000 words, which reveals a deeply depressive personality quite at odds with the exuberant charm which made him so generally beloved.

'Squaring'

Francis Macdonald Cornford (1874–1943), FBA, was a top-line classicist who challenged the prevailing approach to the study of ancient Greece, not by abandoning its classic texts but by trying to get past the texts, as it were, to the mental and moral world from which they had emerged. Drawing insights from the novel insights of archaeology and anthropology, Cornford investigated such phenomena as ritual behaviour and symbolic artefacts, like coins and statuary, which purely textual scholars had previously ignored. He also wrote a very funny – and perceptive – book about university politics. *Microcosmographia Academica, being a guide for the young academic politician*, was first published in 1908. Unlike most satires it has stood the test of time, being reprinted in 1922, 1933, 1949 and 1953. Cornford explains that university politics revolve around 'Jobs', which fall into two categories – 'My Jobs are public-spirited proposals, which happen (much to my regret) to involve the advancement of personal friends, or (still more to my regret) of myself. Your Jobs are insidious intrigues for the advancement of yourself and your friends, speciously disguised as public-spirited proposals.'

The reconciliation of conflicting Jobs – 'squaring' – 'can be carried on at lunch; but it is better that we meet casually', preferably between 2:00 and 4:00pm, somewhere between Pembroke and Caius, on King's Parade. After meeting 'accidentally' and chatting 'about indifferent matters', conversation should be broken off.

> After walking five paces in the opposite direction you should call me back and begin with the words, 'Oh, by the way, if you should happen...'. The nature of Your Job must then be vaguely indicated, without mentioning names; and it should be treated by both parties as a matter of very small importance. You should hint that I am a very influential person, and that the whole thing is a secret between us. Then we shall part as before, and I shall call you back and introduce the subject of My Job, in the same formula. By observing this procedure we shall emphasise the fact that there is no connection whatever between my supporting your Job and your supporting mine. This absence of connection is the essential feature of Squaring.

The ambitious young don is therefore admonished to choose whether or not to become one of 'the men who get things done' because they walk the post-prandial King's Parade beat 'every day of their lives' – 'You can either join them, and become a powerful person; or you can join the great throng of those who spend all their time in preventing them from getting things done, and in the larger task of preventing one another from doing anything whatever.'

Cornford doubtless drew on the frustrations he had himself experienced in trying to promote the suggestions wittily set out in his reformist pamphlet *The Cambridge Classical Course* (1903), which called for a less narrowly philological, more humanistic, approach and an effort to reduce chaotic collegiate teaching arrangements to some sort of coherence. Cornford's gifted son was to sacrifice himself to an altogether more brutal form of politics.

The changing town

By 1914 Cambridge, the university, was noticeably different from its mid-Victorian incarnation and this was even more the case with Cambridge, the town. From 1888 onwards changes were chronicled and commented on in the columns of the *Cambridge Evening News*, the town's first daily newspaper. Civic and commercial, rather than university or collegiate, initiatives began to make their mark on the city. In 1907 Alexandra Gardens opened on the site of old brick-pits. In 1914 a new County Hall opened in Hobson Street. As college fellows were generally granted permission to marry by the 1880s their need for residential housing fuelled a minor building boom which enlarged the city's suburban quarters and in 1911 encouraged Cyril Ridgeon to establish his well-known building materials business, starting from the back bedroom of his house.

From 1875 onwards academics and townsfolk alike had the option of sending their sons to the Leys School, a Methodist foundation. In 1890 the Perse School moved from Free School Lane out to Hills Road. To accommodate the needs of a growing town where everything was no longer within a convenient walking distance, a horse-drawn tram service was inaugurated in 1880 and continued in service until 1914. Horse-drawn buses lasted only until 1902, to be replaced by motor bus services from 1905 onwards. By far the most enduring impact on the mobility of Cambridge residents was, however, the general adoption of the pneumatic-tyre 'safety bicycle' from the 1880s onwards. On the river punting became a favoured pastime.

Motor cars only became legal on the Queen's highways in 1896. The first person to own a motor car in Cambridge, and only the fourth in all of Britain, was the Hon Charles Stewart Rolls (1877–1910), captain of the university cycling team. One of the first graduates in engineering, Rolls went on to partner Frederick Henry Royce (1863–1933) in manufacturing the most famous motor car in the world. A daredevil driver, Rolls set numerous motoring records and made 10 balloon ascents before becoming the first Englishman to die in an aeroplane crash.

Electricity came to Cambridge in 1892 and the installation of a modern sewerage system began the following year. A decade later, however, one in eight children born in Cambridge still died before reaching their first birthday. However, in 1909 Cambridge became the first English town to provide free dental care to its schoolchildren. Rising standards of prosperity among the general population were reflected in new leisure opportunities. The university finally renounced its powers to control theatres in 1894 (at the same time renouncing its power to detain women at random on suspicion of prostitution). The New Theatre opened in 1896. In 1908 the first regular film shows were put on in the Corn Exchange. The purpose-built Playhouse Cinema opened in 1912. From 1908 football fans could cheer on Cambridge Town FC, the ancestor of today's Cambridge City, and from 1912 its rival, Abbey United, was formed, later Cambridge United. The growing popularity of Cambridge as a visitor destination led the University Arms Hotel to add a new wing in 1900.

Cambridge even began to develop an industrial sector. In 1896 William George Pye (1869–1949), a former technician in the Cavendish Laboratory, started up a business in the garden shed of the family home. This evolved into a factory in Newmarket Road which in 1921 began to manufacture radios and by the 1950s would become Britain's largest domestic producer of television sets. In 1909 David Marshall (1873–1942), a former apprentice in the kitchens at Trinity College, founded a chauffeur service; by 1912 he had established his first garage in Jesus Lane. Marshall's would later become a leading force in aviation, opening its own airfield and eventually becoming responsible for producing Concorde's iconic 'drop-nose'. Out at Histon, the farming Chivers family opened a jam factory in 1875 and then diversified into marmalade, jellies, lemonade, mincemeat, preserves and puddings which became standard fare for tea-times and picnics among undergraduates and dons alike.

Landmark

When the architect William Wilkins lived at Lensfield House it was on the very edge of Cambridge. The encroachment of the city eroded its rural charm and in 1879 the whole Lensfield estate was acquired by England's premier Roman Catholic aristocrat, Henry Fitzalan-Howard, the 15th Duke of Norfolk (1847–1917). 1885 saw the construction of the Church of Our Lady of the Assumption and English Martyrs on Lensfield Road, the entire costs of which – £70,000 – were borne by a widow, Mrs Yolande Marie Louise Lyne-Stephens (1812–94). Half a century previously, in 1833, as French ballet dancer Pauline Duvernay, she had bewitched Thackeray on her debut. Her future husband, Stephens Lyne Stephens, was allegedly the richest commoner in England, thanks to his family's glass factories in Portugal. By the time Pauline/Yolande became his mistress she had already had two lovers and was pregnant by the Marquis de La Valette, miscarrying his child. She then became respectable – but, doubtless to her regret, remained childless.

E M Forster noted wryly in *The Longest Journey* (1907):

> [Lensfield House] is the first big building that the incoming
> visitor sees. 'Oh, here come the colleges!' cries the Protestant
> parent and then learns that it was built by a Papist who made a
> fortune out of movable eyes for dolls. 'Built out of dolls' eyes to
> contain idols' – that, at all events, is the legend and the joke.

An inscription recording Mrs Stephens' beneficence can be seen on the Hills Road side of the church, as well as the *Ave Maria*. Putting this prayer on the *outside* of the church galled local Protestant hardliners who had opposed the whole project. Good job they didn't know more about her past...

JEWELS IN THE CROWN: AN ORIENTAL INTERLUDE

Britain's post-war super-spy, James Bond, allegedly took a First in Oriental Languages at Cambridge; but Cambridge has many links with Asia that are far from fictional. Lee Kuan Yew, creator of modern Singapore, read Law at Cambridge. The best-known broadcaster about India, Mark Tully, read History and Theology at Trinity Hall. By 2007 the number of Chinese students at Cambridge outnumbered the Americans by 478 to 435. The university also has a Muslim male-voice choir, *Harmonia Alcorani*, which performs in English, Arabic and Turkish.

From 1878 onwards Cambridge offered a Tripos in Semitic Languages and from 1879 in Indian Languages. Abdullah Yusuf Ali (1872–1953), who graduated from St John's in 1895, produced a translation of the Qur'an which has outsold all others. In 1905 a Cambridge and Oxford Society was founded in Tokyo by young Japanese aristocrats – most of whom had studied at Cambridge. The best-known Urdu poet of the 20th century, Sir Muhammad Iqbal (1873–1938) graduated in Law from Trinity in 1906. In 1907 the future first Prime Minister of independent India, Jawaharlal Nehru (1889–1964), came up to Trinity to read Natural Sciences and passed 'three quiet years with little of disturbance in them, moving slowly on like the sluggish Cam'. He was followed in 1919 by Subhas Chandra Bose (1897–1945), who read Moral Sciences at Fitzwilliam House and during World War Two raised a Japanese-sponsored army to overthrow British rule in India. Another Indian Prime Minister, Rajiv Gandhi (1944–91), read Mechanical Sciences at Cambridge. Abba Eban (1915–2002), sometime Foreign Secretary of Israel, when congratulated on his 'Oxford accent', replied, 'Sir, I would have you know that I went to Cambridge, but in public life you must expect to be smeared.'

Some Arabists

The first Professorship of Arabic in the English-speaking world was established by Sir Thomas Adams (1586–1668), a self-made man from

Shropshire and Lord Mayor of London, who bequeathed £40 a year in perpetuity for its upkeep and also sponsored the translation of the Gospels into Persian. The first occupant of the new chair was another Salopian, the self-taught Abraham Wheelock (1593–1653). A poor man, scarcely much better off for the meagre salary attached to the chair, Wheelock laboured diligently at the University Library on Anglo-Saxon manuscripts and taught to supplement his income but was unable to publish in Arabic for lack of facilities for printing the language.

Born in Cambridge, Edward Palmer (1840–82) learnt Romany as a boy from gypsy tramps and tinkers, then Italian from organ-grinders and French from political exiles, also becoming adept at hypnotism and conjuring. Returning to Cambridge, he dabbled in acting and versifying and befriended resident teachers of Oriental languages who helped him master Arabic, Persian and Urdu. Palmer's gifts as a linguist secured him first admission to St John's in 1863, then a fellowship and membership of an expedition to the Middle East, during which he walked 600 miles of desert from Sinai to Jerusalem, establishing the true site of the Holy Sepulchre and the age of the Dome of the Rock. Appointed Professor of Arabic in 1871, in 10 years he produced an Arabic grammar, a Persian dictionary, a translation of the Qur'an and the complete works of the Egyptian poet Zoheir, qualified as a barrister, served as official interpreter for a visiting Shah of Persia, examined candidates in Indian languages for the civil service, scribbled off burlesques for the local stage, edited a college magazine and helped colleagues work on manuscripts in Finnish and Danish. Recruited to work for the army as a secret agent among the Bedouin during the British invasion of Egypt in 1882, Palmer was ambushed in the desert, robbed and murdered. The government went to extraordinary lengths to discover and punish his killers and recover his remains, which were buried in the crypt of St Paul's cathedral. A portrait of Palmer in Arab dress is in the hall of St John's.

The Russo-Turkish war of 1877–88 inspired Edward Granville Browne (1862–1926) to start learning Turkish at 15. After passing the Natural Sciences Tripos to become a doctor, he took the Indian

Languages Tripos in two years, spent a long vacation in Constantinople, qualified in medicine at Bart's Hospital in London, then travelled in Iran for a year, recounting his experiences in *A Year Amongst the Persians* (1893). Browne's *magnum opus* was a four-volume *Literary History of Persia* but he also made a pioneering study of Arab medicine. Browne occupied Pitt's rooms at Pembroke.

Arthur John Arberry, FBA (1905–69), another Pembroke man, took a first in Classics, then a second degree in Arabic and Persian in two years. He also mastered Maltese. After two years in Cairo, Arberry worked in the India Office Library, the wartime Ministry of Information and the University of London. Returning to Cambridge in 1947 after an absence of 15 years, Arberry introduced the study of Turkish and modern, as opposed to classical, Arabic and established the Middle Eastern Centre to provide a focus for the work of scholars scattered in different colleges and faculties. Habitually working a 12-hour day, with football and philately his only diversions, in 1955 Arberry produced a rendering of the Qur'an in English, which set a new standard of literary elegance – but broke his health and hastened his death.

Number one

Cambridge recognised the extraordinary talent of self-taught mathematician Srinivasa Ramanujan (1887–1920), but failed quite literally to nourish him. A humble clerk of a high caste but impoverished background, Ramanujan sent a letter to Godfrey Harold Hardy FRS (1877–1947) of Trinity, querying some of his work and enclosing examples of his own, and Hardy subsequently arranged for Ramanujan to come to Cambridge for a collaboration which was 'the one romantic incident in my life'. In 1918 Ramanujan became the first Indian to be elected a Fellow of the Royal Society; but by then his delicate health was undermined by tuberculosis, worsened by a wartime diet quite unsuited to him. Ramanujan recovered just enough to return home, dying at 32, unknown but recognised by fellow mathematicians as the most original genius for a century.

Hardy's associate Neville Watson (1886–1965) spent 10 years working through Ramanujan's insights, deriving 25 scholarly papers from them and transcribing all of his notebooks with painstaking penmanship. Hardy edited Ramanujan's collected works and wrote his biography.

Asian odyssey

As a Magdalene undergraduate, the future Sir William Empson, FBA (1906–84), excelling in both Mathematics and English, asked his supervisor Ivor Armstrong Richards if, instead of the usual weekly essay, he could work on a sustained theme – the notion that ambiguity might not be a blemish in a poem, as conventional criticism often held, but one way that poetry worked. The resulting 30,000 words became the core of Empson's first book *Seven Types of Ambiguity* (1930), securing him a fellowship, of which he was immediately deprived when a college servant, moving his effects into his new rooms, found condoms among his possessions. This was taken as *prima facie* evidence of unchastity, then an offence against university regulations. Cambridge thus lost a pre-eminent critical and poetic talent for good.

Empson broadened his horizons as a Professor of English in Tokyo (1931–4) and then in war-torn China (1937–40), where the chaos of academic life on the run from the Japanese led him to write out *Othello* entirely from memory. Empson then headed the Chinese section of the BBC's Far Eastern Service and finally took a chair at Sheffield. Cambridge belatedly awarded him an honorary degree in 1977. The *Oxford Companion to English Literature* notes that 'Empson's poetry is extremely difficult, making use of analytical argument and imagery drawn from modern physics and mathematics; a technical virtuoso, he offered (in his own words) "a sort of puzzle interest"'. If ever there was a plausible representative of C P Snow's 'Two Cultures' it was surely Empson. Unfortunately, Cambridge spat him out.

'The Erasmus of the 20th century'

At the time of his death, Joseph Needham (1900–95) was the only Fellow of the Royal Society who was also a Fellow of the British Academy, a Companion of Honour and the holder of the Chinese Order of the Brilliant Star. Polymath George Steiner ranked Needham's intellectual stature alongside Voltaire and Goethe. He certainly had a life quite as extraordinary as either of them.

Initially a research biochemist at Caius, Needham was also master of seven languages and author of two major academic works when his life was turned around in 1937 by the arrival in Cambridge of three Chinese scientists, one of whom, Lu Gwei-Djen, became his mistress, life-long collaborator and, in their 80s, briefly his second wife. In a moment of post-coital repose she wrote out the Chinese character for 'cigarette' (literally 'fragrant smoke') and Needham was hooked on China for the rest of his life.

In 1942 Needham got himself appointed Director of the Sino-British Science Co-operation Office, a political goodwill gesture to help Chinese universities deal with massive wartime disruption. Needham used his posting to travel 30,000 miles, at great personal risk, through ravaged China, visiting 296 universities, institutes and cultural sites, and amassing a priceless collection of books and manuscripts.

Returning to the West, Needham put the Science into the UN's new cultural arm, UNESCO, acting as the first director of its Science Division. In 1954 he began the project which would dominate his life and continue after his death. Needham's study of *Science and Civilization in China*, originally intended as a single volume, expanded to seven, then 17. It is still in progress at the Needham Research Institute, established in 1985, and now stands at 24 volumes of 3,000,000 words.

Most educated people know the Chinese invented or discovered paper, gunpowder and the compass and, on further reflection, would concede the abacus, acupuncture, lacquer, porcelain, tea, chopsticks and noodles. Needham also gave them credit for the umbrella, the fishing reel, chess, clockwork, coinage, the crossbow, asbestos cloth, decimals, dials, dominoes, ball bearings, belt and chain drives, the blast furnace, suspension bridges, the kite, the wheelbarrow, the folding chair, stirrups, the seed drill, the toothbrush, dental fillings, artificial pearls, printing, playing cards, toilet paper, coal dust briquettes, vinegar, the water wheel, the weather vane and air conditioning. Needham was, however, criticised for a) giving rather *too* much uncritical credit to the Chinese and b) failing to answer 'the Needham question' – if the Chinese were so amazingly inventive, why didn't they have a scientific and industrial revolution?

Needham's other activities included founding the Society for Anglo-Chinese Understanding in 1965 and a decade as Master of Caius. His personal enthusiasms included the accordion, fast sports cars, steam railways, morris dancing, nudism and serial philandering. Despite worshipping as a High Church Anglican, Needham consistently refused to condemn the brutal excesses of the Chinese Communist regime. A chair in Chinese studies was endowed in his memory in 2008, the year in which Simon Winchester published his riveting biographical study *Bomb, Book and Compass: Joseph Needham and the Great Secrets of China*.

8

The Great War

> The melancholy of this place nowadays is beyond endurance –
> the Colleges are dead, except for a few Indians and a few pale
> pacifists and bloodthirsty old men hobbling along victorious in
> the absence of youth.
>
> Bertrand Russell, March 1916

When war broke out in August 1914 the rush to the colours was, if any-thing, even more marked in the university than in civilian society as a whole. Max Woosnam (1892–1965) of Trinity, who had won Blues at football, golf, lawn tennis and real tennis, had just landed in Brazil to tour with Corinthians FC when he learnt of the outbreak of hostili-ties. The entire touring party returned straight home the following day and within 24 hours of docking at Tilbury every man had joined up. Woosnam would serve in France with the Royal Welch Fusiliers and survive to compete in the 1920 Antwerp Olympics, where he would win gold in the lawn tennis men's doubles and silver in the mixed doubles. In 1921 he went on to victory in the men's doubles at Wim-bledon, to captain Manchester City FC as First Division runners-up and also to captain the England football team against Wales. But, of 70 undergraduates who came up to St John's in 1913, only four would return to resume their interrupted academic careers and, of those, one would die almost immediately in the post-war influenza pandemic.

By the end of the hostilities some 14,000 former Cambridge students and staff would have fought in active service. Almost one in six would be killed, an amount nearly equal to the entire undergraduate body at any one time in the pre-war decade.

By October 1914 the colleges had fewer than half the usual number of men in residence. By 1915 the figure had halved again to 825; by Easter 1916 it stood at 575. Their places would be taken by serving soldiers, temporarily billeted in colleges, while others were encamped in fields around the town, on Parker's Piece, Midsummer Common and Grantchester Meadow. Refugees were taken in from Belgian universities. The children's ward at Addenbrooke's was converted to receive casualties. Part of the Leys School became a military hospital. The First Eastern General Hospital would occupy King's and Clare's cricket ground, where the University Library now stands, its nurses housed in a whole block at King's. Over the course of the war it would deal with more than 62,000 casualties, of whom only 437 died.

College fare became 'decently frugal'. At night the town was plunged into darkness for fear that German airships might bomb King's College Chapel. Every college chapel held seemingly endless memorial services. Barbara Wootton (1897–1988), later a distinguished social scientist but then a teenager, was profoundly disturbed by the, to her, unprecedented sight of 'distinguished professors and famous men whom I had been brought up to regard with awe openly crying in church.'

'The most handsome man in England'

The name that became synonymous with the idealism and sacrifice of the Great War was Rupert Brooke (1887–1915), once described by Henry James as 'a creature on whom the gods had smiled their brightest'. Brooke had revelled in undergraduate life at King's, becoming a member of the Apostles, President of the University Fabian Society and a founder member of the Marlowe Society. From 1909 to 1912 he lived in a rural idyll at Grantchester, initially at The Orchard in a room opening 'straight out onto a stone verandah covered with creepers and a little old garden full of old-fashioned flowers'. Latterly he was at the Old Vicarage, 'a deserted, lonely, dank, ruined, overgrown, gloomy, lovely house'. Brooke's research on Elizabethan drama was punctuated by meandering riverside walks and bathing in the river. In 1911 he published a well-received volume of *Poems* and in 1912 was elected to a Fellowship at King's, but then suffered a serious breakdown and to recuperate undertook a world tour, which inspired some of his best poetry.

At the outbreak of war Brooke produced a five-sonnet sequence, including 'The Soldier', which included the much-anthologised and personally prophetic lines:

> If I should die think only this of me
> That there's some corner of a foreign field
> That is for ever England.

The public reception of this work immediately marked Brooke as *the* 'war poet'.

Commissioned into the Royal Naval Division, he took part in the attempted relief of Antwerp in October 1914 and was then in the abortive expedition to seize the Dardanelles. Contracting blood-poisoning en route, he was buried on the Greek island of Skyros. An edition of Brooke's *Collected Poems*, published in 1919, is prefaced by a portrait and title-page, featuring two naked youths under a stylised tree – 'Cut On The Wood' by Gwen Raverat. Brooke's name appears on the village war memorial at Trumpington, the work (1921–2) of the supreme modern master of carved lettering, Eric Gill (1882–1940).

Siegfried Sassoon (1886–1967), Brooke's near contemporary, also of striking appearance, had left Clare without taking a degree and had devoted his time to the leisure pursuits of a country gentleman, publishing his poetry privately in pamphlet form. Enlisting as a trooper, he became an infantry officer renowned as 'Mad Jack' for his daring, awarded the Military Cross for rescuing a man under heavy fire and recommended for the Victoria Cross for taking a German trench single-handed. Twice seriously wounded, Sassoon made national news by denouncing the war but, diagnosed with 'shell shock', was invalided to Craiglockhart Hospital and the care of William Halse Rivers, whom he came to revere. Sassoon survived the war to become an acclaimed poet and memoirist. Clare made him an honorary fellow. A portrait by Glyn Philpot is in the Fitzwilliam Museum.

On the front line

The young historian George Macaulay Trevelyan agonised about supporting the war before committing himself. Defective eyesight excluded him from combat but he became Commandant of the first British Red Cross ambulance unit sent to Italy, where he served on the mountainous Isonzo front. Honoured for his efforts by both the Italian and British governments, he wrote a characteristically self-effacing memoir, *Scenes from Italy's War*.

Conscientious objection to combat similarly prevented the distinguished economist Arthur Cecil Pigou (1877–1959) from joining up, but he spent every vacation driving an ambulance with a Quaker medical unit. Other Quaker ambulance drivers included the King's philosopher Richard Braithwaite (1900–90) and Frank Raymond Leavis who was left with a lifetime of insomnia and disordered digestion.

The Greek scholar Francis Macdonald Cornford became a Sergeant-Instructor of Musketry. Economist Dennis Robertson (1890–1963) served with the 11th Battalion of the London Regiment in the Middle East and was awarded the Military Cross. D S Robertson (1885–1961) ignored congenital lameness to become a major in the Army Service Corps and returned to become Regius Professor of Greek. Historian Sir James R M Butler (1889–1975) served at Gallipoli and in Egypt and was twice mentioned in dispatches before being promoted to the General Staff in France. Another historian, Harold Temperley (1879–1939), served with the Serbs in Salonika and was subsequently a member of the British delegation at the Versailles Peace Conference. Eric Milner-White, future Dean of King's, earned himself a severe reprimand from the Chaplain-General for abandoning his non-combatant status by assuming battlefield command of a unit when all its officers were killed. Future Professor of Music Patrick Hadley, younger son of the Master of Pembroke, lost a leg within weeks of entering active service with the Royal Field Artillery yet subsequently managed to cycle, drive and play tennis with the prosthetic limb which he sometimes wore back to front to amuse his pupils. His eldest brother, however, did not return.

In 1915 the future Sir (William) Lawrence Bragg FRS, CH (1890–1971) shared the Nobel Prize with his father for work on X-rays, thus becoming the youngest-ever recipient of that honour. Three years later he was awarded the Military Cross and an OBE. Born in Adelaide, Bragg had entered the local university at 15 and graduated with a First at 18. While serving with the artillery he was three times mentioned in dispatches and developed a method of locating enemy guns by the sound of the firing, which was used during World War Two against V-2 rockets. Bragg later returned to Cambridge as Cavendish Professor of Physics (1938–54). Another future adornment of the Cavendish Laboratory was future Nobel Laureate (Sir) John Cockcroft, who served as a signaller with the Royal Field Artillery and was twice mentioned in dispatches.

Ever eager for assignment to the most challenging locations, Alexander Wollaston (1875–1930) served as a Royal Navy surgeon from East Africa to Murmansk and was awarded the Distinguished Service Cross. Scion of a distinguished dynasty of scientists, Wollaston had made his name as a man of action, an explorer, ethnographer, photographer and plant-hunter in the Sudan, Colombia and New Guinea. After the war he accompanied the first attempt on Mount Everest as its medical officer. He was then delighted to be made a fellow and tutor of his old college, King's, despite his lack of scholarly qualifications. In June 1930 a deranged student came to Wollaston's college room, shot him dead and then killed himself. A stunned Cambridge mourned 'a Prince among Men'. Wollaston's ashes were buried in King's chapel.

Despite the official line that officer status was denied to anyone 'not of pure European descent', a few Cambridge men managed to circumvent this barrier. Kershap Naoroji, grandson of Britain's first Asian MP Dadabhai Naoroji, initially served in France as a private in the Middlesex Regiment and attained commissioned rank serving with the Hazara Pioneers in Iraq. Shrikrishna Chandra Welinkar of Jesus managed to become a second lieutenant in the fledgling Royal Air Force and was killed in combat in June 1918.

Sporting heroes

Henry Macintosh (1892–1918) of Corpus Christi won a gold medal at the Stockholm Olympics in 1912 as a member of the 4 × 100 metres relay team. As president of the Cambridge University Athletics Club in 1913 he won the 100 yards against Oxford, won the Scottish 100 yards title and equalled the British record of 9.8 seconds. The outbreak of war saw him return from colonial administration in South Africa to take a commission in the Argyll and Sutherland Highlanders. Captain Macintosh was killed in action on the Somme in July 1918.

Ronald Rawson (1882–1952) of Trinity just failed to get a cricketing blue but took up inter-varsity boxing successfully in 1913–14. As a captain in the Royal Engineers, Rawson achieved the rare distinction of winning the Military Cross with two bars. In a postwar amateur boxing career which lasted little more than a year, Rawson won 27 out of 28 heavyweight fights by knock-out and collared the Gold Medal at the 1920 Antwerp Olympics, where none of his opponents managed to last the scheduled three rounds.

Australian-born Arthur Leighton (1889–1939) of Caius captained the Cambridge hockey team in 1910. As a lieutenant of artillery Leighton won the Military Cross, and despite being severely gassed continued to play top-class sport after the war, winning 27 England caps and a Gold Medal for hockey at Antwerp in 1920.

Gordon Thomson (1884–1953) didn't go up to Trinity Hall until he was 25, having won a rowing gold in the coxless pairs and a silver in the coxless fours at the 1908 London Games. During the war Thomson served with the infant RAF and was awarded the Distinguished Service Cross for low-level photographic reconnaissance over enemy lines at Gallipoli. He also won the Distinguished Flying Cross, a rare 'double'.

At 36, Lord John 'Jack' Wodehouse (1883–1941) was the youngest member of the polo team which took Olympic gold in 1920. At Trinity Hall he had captained the victorious varsity team in 1904 and 1905. An MP at 23, he won silver for polo at the 1908 London Games. Serving with the 16th Lancers he won the Military Cross, the Croix de Guerre and the Italian War Cross. He was to be killed in an air raid in the Blitz in 1941, making a rare visit to London from his Norfolk estates.

Backroom boys

The contribution made to the war effort by the King's College classicist F E Adcock (1886–1968) was described as 'armchair but distinguished'. As a member of the staff of the Admiralty's 'Room 40', responsible for decoding German naval and diplomatic messages, he was awarded an OBE for his work on codes and ciphers.

Economic historian John Harold Clapham (1873–1946) was appropriately seconded to the Board of Trade and made CBE for his services. At the Treasury, J M Keynes, with a characteristic mixture of intellectual ingenuity and artistic flair, came up with a scheme to help the French with their balance of payments problem by buying works of art from the Degas collection for the National Gallery. Mathematician John Edensor Littlewood (1885–1977) used his expertise to work out the trajectories of anti-aircraft projectiles. Geoffrey Ingram Taylor (1886–1975) brought a novel scientific rigour to the design of aircraft and parachutes. Another physicist, (Sir) James Chadwick (1891–1974), an expert on radioactivity, had the misfortune to be involved in a research project in Berlin when the war broke out and was interned for its duration. At the cost of permanently impaired digestion he survived to play a key role in the development of the atom bomb in World War Two and serve as Master of Caius.

Mending broken men

Few Cambridge academics made a more original contribution to the war effort than W H R Rivers (1864–1922). Having graduated as the youngest-ever doctor in history to qualify from St Bartholomew's Hospital in London, Rivers had been appointed as the first-ever lecturer in psychology at Cambridge in 1897. In 1898 he accompanied the celebrated anthropological expedition to the Torres Straits where he undertook pioneering experiments in cross-cultural psychology. Rivers subsequently wrote a definitive monograph on the Toda people of south-west India before Cambridge appointed him director of Britain's first psychological laboratory in 1907. He was elected FRS the following year and awarded the Royal Society's Gold Medal in 1914. Rivers's research interests included the effects of alcohol and caffeine on fatigue – a topic for which a university would provide endless first-hand subjects.

The unprecedented conditions of combat created by the Great War, most notably the development of massive and sustained artillery barrages, created a novel problem for military medicine, soon to be dubbed 'shell shock': a crippling psychological condition which afflicted men of proven courage to the point where they were quite unable to perform frontline duties. Serving with the Royal Army Medical Corps, Rivers was one of the very few people capable of bringing not only a sympathetic intelligence but also a degree of informed understanding to the treatment of victims. Painfully shy himself and afflicted with a stammer, Rivers's most notable placement was at Craiglockhart Hospital in Edinburgh, where his patients included the celebrated 'war poet' Siegfried Sassoon. Pat Barker's prize-winning novel *Regeneration,* based on Rivers's own case-notes, brilliantly recreates this passage of his remarkable life. For Rivers himself the experience proved transformational, liberating him personally and socially so that when the war ended he actively sought out public-speaking engagements and set out to launch himself on a political career as a Labour supporter – only to die shortly afterwards.

One of the special collections of the University Library is a cache of contemporary pamphlets and ephemera relating to the effects of combat on soldiers of the Great War.

Cause célèbre

Very few faculty members resolutely refused to 'serve'. The classicist and historian Goldsworthy Lowes Dickinson (1862–1932) deplored the 'blindly patriotic, savagely violent' mass sentiment to which it seemed to him he alone was immune – 'All discussion, all pursuit of truth ceased, as in a moment. To win the war or to hide safely among the winners, became the only preoccupation.' Dickinson campaigned for a post-war 'League of Nations' – a phrase he may well have invented – to prevent further outbreaks of conflict and subsequently published *The International Anarchy 1904–14* in 1926 in an effort to uncover the causes of global conflict and sketch out the conditions for their avoidance.

In 1916, Trinity philosopher Bertrand Russell (1872–1970), who had signed up for the No-Conscription Fellowship, was fined £100 for issuing a leaflet deemed to be seditious, contrary to the Defence of the Realm Act. He was then deprived of his college lectureship. Twenty-two fellows protested against this decision but took no further action. Russell, who 'felt that Cambridge was the only place on earth that I could regard as home', was then offered the chance to lecture in the USA but was denied a passport by the Foreign Office. Having subsequently fallen out with the No-Conscription Fellowship, Russell then wrote a piece suggesting that American troops might usefully be employed as strike-breakers in Britain since they were clearly used to doing this in their own country. This outburst earnt Russell six months in Brixton prison for sedition, during which he composed his *Introduction to Mathematical Philosophy*, an admirably polished work which would one day lead an obituarist, the philosopher Anthony Quinton, to observe that, in the light of his many later publications, often dashed off under the influence of passion or penury, 'one might wish he had been imprisoned more often.' Russell was restored to his lectureship in November 1919, thanks to the votes of junior colleagues, returned from war service, who proved far less vindictive than their bellicose, stay-at-home seniors. His tenure, however, proved short-lived. Russell went on leave for the Far East, resigning his lectureship because his private life was passing through one of several untidy phases and he wished to avoid embarrassing his supporters. Russell would marry four times, the last time at 80, and be imprisoned again in 1961, for civil disobedience while campaigning for nuclear disarmament. Awarded the Nobel Prize for Literature in 1950 for his best-selling *History of Western Philosophy* (1945), he wrote more than 70 books and penned some 60,000 letters.

Armistice

Newnham undergraduate Dora Lawe remembered that when news of the ending of the war reached Cambridge 'Town and Gown went mad and everything went chaotic'. I A Richards described the scene as pandemonium, personally witnessing 'twenty or thirty drunken medical students' sacking the picture gallery owned by the pacifist don Charles Kay Ogden, who stood helplessly by as works of art by the avant-garde luminaries of Bloomsbury were hurled through its smashed window. A horde of undergraduates stormed out to Girton, lit a bonfire in the quad and yelled 'Where are the women we have been fighting for?' Katherine Jex-Blake (1860–1951), the Principal, fearlessly faced them down – then invited them to return the following Saturday for a dance.

Lest we forget

As early as October 1914 Sir Arthur Quiller-Couch was stopped by a Head of House before the window of a Cambridge photographer, displaying group portraits of volunteers prior to their departure; he 'ticked off the cheerful, resolute faces of those fallen ... since he had entertained them a few weeks ago. In one row of a dozen West Yorks, he could find two survivors only'.

Five years later in a Commemoration sermon H F Stewart (1863–1948), Dean of Trinity, said:

> I take the War List and I run my fingers down it. Here is name after name which I cannot read ... without emotion – names which are only names to you, the new College, but which to us, who knew the men, bring up one after another pictures of ... the flower of a generation, the glory of Israel, the pick of England; and they died to save England and all that England stands for.

A lifetime later film director Lindsay Anderson (1923–94) would quote this passage almost verbatim in one of the opening scenes of *Chariots of Fire* (1984), himself assuming a cameo part as Stewart to skilful and memorable effect.

Recent music graduate Arthur Bliss (1891–1975), an early volunteer, had been twice wounded, gassed and mentioned in dispatches; his allusively-titled *Morning Heroes* (1930), a strikingly original symphonic composition combining speech, chorus and orchestra, was written as a belated act of exorcism and a tribute to a brother and 'all other comrades killed in battle'.

College chapels, or the cloisters leading to them, bear the names of the 2,162 members of the university killed in 'The Great War for Civilisation'. A further 2,902 were wounded. At Pembroke the inscription records – in Latin, the conventional lapidary language for most memorials – 'The memory still lives of the three hundred sons of the House who laid down their lives fighting for their country.' The poignancy of 'sons of the House' is not misplaced. Pembroke suffered exceptionally high losses – more than a quarter of those who served, twice the average for the university as a whole.

Magdalene's chapel inscription is an injunction to the living; 'Remember your brothers in the Lord who, by going to meet Death, earned Life.' At Trinity the metaphorically allusive inscription was taken from Hebrews 11:13: 'All these people died in faith. They had not yet received the things promised, but seeing them afar off and greeting them, they confessed that they were strangers and pilgrims on earth.' At St Catharine's College, just before the outbreak of the Second World War, it was belatedly decided that the comradeship of college transcended national loyalties and a single additional name – L H Jagenberg – was acknowledged on the Roll of Honour as '*Hostis amicus*' – 'A friend among enemies'.

Clare College combined elegy with practicality by building its neo-Georgian Memorial Court to cope with the enlarged number of new entrants after the conclusion of hostilities. In doing so it took the then momentous step of building beyond the former 'frontier' of the Backs, a decision much criticised at the time. Erected between 1923–34 to the designs of Sir Giles Gilbert Scott (1880–1960) (he of the adjacent University Library and the red London telephone kiosk), it bears a quotation from Virgil's *Aeneid* (Book VI line 664) – 'By their merits they made others remember them.'

Of the £4,000 raised for the city war memorial at the corner of Station Road, the colleges contributed only 5%, but the site and subject were chosen by the Vice-Chancellor Sir Arthur Shipley (1861–1927), a world-ranking expert on parasitic worms, who in 1915 had published an unexpected bestseller on his subject, *The Minor Horrors of War,* and generously housed and entertained a succession of convalescing officers in the Master's Lodge at Christ's. Shipley was also a bachelor with an eye for the masculine form and nominated as the model a handsome Christ's undergraduate, Kenneth Hamilton. He also chose the sculptor, the remarkably multi-talented Canadian Robert Tait McKenzie (1867–1938), an athlete, doctor and pioneer of physical education, physiotherapy and reconstructive plastic surgery, who had himself assisted in the restoration of the faces of disfigured soldiers.

The Duke of York (later King George VI) came to unveil the figure in July 1922 but, as it had yet to be cast, what he actually revealed to the packed ranks of onlookers was a plaster version, painted to look like bronze. The final statue was, in the sardonic words of Peter Richards, editor of the Cambridge alumni magazine, 'more recruiting advertisement than memorial ... a mildly erotic public school athlete bestriding the traffic as if auditioning for a bit part in *Triumph of the Will*.' Bareheaded, the triumphant Tommy carries his tin hat and an English rose in his right hand, a trophy German 'coal scuttle' helmet dangling from his rifle, framed by a laurel wreath of victory. Unusually, the figure glances to the side, gazing down the long straight approach road to Cambridge railway station. One wonders why. In memory of those who returned that way – or departed, never to return?

CLUBS AND CLIQUES: A FRATERNAL INTERLUDE

Cambridge Union

The Cambridge Union was founded by amalgamating three existing student debating clubs. It first met in 1815. Banned in 1817 for daring to discuss current politics, it was re-established in 1821, subject to avoiding any discussion of political issues less than 20 years old, a prohibition which lasted about a decade. Initially meeting at the Red Lion in Petty Cury, in 1866 it finally settled in purpose-built headquarters at the rear of the Round Church. These were designed by Alfred Waterhouse (1830–1905) as his first Cambridge commission. The Union thus took on the character of a private members' clubhouse and refuge from college and remains the only central student venue.

In the 1880s the Union began to invite guest speakers from outside the university. A century later they became the most notable feature of its formal debates. A training-ground for budding politicians

– though not on anything like the same scale as its opposite number at Oxford – the Cambridge Union has numbered among its presidents J M Keynes and, more recently, the Tory politicians Kenneth Clarke, John Gummer, Michael Howard and Douglas Hurd. The Union has produced dozens of MPs but no prime minister, and since its foundation no Cambridge prime minister has ever spoken there as an undergraduate. A different measure of the Union's stature might, however, be the turn-out for the celebration of its 175th anniversary in 1990, when guest speakers included MPs Charles Kennedy, David Steel, Norman Lamont (another past president of the Union), Sir Clement Freud, Rajiv Gandhi, KGB defector Oleg Gordievsky and former US President Ronald Reagan.

The Students' Union

The Cambridge Union, a debating society, is not to be confused with the Cambridge University Students' Union, which represents the interests of students at large. Cambridge students took part in the foundation of the National Union of Students in 1922 but at Cambridge itself student representation evolved on a collegiate basis, through the development in each college of a Junior Combination Room. In 1964 a Student Representative Council was established with one member from each JCR. In 1975, as the Cambridge Student Union, it gained a foothold in the University Council, achieving formal recognition in 1984.

The Apostles

Founded in 1820 as the Cambridge Conversazione Society, the membership of this club was initially earnest but undistinguished and limited to a dozen – hence the later nomenclature of 'Apostles'. No topics of discussion were to be off-limits, except 'Mathematics and Classics, professionally considered'. Members could present a paper on any subject they wished, provided only that they genuinely held the views they put forward. As Henry Sidgwick recalled on his deathbed – 'Absolute candour was the only duty that the tradition of the society enforced.' To evade the pestering of would-be members not up to snuff, from the 1850s the Apostles acquired a semi-secret existence, meeting at midnight behind locked doors at Trinity or King's. Membership remained highly restricted, neophytes regarding their acceptance as the highest compliment imaginable. Past members retained the honorary status of 'Angels'. Apostles mentioned elsewhere in this book include J M Keynes, Rupert Brooke, G M Trevelyan, Bertrand Russell and Ludwig Wittgenstein. A meeting of the Apostles is described in the opening chapter of E M Forster's *The Longest Journey* (1907).

The University Pitt Club

The socially exclusive and still all-male Pitt Club was founded in 1835 to honour the memory of William Pitt the Younger, and certainly did much to honour his taste for alcohol. As Master of Trinity, Whewell strongly disapproved of undergraduates attending its bibulous dinners. Members also undertook to work for the election of Tory Members of Parliament, until allegations of bribing voters brought this activity into disrepute. In February 1863 the Roman Bath Company opened a public bath the size of a swimming pool for the benefit of the people of Cambridge, whose indifference led to its closure in December. Bought at auction by the architect who designed it, Sir Matthew Digby Wyatt (1820–77), the building at 7A Jesus Lane was then converted to be leased out, half to the Pitt Club and half to Orme's Billiard Rooms. The Club eventually took over the whole building until financial difficulties led to it leasing the ground floor to Pizza Express, a chain founded by Peter Boizot, an alumnus of St Catharine's. It became a Grade II listed building in 1950. Past members of the Pitt Club have included J M Keynes, Anthony Burgess, Anthony Blunt and Sir David Frost.

The Hawks

The Hawks was founded in 1872 as a social club for 'Blues'; membership to be by election only. A 'Blue' is a sportsman who has represented the university with distinction in a 'major' sport against Oxford. Recipients may wear distinctive regalia in the form of ties, badges, scarves, sweaters, blazers etc. The first association between Cambridge and light blue as a sporting favour dates from the second Boat Race in 1836. Blues were originally awarded by the presidents of the university clubs for rowing, athletics and cricket. Rugby, football and hockey challenged this monopoly by awarding their own blues until a coordinating committee was established in 1912. 'Full Blue' status was subsequently awarded to lawn tennis (1922), golf (1938), boxing (1948), squash (1960), swimming (1966), cross country (1977) and basketball (1996). 'Half Blues' are awarded to minor sports, including chess and dance. Given the annual turnover of university athletes, membership of the Hawks may stand at around 60 at the beginning of the year, rising to 200 by the end as varsity matches are played.

In 1936 an annual London dinner was inaugurated, held on the eve of the Varsity rugby fixture. In 1985 the Hawks was joined by its sister organisation for female athletes, the Ospreys. In 1992 the club acquired its own building at 18 Portugal Place and in 1996 established its own charitable trust, currently the university's single largest source of sporting sponsorship for individual athletes.

The Heretics

The Heretics Society was founded in 1911 by C K Ogden, who became its president. Members were required to have renounced obedience to any external authority in religion. The increasing secularisation of the university was mirrored in the fact that the founding 15 members included two professors and four future Heads of Houses. The Heretics met to hear provocative papers, some of which were subsequently published. Guest speakers included Newnham archaeologist Jane Harrison, classicist F M Cornford and historian G M Trevelyan, and from outside the university such literary luminaries as G K Chesterton (1874–1936) and George Bernard Shaw (1856–1950).

Granta

Initially an imitation of the long-established satirical miscellany, *Punch*, *Granta* was founded in 1899 as 'A College Joke to Cure The Dumps' and to fill the gap left by the demise of *Gadfly*, sunk 'owing to an article of a personal character.' Over the years *Granta* attracted the varying talents of both the ambitious and the established, despite being periodically in severe financial difficulties. A *Best of Granta* anthology, compiled in 1967 by future BBC World Affairs editor John Simpson and poet Jim Philip, featured contributions from E M Forster, society photographer Cecil Beaton (1904–80), veteran musical star Jack Hulbert, comedians Peter Cook and Jonathan Miller, polymath Jacob Bronowski (1908–74), cartoonist Ronald 'St Trinian's' Searle, formerly of the *Cambridge Evening News*, and poets Thom Gunn and Stevie Smith. Editors have included A A 'Winnie-the-Pooh' Milne (1882–1956), Alistair Cooke, cartoonist Mark Boxer (sent down for publishing a blasphemous poem) and Sir David Frost. Eventually a tough and talented American, Bill Buford, turned *Granta* into a seriously successful vehicle for new literary talent (luminaries including Angela Carter, Salman Rushdie, Martin Amis and Ian McEwan) spawning its own publishing house in association with Penguin Books – until Buford left.

Varsity

A student newspaper, founded in 1947, *Varsity* was variously edited by future film producer Michael Winner (1935–2013), fashion guru Suzy Menkes, TV quizmaster Richard Whiteley (1943–2005) and heavyweight TV interviewer Jeremy Paxman. As so often with student journalism, despite repeatedly winning the National Union of Students' prize for best student newspaper, it was undone by its financial failure and in 1973 merged with a new rival, *Stop Press*. The title reverted to *Varsity* in 1987. New computer technology enabled a *Daily Varsity* to appear in 1992, succeeded by *Varsity Online*. In 1999 the Cambridge University Students' Union launched its own publication *The Cambridge Student* (TCS). Both university newspapers are now distributed free.

Night climbers

Should those who indulge in 'night climbing' be regarded as a club or a conspiracy? Given that the authorities are more or less bound to disapprove of people clambering in the dead of night at risk of life and limb over buildings, often venerable and vulnerable ones, those who indulge in this 'sport' could scarcely flaunt their activities. It nevertheless became sufficiently popular to generate its own genre of practical handbooks.

The Roof-Climber's Guide to Trinity, published in 1899, noted that an entire circuit of the Great Court should be feasible in two hours, but had only once been accomplished because it presented 'every variety of roof-climbing difficulty', compounded by 'every form of authoritative residence'. Even that single success excepted the Great Gate – an 'as yet unconquered barrier.' Apart from being offered suggested routes, would-be participants were also given highly specific advice regarding the hazards of lead gutters, loose drainpipes and 'ankle-wringing drain-holes'. The naturalist Peter Scott (1909–89) claimed to have been 'one of the party which made the first complete circuit of Trinity Great Court' but confessed that 'the climb that frightened me most was the ascent of St John's College Chapel. There was an overhanging cornice about sixty feet from the ground which required the most determined disregard of my indifferent head for heights.'

It must be conceded, however, that the practical requirements of night-climbing put the university's architecture in quite a novel perspective: 'St John's Chapel ... is basically a large square tower, with four corner pinnacles. The whole effect is singularly unattractive ... The beauty of the chapel lies essentially in its climbing. It is a climber's building' (Hederatus, *Cambridge Nightclimbing*, 1970). The same source emphasises that hazard and height are not directly related. Would-be conquerors of the Porter's Lodge at King's College are warned that it represents 'a strenuous climb, particularly on the hands' and that 'few people have been known to finish it without arousing some interest from below.'

The 1937 account of *The Night Climbers of Cambridge* was reprinted in 2007.

9

Bright Young Things?

The terrible hiatus of World War One ensured that the post-war intake of undergraduates was more varied than the customary influx. The writer J B Priestley (1894–1984), wounded twice and commissioned from the ranks, recalled a 'crowded and turbulent' Cambridge where 'men who had lately commanded brigades and battalions' were mixed up with 'nice pink lads'. The Caius entry included athlete Harold Abrahams, who had been commissioned, but too late to see action, and a future Master, Joseph Needham, straight out of public school. Kipling realised the veterans deserved special consideration:

> Tenderly, Proctor, let them down, if they do not walk as they
>   should;
> For, by God, if they owe you half-a-crown, you owe them your
>   four years food.

Others had been flotsam on the tides of war. A 'White Russian' exile, the son of a minister in the short-lived Kerensky government, Vladimir Nabokov (1899–1977) inhabited 'intolerably squalid' lodgings while at Trinity, 'trying to become a Russian writer'. Devoting much time to tennis, goalkeeping and punting, he breezed effortlessly through his degree studies in French and Russian literature and found the spare time to translate poems by Rupert Brooke into Russian and to compose a scholarly essay on the butterflies and moths of the Crimea. As he later confessed:

> I had no interest whatever in the history of the place and was quite sure that Cambridge was in no way affecting my soul, although actually it was Cambridge that supplied ... the very colours and inner rhythms for my very special Russian thoughts.

For Xu Zhimo (1897–1931), a much briefer bird of passage, the impact of Cambridge at that very same time was, by contrast, a self-acknowledged turning-point, both in terms of what he learnt and what he felt. Having studied in the USA, which he found 'intolerable', Xu spent much of 1922 at King's, where the poetry of Keats and Shelley came as a revelation to him. Returning to a troubled China, he flourished as a poet, editor, translator and teacher until he was killed in a plane crash, not yet 35. Xu's poem, 'Saying Farewell to Cambridge Again', drafted on the Backs, became a standard choice for school anthologies, known to millions and therefore 'arguably the most famous Chinese poem of the twentieth century.' In July 2008 a two-ton block of white Beijing marble was placed as a memorial to the poet at the western end of King's bridge over the Cam, inscribed in Chinese characters with the first and last two lines of Xu's subdued lament:

> I leave softly, gently
> > Exactly as I came –
> Gently I flick my sleeves,
> > Not even a wisp of cloud will I bring away.

Right face

Despite the upheavals of revolution in Russia, the accession to power of Fascism in Italy and the advent of the first, if short-lived, Labour government in Britain, the mass of Cambridge undergraduates remained instinctively conservative in outlook, though in a largely apolitical sort of way. During the General Strike of 1926, when the organised labour movement paralysed transport, power and newspapers in support of the miners' attempts to resist wage cuts, some 2,000 students volunteered to serve as special constables or seized the chance, as unique as it was unexpected, to realise a childhood fantasy by driving a bus or, better still, a train – less as an expression of class hostility than from an eagerness to shirk their studies for 'a lark'.

Making a new man of himself

It was during his years at Jesus (1927–32) that Alfred Alistair Cooke (1908–2004) from Blackpool reinvented himself as Alistair Cooke of Manchester, growing a moustache and grinding out all trace of a Northern accent. Talented as a caricaturist and composer, Cooke edited *Granta* and established The Mummers, the first Cambridge drama group to accept women. Unsurprisingly, given these distractions, Cooke failed to get the expected First. Elizabethan literature expert E M W Tillyard (1889–1962) spoke more truly than he knew when he dismissed Cooke for his 'journalist's mind'. His tutor noted likewise – 'very much out for himself, a clever careerist'. Desperate to stay on, Cooke failed to survive by tutoring and writing, but avoided schoolmastering thanks to the newly established Harkness Scholarship scheme, which enabled him to escape to Yale to study theatre production. The rest is, indeed, history, much of which Cooke witnessed and reported first-hand and some of which, in broadcasting terms, he made. Cambridge eventually revised its jaundiced impressions but waited until he was 79 to award him an honorary degree.

'The Great George'

George Macaulay Trevelyan (1876–1962) was to become the most well-known British historian of his generation. Born of a distinguished lineage, the great-nephew of Thomas Babington Macaulay, Trevelyan became an 'Apostle' and a Fellow of Trinity. Proclaiming history as a branch of literature, he believed it should be written not for fellow academics, but for the public. His own dissertation was sufficiently readable to be published as *England in the Age of Wycliffe* (1899). By the time his equally popular *England Under the Stuarts* (1904) was published he had abandoned Cambridge for London and a literary career. An Italophile, he made his name with a three-volume biography (1907–11), of Giuseppe Garibaldi, hero of the Risorgimento.

Trevelyan then played a leading role in the 1922–6 Royal Commission, which reorganised the governance of Oxford and Cambridge. Returning to Cambridge in 1927 as Regius Professor of History, he produced his *magnum opus*, a three-volume account of *England Under Queen Anne*. A Northumbrian squire by background, the tall, wiry Trevelyan was a formidable walker and like his hero, Macaulay, believed passionately in treading the very soil where Garibaldi had bled and Marlborough had directed his great victories. In 1940 Trevelyan was chosen by Churchill to become Master of Trinity. His popular masterpiece, *English Social History* (1944), written against the background of a struggle for national survival, was a reassuring account in which England itself is the silent hero – in the words of a medieval poet, 'a fair field full of folk'. Trevelyan's tenure as Master of Trinity was extended by his colleagues to the maximum permissible. He could have been Director of the London School of Economics, President of the British Academy or Governor-General of Canada, but was content enough to remain as a Fellow of the Royal Society, a Fellow of the British Academy and holder of the Order of Merit.

An English revolution?

'[A] general insensitivity to poetry does witness a low level of general imaginative life ...'

Ivor Armstrong Richards

Between them, two Magdalene dons, C K Ogden (1889–1957) and I A Richards (1893–1979), transformed the teaching of English as both a language and a body of literature.

Both a linguist and a psychologist, Ogden, founder of the Heretics Society, also established the highly influential *Cambridge Magazine*, a penny weekly journal of comment that had sold 20,000 copies by 1918. In 1922 he translated Wittgenstein's *Tractatus* and, jointly with Richards, published *The Meaning of Meaning* (1923), an enquiry into how language can be used with greater precision and understanding. Inspired by the little-known contribution of the philosopher Jeremy Bentham (1748–1832) to linguistics, Ogden, with Richards's aid, created Basic English as 'an auxiliary international language comprising 850 words arranged in a system in which everything may be said for all the purposes of everyday language'. The vocabulary, 60% of which consisted of single syllable words, included just 18 verbs. During World War Two Churchill pledged to promote its use, via the British Council and the BBC, as an element of British cultural policy, arranging for the Crown to buy out the copyright, thus enabling Ogden to indulge his bibliomania. After selling off his *valuable* collections, Ogden still left 100,000 volumes at his death.

Richards, a celebrated mountaineer despite a severe early bout of tuberculosis, made his reputation with *Principles of Literary Criticism* (1924) and *Practical Criticism* (1929), which, according to the *Oxford Companion to Literature* 'revolutionised the teaching and study of English'. Both derived from Richards's key teaching technique of distributing unattributed poems to students and analysing their written reactions to 'the words on the page' – sounds, rhythms, sentence structures. He was appalled to discover that many found the works of Donne or Gerard Manley Hopkins less appealing than the effusions of the Bard of the Trenches, 'Woodbine Willie'. George Orwell – an Etonian but not a university man – found this revelation hugely amusing – 'For anyone who wants a good laugh ... I recommend I A Richards's *Practical Criticism*.'

Richards became a crusader against the critical failings of vagueness, laziness and sentimentality and for an appreciation of complexity, allusiveness, irony and ambiguity. Emphasising close reading to the exclusion of biographical, social and historical context, Richards became the father of 'textual studies', whose doctrines were to be developed by his student William Empson and partial disciple F R Leavis (see below). Richards's later career included extended periods teaching in China and at Harvard and writing works on Mencius, Coleridge and Plato, as well as his own, late, poetry. A Senate House memorial ceremony in 1979 featured white silk funeral banners sent in respect by the Chinese government.

English with attitude

'[A] magnificent, acid, malevolently humorous little man who looks exactly like a bandy-legged leprechaun.'

Sylvia Plath, 1955

The achievement of F R Leavis (1895–1978) was not so much to revolutionise literary criticism as to make it a quasi-religious cult. Born in Cambridge and educated at the Perse School, Leavis won a history scholarship to Emmanuel, switched to English, took a First and completed a doctorate on journalism and literature. In 1929 Leavis married the formidable Queenie Roth, a ferociously bright product of Jewish North London's intellectual enclave, Hampstead, and an expert on the history of working-class readership. Together they produced (1932–53) the literary journal *Scrutiny* as a vehicle for their views.

Scorning neckties and carrying his battered texts in a garden sack rather than a briefcase, Leavis was as much preacher as teacher; as concerned with what one should *not* read as with what one should. Rupert Brooke, he dismissed as exhibiting 'Keats's vulgarity with a public school accent'. Part of Leavis's attraction was that, in contrast to the languorous ambivalences of so many dons, he offered burning certainties, attracting not pupils but disciples – on whom he often turned with venom. As Clive James (1939–2019) has noted, 'the Leavisite brand of *odium theologicum* had all the characteristics of totalitarian argument, right down to the special hatred reserved for heretics.'

As a disciple of I A Richards, Leavis discarded the narrative tradition of literary history in favour of close textual analysis. Loathing Marxism, materialism and mass media, contemptuous of advertising and technology, he believed that the true history of the English had been written by its great novelists, notably George Eliot (1819–80). This was still true for authors such as Henry James and Joseph Conrad (1857–1924), who were not even English. Through appreciative analyses in *Scrutiny*, in the lecture room and as a provocative speaker at student literary gatherings, Leavis promoted the work of James Joyce (1882–1941), T S Eliot (1888–1965) and D H Lawrence (1885–1930) when their names were scarcely known, let alone part of any canon; likewise the poetry of Gerard Manley Hopkins (1844–89), W B Yeats (1865–1939) and Ezra Pound (1885–1972).

Leavis remained controversial in Cambridge to the end, excluded from the English faculty until he was past 40 and from its board until almost 60, and only appointed Reader on the eve of retirement. Outside Cambridge it was different. Leavis's impact on generations of teachers of English was incalculable. He was awarded five honorary degrees and made a Companion of Honour. To the end he remained unshaken in his belief that in an age of cultural barbarism the university must be 'more than a collocation of specialist departments ... a centre of human consciousness: perception, knowledge, judgment and responsibility'; and at the heart of the university must be 'a vital English school'. Though Leavis, of course, believed that that school was to be found in the pages of *Scrutiny* – 'the essential Cambridge, in spite of Cambridge'. The music shop of Leavis Senior, opposite the gates of Downing College, is now a branch of Pizza Hut.

Young Turks

The interwar years were a golden age for Cambridge science. Professorships were established in newly recognised fields including aeronautical engineering, mineralogy and petrology, animal pathology and biochemistry.

At the Cavendish, J J Thomson was succeeded as Head by his first-ever research student, the New Zealander Ernest Rutherford (1871–1937), who is claimed by *The Cambridge Dictionary of Scientists* to have 'founded nuclear physics'. He had already been awarded the Nobel Prize for Chemistry in 1908. Rutherford was the first to describe the structure of the atom correctly, to predict the existence of the neutron and to collaborate with colleagues to bring about the first nuclear fusion reaction. Energetic and charismatic, Rutherford attracted a galaxy of young talent to Cambridge, making it the world centre for what he called, in the title of his last book, *The Newer Alchemy*.

If the younger Leavis can be said to have had a scientific counterpart it was J D Bernal (1901–71), nicknamed 'Sage' while still an undergraduate at Emmanuel. In a decade at the Cavendish, he played a major role in the development of crystallography, with groundbreaking investigations into the structure of viruses and proteins, and became 'the founding father of molecular biology'. Bernal's extraordinary range of interests also led him to undertake pioneering work in the history of science. Max Perutz remembered Bernal's sub-department – 'housed in a few ill-lit and dirty rooms ... These dingy quarters were turned into a fairy castle by Bernal's brilliance'. Nobel Laureate Dorothy Hodgkin (1910–94) recalled lunchtime picnics in the lab when the conversation ranged from anaerobic bacteria to Romanesque architecture or Da Vinci's 'engines of war'. Elected a Fellow of the Royal Society at 36, Bernal, a lifelong Communist, played a key role as a top-level scientific adviser during World War Two and earnt the unusual distinction of being the recipient of both the United States Medal of Freedom and the Lenin Prize for Peace.

The Westminster Abbey memorial to Paul Dirac (1902–84) was the first to carry an equation as part of its inscription and lies next to that of his predecessor as Lucasian Professor of Mathematics, Sir Isaac Newton. Dirac is the founding father of quantum mechanics, which explains phenomena as various as why the stars shine and how transistors work. It was also Dirac who predicted the existence of 'antimatter'. Appointed to the Lucasian chair at just 30, a year later Dirac shared the Nobel Prize for Physics with Erwin Schrödinger (1887–1961).

'And I remember Spain'

Born in December 1915, Rupert John Cornford (1915–36) was named after Rupert Brooke, who had died in April of that year. Cornford's mother, the poet Franc*es* Cornford (1886–1960), was a granddaughter of Charles Darwin; his father, confusingly, was the classicist Professor Franc*is* Cornford. Frances Cornford was an admirer of Brooke's poetry, as well as a personal friend. Her son came to despise the whole 'Georgian' school of poetry and, rejecting the association with Brooke, insisted on using his second given name. During three years at Trinity, Cornford devoted most of his waking hours to Communism but still managed to collect a First in both parts of the historical Tripos. He also fathered an illegitimate son but abandoned both the child and its mother on discovering the love of his life in Newnham history student Margot Heinemann (1913–92).

When civil war broke out in Spain in July 1936, Cornford, with no Spanish, left at once, without telling even his family, to become the first Englishman in the International Brigade. A serious head wound during the battle for Madrid curiously rekindled his impulse to write and over a few weeks he produced memorable work, notably *Heart of the Heartless World*. John Cornford was killed in a shambolic skirmish near Lopera, probably on his 21st birthday.

Britain's leading Communist agitator, Harry Pollitt (1890–1960), observed brutally, if rationally, that Cornford's death was a great loss to the Communist cause as it had Welsh miners to spare but precious few first-class intellectuals. Cornford's son, James, was adopted and brought up by his own parents. Margot Heinemann eventually had a daughter with J D Bernal, remained a Communist until the dissolution of the Communist Party of Great Britain and was still teaching at New Hall at 76.

Cornford's sacrifice was not unique. Julian Bell (1908–37), nephew of Virginia Woolf, returned from teaching English in China to take up the Spanish cause. Whereas Cornford had lived in bare-light-bulb austerity, Bell had enjoyed having 'a car, and my own rooms, furniture, pictures – all the amenities of Cambridge at its best'. When he was invited to join the Apostles he felt he 'had reached the pinnacle of Cambridge intellectualism'. He had. Four years dissipated on two dissertations failed to secure him a King's fellowship – hence the odyssey to Wuhan. Respect for his mother's pacifist principles led Bell to become an ambulance driver in Spain but he was killed at the Battle of Brunete, aged 29.

David Haden-Guest (1911–38), a leading light of the Moral Sciences Club, decorated his Trinity room with a picture of Lenin. Studying in Germany, he became an active anti-Nazi, and later taught mathematics in Moscow. Haden-Guest was also killed in action with the International Brigade in Spain. *A Textbook of Dialectical Materialism*, based on notes from his lectures to workers at a Marx Memorial School, was published posthumously.

The enemies within

While the Communist Cornford fought Fascism to die in a foreign country, a clique of his Cambridge contemporaries opted to fight Fascism by betraying their own. Self-assigned servants of a supposedly larger patriotism, they were recruited as agents of the USSR. Flamboyant Etonian and Apostle, Guy Burgess (1910–63) of Trinity penetrated the British establishment via the BBC, MI6 and the Foreign Office until he arranged to be recalled from the British Embassy in Washington DC for 'serious misconduct' in 1951 when he believed himself to be under suspicion. Burgess then 'disappeared', only to re-emerge in 1956 in Moscow, where he died of alcoholism in 1963. Burgess's closest collaborator, Donald Maclean (1913–83), recruited as a spy by

Anthony Blunt while still an undergraduate, took a First in Modern Languages at Trinity Hall and rose through the Foreign Office ranks to betray secrets about Britain's atomic programme and the formation of NATO before fleeing with Burgess in 1951, also turning up in Moscow where he became a colonel in the KGB. As head of British counter-espionage, charged with combatting Soviet subversion, 'Kim' Philby (1912–88) was uniquely placed to betray many agents and pass on CIA secrets to the USSR. He also tipped off Burgess and Maclean that they had come under suspicion and should flee. Sacked in 1955, Philby evaded arrest, eventually fleeing to the USSR in 1963, where he was granted political asylum. The mannered Anthony Blunt (1907–83), another Apostle and a Fellow of Trinity, limited his betrayals to wartime service with MI5 and pursued a glittering career as Britain's leading art historian. Appointed to take charge of the royal picture collection in 1945, he also became the director of the Courtauld Institute of Art in 1947, a post he held for the subsequent 27 years. Having made a secret confession in return for immunity from prosecution in 1964, Blunt was not publicly unmasked until 1979, when he was stripped of his knighthood. A 'fifth man' was eventually identified as John Cairncross (1913–95), another brilliant linguist who worked as a code-breaker at Bletchley Park and passed almost 6,000 documents to the USSR. Cairncross, a Scot who did not share the public-school background of the other four, worked independently of them. His exposure obliged him to reinvent himself as a professor of French literature in the USA and then a translator in Italy before marrying an opera singer in the year of his death at the age of 82.

Quest for certainty

The intellectual odyssey of Ludwig Wittgenstein (1889–1951), seeking the limits of the thinkable, was mirrored in a life bereft of stability. Austrian by birth, originally trained in mechanical engineering, he studied aeronautics at the University of Manchester until a deepening interest in mathematics led on to philosophy and Cambridge in

1912 to study under Bertrand Russell. After five terms Wittgenstein left to become a recluse in Norway, a decorated artillery officer in the Austro-Hungarian army, a prisoner of war, a village primary school teacher, a gardener's labourer and a self-taught architect. Returning to Cambridge in 1929, Wittgenstein offered for his PhD thesis his most celebrated work, the *Tractatus Logico-Philosophicus*, running to just 75 pages. This gained him both a doctorate and a fellowship at Trinity. In 1939 he succeeded to the chair of philosophy previously occupied by George Edward Moore (1873–1958).

Wittgenstein's attempts at a clarification of thought through a critique of language led to a questioning of such basic philosophical terms as 'proposition', 'rule' and 'knowledge'. His teaching was an agonised process of self-interrogation and self-accusation which left his listeners enthralled or bewildered, and Wittgenstein himself drained; the ordeal immediately exorcised by a trip to one of the Cambridge flea-pit cinemas and a hasty pork pie. Interestingly, while he taught in English he still wrote in German – beautifully. Having become a British citizen in 1938, on the outbreak of war Wittgenstein forsook the comforts of Trinity to work as a porter in Guy's Hospital in Blitz-torn London and as a laboratory assistant in Newcastle. He returned briefly to Cambridge after the war but quit teaching in 1947. His *Philosophical Investigations,* published posthumously in 1953, essentially contradicted the position he presented in the *Tractatus*.

'... little more than a towering bookstack'

Described as looking like a cross between a 'warehouse and an Assyrian palace', a 'motor factory or steam laundry', the University Library was built between 1931 and 1934 to the designs of Sir Giles Gilbert Scott. The 156-foot tower which looms over the surrounding country-side was imposed on the original design at the insistence of the American benefactor who stumped up half the cash needed for the project. As its steel skeleton rose inexorably higher, contemporaries discussed whether or not it was 'a Mistake', opinions varying from 'eye-sore' to 'beautiful – in its own way of course but definitely beautiful' to 'admirable in any place but this.' The entire stock of the University Library – 1,142,000 books – was transferred from the Old Schools site in 689 loads, during eight weeks of the Long Vacation of 1934, by Library staff and porters hired from Eaden Lilley's department store. Horse-drawn vans were preferred over motor trucks to maintain an even pace between those loading and those unpacking.

Cambridge University Library prides itself on being the largest open-access library in Europe, with some two million volumes available to readers. Placed end to end, the shelves would stretch from Cambridge to Brighton. As the historian Piers Brendon notes, the freedom to browse creates endless opportunities for 'that incomparable tool of academic research, serendipity', whereas in Oxford's Bodleian library 'you have to know what you are looking for in order to request it and it takes time to arrive.' The UL also accommodates the entire libraries of Peterborough Cathedral and the Royal Commonwealth Society and the 70,000 volumes collected by Lord Acton. Its other treasures range from Chinese oracle bones dating from 1200 BC to the 14,000 letters of the Darwin Archive. And *every week* as a result of its status as one of six 'copyright libraries' in the British Isles it receives some 1,500 books, 2,000 issues of periodicals and hundreds of maps and pieces of sheet music to add to its collections ... plus 70,000 monographs and dissertations a year ... plus any purchases that might be made around the world. Once an item comes into the possession of the Library it is *never* for sale.

New buildings, not noticeably new architecture

Despite the unfavourable economic background of the interwar depression, many colleges undertook building projects, Clare's Memorial Court being perhaps the boldest and most coherent. In 1922–3 Jesus added a small corner range to Second Court. Garden Court was built at Sidney Sussex in 1923–5. In 1925–6 Magdalene undertook one of the most imaginative and successful schemes in the city, creating Mallory Court by adding new buildings to existing medieval cottages. In 1927 King's removed the railings along its frontage and replaced them with the low wall that generations of tourists have sat on ever since. In 1930–2 the doyen of the British architectural profession, Sir Edwin Lutyens, designer of celebrated country houses and the Cenotaph, added a range to Benson Court at Magdalene. In 1929–32 his collaborator in designing New Delhi, Sir Herbert Baker, added the north range to Downing College.

The pace of construction quickened in the 1930s. Selwyn built a library (1930), Jesus a south range to Chapel Court (1931), Girton Woodlands Court (1931), Pembroke a new Master's Lodge (1932–3) and Trinity Hall two new ranges in North Court (1934). In 1934 Caius's new hostel facing onto Market Hill became one of the earliest modern buildings in the city centre. At Queens', Fisher Court (1935–6), west of the Cam, employed a conventional architectural style ('suburban Tudor') but followed an unconventional curving plan to create unforeseen restrictions on the future development of the area to its north; it is notable, however, as the first college building with the luxury of bathrooms and lavatories near students' rooms, rather than across some chilly courtyard. In 1936 St Catharine's added a west range to Sherlock Court. Sidney Sussex built a range along Sussex Street in 1937–9. Newnham put up its Fawcett Building (1938) and St John's finally (1938–40) completed its Chapel Court, North Court and Service Court. Along the west side of Bridge Street the college also demolished 18 houses and shops, Warren's Yard, Sussum's Yard and Coulson's Passage to make way for a new music school – and bike sheds.

University projects were limited to the Department of Pathology (1927) and the Scott Polar Research Institute (1933–4), another effort by Sir Herbert Baker.

The most significant municipal undertaking was the rebuilding of the Guildhall (1939) to the designs of Charles Cowles-Voysey – perhaps a riposte to the county's new (1932) Shire Hall on Castle Hill on the site of the old County Gaol. In 1934 the borough boundaries were extended to embrace both Cherry Hinton and Trumpington. In 1936, as if in acknowledgment of the demolitions wrought in the name of progress, the 16th-century White Horse Inn was converted into a museum of folk history. A Cambridge Preservation Society had come into existence in 1928.

In 1922 the *Cambridge Evening News* complained that 'for three months of the year Cambridge is almost a deserted city and trade dwindles to a mere trickle.' A rapid expansion of motor traffic was, however, soon to promote both prosperity and problems. The town undertook numerous road-widening schemes, as at Jesus Lane (1922) and along Bridge Street (1938). Drummer Street was redeveloped in 1925 to create a major bus depot and space for car parking. Other measures included the introduction of one-way streets from 1925, and the provision of more parking space in New Square in 1932. The river crossing at Fen Causeway was undertaken in 1926, providing 90 jobs for recruits from the ranks of the unemployed. The university made its own, characteristically negative, contribution by imposing severe limitations on the ownership of motor cars by the student population.

To cope with the increasing number of visitors to Cambridge the University Arms Hotel added a large extension to its rear. National retailing chains in the form of Woolworth's, Marks & Spencer, Boot's and Sainsbury's also opened branches in Cambridge. Local businesses succumbed to the competition; the 16 breweries existing in 1900 were reduced to six by 1925. Stourbridge Fair finally petered out. In 1931, as the nation entered the depths of depression, Cambridge acquired a quite novel entertainment venue – The Dorothy. In its basement was a pub, The Prince of Wales, on the ground floor a shop and restaurant, on the first floor a dance hall, on the second a dining hall and at the top a roof garden.

The movies increased in popularity among both students and townsfolk. In 1925 a second purpose-built cinema, the Tivoli, was opened on Chesterton Road and in 1930 the Central cinema on Hobson Street was rebuilt. In 1931 the Victoria cinema opened where Marks & Spencer now stands and in 1937 another establishment, the

Regal, was opened. In the same year Cambridge elected its first-ever Labour Mayor, who bore the uncompromisingly proletarian name of Bill Briggs. Communists in the university surprised few – but a *Labour* mayor!

ACTING IT OUT: A THESPIAN INTERLUDE

In 1575 William Soone, formerly Regius Professor of Civil Law, recorded that 'to beguile the long evenings' in the depths of winter, students 'amuse themselves with exhibiting public plays, which they perform with so much elegance, such graceful action, and such command of voice, countenance and gesture, that if Plautus, Terence or Seneca, were to come to life again, they would admire their own pieces and be better pleased with them than when they were performed before the people of Rome.'

In 1579 *Richardus Tertius*, a play about Richard III, written by Thomas Legge (1535–1607), Master of Caius, was performed in the hall of St John's. The great dining hall at Trinity, built in 1608 by Thomas Nevile, was clearly intended for periodic use as a theatre. Historian Patrick Collinson, indeed, claims it as 'England's oldest surviving theatre', no less. The most common Tudor and Jacobean fare was comedy – in Latin – mostly by Terence. In 1614 James I braved wintry weather to trek over from Newmarket to see four plays on four nights, including *Ignoramus*, a satire on lawyers. Despite the fact that the piece took six hours to get through, James loved it, and came back two months later for an encore performance.

Thomas Heywood (c.1570–1641), himself a Cambridge undergraduate in the 1590s, argued in *An Apology for Actors* (1612) that performing in plays was a useful training for the world of public affairs 'emboldening ... junior scholars, to arm them with audacity, against they come to be employed in any public exercise'. The commercial stage, however, was frowned on by the university authorities, who even banned the townspeople from watching puppet shows, although Stourbridge Fair offered the more exotic attractions of rope-dancers, fireworks and freak shows. Touring companies of actors trying their luck in Cambridge were either paid off or seen off. Since the repeal in the 1850s of statutes banning drama, the atmosphere has changed somewhat...

The ADC

Cambridge University Amateur Dramatic Club was founded in 1855, making it England's oldest university theatre group. It is still the largest in Cambridge. The core support came from Trinity, its leading light 19-year-old Francis Cowley Burnand (1836–1917), the first of many subsequent students to devote more time to the stage than study. In his case it paid off. Scotching family plans for the Anglican priesthood by becoming a Catholic, qualifying for the bar but declining to practise, Burnand wrote over 100 pieces for the stage, enjoyed a great hit with *Black-Eyed Susan* (1866), edited *Punch* for 26 years and ended his days as Sir Francis Cowley Burnand, patriarch of 13 offspring.

The ADC was fortunate early in its existence to find permanent premises in the Hoop, a former coaching inn on Park Street, whose business had been badly hit by the coming of the railways. Until the 1920s the standard theatrical fare was the sort of lightweight stuff that Burnand had proved so adept at turning out. After it became home to the Marlowe Society (see below), the Club began to engage with Elizabethan texts and other classic works.

The ADC was burnt down in 1933 but, thanks to widespread popular support, rebuilt within 18 months. Women were permitted on the stage from 1935 onwards. Threatened with bankruptcy in 1974, it was taken over by the university and nowadays is technically its smallest department. Membership is not, however, limited to members of the university but is open to all full-time students in Cambridge.

ADC alumni have included four Directors of the Royal National Theatre (Sir Peter Hall, Sir Trevor Nunn, Sir Richard Eyre and Sir Nicholas Hytner) as well as the late Sir Michael Redgrave (1908–85),

Sir Derek Jacobi, Sir Ian McKellen, Sam Mendes, Simon Russell Beale and Rachel Weisz.

The Marlowe Society

The Marlowe Society was founded in 1907 to revive interest in the Elizabethan and Jacobean theatre, no Shakespeare having been performed in Cambridge since 1886. The Society's first production was *Dr Faustus,* featuring the newly arrived Rupert Brooke. In 1922 the Society presented a milestone production of *Troilus and Cressida.* Soon after it became the special directorial province of the charismatic 'Dadie' Rylands (see below). James Mason (1909–84) of Peterhouse took a First in Architecture in 1931 but it was the reception given to his performance that year as Flamineo in the Society's production of *The White Devil* that encouraged him to abandon the drawing-board for the boards. By 1944 James Mason was Britain's top box-office star and would eventually appear in more than 100 films. In 1948, at the height of the Berlin Blockade, when Stalin sent the Red Army Choir to the German capital on a propaganda tour, the British Council riposted by dispatching Rylands and the Marlowe Society to play *Measure for Measure* and *The White Devil.* Between 1957 and 1964 Rylands and the Society responded by obliging the BBC to record *all* of Shakespeare's works to mark the 400th anniversary of his birth. In 1977 Griff Rhys Jones enjoyed spectacular success with Ben Jonson's *Bartholomew Fair,* as Sam Mendes did with Rostand's *Cyrano de Bergerac* in 1988. In 1993, to mark the 400th anniversary of Marlowe's murder, Robin Chapman produced *Chistoferus or Tom Kyd's Revenge.*

Footlights

Footlights' alumni have included John Cleese, Sir David Frost, Michael Frayn, Sir Jonathan Miller, Peter Cook, Bill Oddie, Clive Anderson, Tim Brooke-Taylor, Stephen Fry, Hugh Laurie, Nick Hancock, Steve Punt, David Baddiel, David Mitchell and Sacha Baron Cohen, not to mention numerous bishops and MPs, several Professors of Music, one of Mrs Thatcher's speechwriters, an Attorney-General, a Chairman of the International Olympic Committee, a Lord Keeper of the Great Seal of Scotland and the author of *The Hitchhiker's Guide to the Galaxy*. Since the 1960s, at least, dozens of applicants have applied to Cambridge less to get into the university than to get into Footlights.

Footlights was established in 1883 and gave its first public performance – which included a cricket match – to the inmates of a Cambridge pauper lunatic asylum. In 1885 it put on its first original operetta *Uncle Joe at Oxbridge*. Since 1892 it has only staged original material. In 1897 Footlights presented an imaginative spoof portraying Cambridge in the year 2000, *The New Dean*. A rich American benefactor saves the university from ruin at the cost of imposing a feminist regime and himself marries the female Vice-Chancellor. The new – female – Dean breaks all the rules by marrying an undergraduate. The Bedmakers Union protest at this breach of propriety by striking until their leader replaces the Dean and employs her as her maid. Male dons meanwhile are redeployed as college servants. This vision of the future was, however, too fantastical to survive even its own denouement, as the opera ends with all the female university officials resigning voluntarily to embrace marriage instead.

Early (1910–14) Footlights excursions onto the London stage lampooned socialism and vegetarians but donated takings to children's charities and the blind. In 1913 a Caius oarsman, Jack Hulbert (1892–1978), notched up an early success with his musical comedy, *Cheer-Oh Cambridge!*, and went on to become a major interwar star of stage and screen. In 1936 Footlights staged the first of 53 revues at the Arts Theatre. By the 1950s, BBC TV and Radio were broadcasting extracts from Footlights productions and transfers to the London stage were regularly lasting three weeks. In 1957 women were at last admitted – since when the names of Miriam Margolyes, Eleanor Bron, Julie Covington, Germaine Greer, Emma Thompson, Sue Perkins and Sandi Toksvig have been added to the roll-call of alumnae. In 1963 *Cambridge Circus* made it to New York and New Zealand. Clive James led a successful assault on the Edinburgh Fringe in 1967.

Footlights has had various homes, all more or less cramped and scruffy. In Clive James's day it was above a fish shop in Petty Cury. Stephen Fry remembers 'a dank, pine-clad hovel in the Union Society's bowels'. Now it has no specific home of its own, but regularly mounts 'smokers' (from informal revues where smoking was allowed), a Christmas pantomime, a spring revue and a summer touring show. For a more extensive account see www.cambridgefootlights.org and Robert Hewison, *Footlights: A Hundred Years of Cambridge Comedy* (1983).

The Arts Theatre

The Arts Theatre, opened in 1936, was the brainchild of J M Keynes, who also saw to its financing and establishment. Of the £32,000 required, Keynes provided nearly £30,000 and eventually got only £17,000 of it back. In the opening season Keynes's wife, the Russian ballerina Lydia Lopokova, took the leading parts in Ibsen's *A Doll's House* and *The Master Builder*. As a small boy, Sir Peter Hall stood at the back, for sixpence, watching Sir John Gielgud (1904–2000) play *Hamlet*. The Arts has not only provided a venue for Footlights and the Marlowe Society, but also for visiting companies, opera, ballet and previews of London productions. It was completely rebuilt in 1995–7 at a cost of some £10,000,000.

'Dadie' Rylands: 'not merely a performer, but a celebrity' – Lord Annan

There was once a don at King's whose pupils and protégés included the ADC's roll-call of theatrical knights (Hall, Nunn, Jacobi, McKellen) and whose talents as a director or lecturer were sought out by the Old Vic, the BBC and the British Council. George Humphrey Wolferstan Rylands (1902–99) was universally known as 'Dadie', from his childhood mispronunciation of 'baby'. A stylish rather than a penetrating lecturer, whose subject matter ranged from Shakespeare, Dryden and Pope to problems of translation and the influences of Greek and Latin on English style, Rylands was also an inspiring teacher in tutorials. Himself the son of a West Country land agent, he proved an unexpectedly capable wartime administrator of King's complex property portfolio, as well as being for decades a mainstay of the Marlowe Society and the Arts Theatre. Having made a stunning debut in 1921 in King's annual Greek play, 20 years later he would astonish donnish colleagues playing the title roles in wartime productions of *Othello* and *King Lear*. As a director Rylands's preoccupation was, in Ian McKellen's words, to instill in actors 'the most scrupulous attention to the classic texts, transforming their understanding' and to set an impeccable standard for the speaking of blank verse.

Rylands's doctoral thesis became his first book, *Words and Poetry* (1928), in which he argued that the impact of verse is on the ear before the brain, making it a matter of music, rather than of morals; he consequently detested the brutal judgmentalism of Leavis. 1928 was also the year in which Rylands moved into the rooms at the Old Provost's Lodge which were to be his home until his death. Bloomsbury artist Dora Carrington (1893–1932) decorated the doors and fireplaces. Despite her judgment that they looked like the work of a sick mouse (blaming too many cocktails), they are now lovingly treasured. Rylands entertained Virginia Woolf to lunch there that same year, a crucial incident recorded in her famous essay *A Room of One's Own*.

Rylands's most influential book was a Shakespeare anthology, widely carried by servicemen during World War Two, which subsequently became the basis for Gielgud's *bravura* one-man stage show, *The Ages of Man*. Etonian, Apostle, CBE and Companion of Honour, in youth 'miraculously blond', in old age wealthy enough to give a fortune to his college, university and beloved Arts Theatre, Dadie Rylands was also prone to self-destructive drunkenness, devastated by the death of his adored mother, guilt-ridden by his homosexuality and allegedly aged 10 years by the exposure of his friend Anthony Blunt as a spy. As Lord Annan pointedly asked the year after Rylands's death – what would the government's new-fangled assessment exercise have made of his 'academic career'? – 'Where were the books ... what had he been doing? Play-acting? Surely we want stout volumes ... not a succession of ephemeral activities.' Would the idea that he had not only have exerted a seminal influence on English theatre, but enhanced the culture of the entire country, even have crossed their minds?

10

The People's War

Anticipation

Few in 1914 had foreseen the nature of the ordeal before them. Few in 1939 had any illusions about the trial they were about to face. The greatest treasures of the Fitzwilliam Museum and of the University Library were moved to safety in remote locations in Wales and Cornwall. The celebrated stained-glass windows of King's College Chapel were removed at a cost of £75 each, though the vast Victorian west window was left in place to take its chances. Members of Berkeley College, Yale met the costs of this precautionary exercise, the glass being partly stored in the cellars under the neighbouring Gibbs Building and in other safe underground locations in the city. It had long been customary for the bells of Great St Mary's to be rung nightly between 9:00 and 9:15 p.m. to summon students home to their colleges. This ceased in 1939, as the ringing of church bells was to be the signal for an enemy invasion.

The war in the air

The threat from the air was seen as menacing and imminent. Members of the University Officers' Training Corps and University Air Squadron were called up immediately. Of the pre-war members of the University Air Squadron, 128 would be killed in action. 70 would be awarded the Distinguished Flying Cross, 17 the Distinguished Service Order and four the Victoria Cross.

As Director of Air Defence Research, John Cockcroft (1897–1967) was the mastermind behind the radar system which was crucial to the victory of the RAF in the Battle of Britain. Awarded the Nobel Prize for Physics in 1951, he became the first Director of the Atomic Energy Research Establishment at Harwell, pioneering the peaceful use of atomic energy for power generation.

Despite the importance of its railway yards to freight movement in a region with a massive military presence, Cambridge suffered only the intermittent attentions of the Luftwaffe, although, being on the flight path to industrial Coventry, it experienced some 424 air raid alerts and received hits from 118 high explosive bombs and more than 1,000 incendiaries. In June 1940 an air raid flattened Vicarage Terrace, Barnwell, killing nine. In 1941 Mrs Robertson, wife of the Regius Professor of Greek, was killed by a bomb while on duty as an air-raid warden. In 1942 bomb damage was inflicted on the Union Society, the Round Church, the Catholic Church, Whewell's Court and in Jesus Lane, where 10 buildings were demolished and more than 120 damaged. There are still visible bomb-damage scars on the walls at the junction of Jesus Lane and Bridge Street. The worst damage was, however, inflicted by a fire in 1941 which devastated some 80 yards of Pembroke's new buildings along Downing Street – started by a cigarette smoked by a member of the RAF Training Wing accommodated there. The total Cambridge toll for the war was 29 dead and 70 injured.

Participation

In terms of mobilisation, humanities students – judged to be the most expendable – went first. Students of science, engineering and medicine were more likely to be assigned to 'reserved occupations'. This category also included university teachers, though many ignored this exemption to serve in the armed forces or in the greatly expanded ranks of the state's wartime bureaucracy. Dons left behind consequently took on additional burdens of teaching, administration and academic supervision as well as such novel challenges as firewatching. To minimise hazards to men moving around in the pitch dark, ornamental chains and posts were removed from college courts.

Extraordinary times require extraordinary measures. In January 1940 the *Cambridge Review* reported in apparent wonderment that following the closure of the regular military academies at Woolwich and Sandhurst, the university was prepared to admit numbers of aspirant students who would otherwise have gone there – 'thus for the first time there may be members of the University who have never studied a word of Latin in their lives.' Short specialist courses were designed for members of the armed forces, especially the Navy, signallers and the RAF, who occupied billets in nine colleges. The university also exercised its administrative ingenuity to formulate a course in military studies by which its own undergraduates, who had broken off their courses to serve, could be awarded an ordinary degree on the strength of their contributions to the war effort.

A Home Guard contingent attracted both college staff and servants, many of them veterans of the First World War, like Hugh Heywood (1897–1987), Dean of Caius, who had been an army chaplain. Some 12,000 'evacuees' descended on the city and university. Apart from bewildered children these also included staff and students from the London School of Economics, Queen Mary College, London and Bedford College, London. Bart's Medical School was lodged at Queens', the University of London's School of Oriental Studies at Christ's, and civil servants at Caius, Corpus, Trinity and Sidney. The population of Cambridge thus rose from 78,000 to 90,000. Newnham accepted mothers and children from London's raffish Soho district, which must have been something of a revelation for both sides of the arrangement. Newnham undergraduates' war work ranged from the simple task of fixing coloured rags to camouflage netting to assembling transmitters for paratroopers. By May 1940, 60 enemy aliens had been interned. Having run out of money and fearing arrest, Dutch Nazi agent Jan Ter Braak shot himself dead in an air-raid shelter on Christ's Pieces; a subsequent search of his lodgings revealed a portable radio transmitter and forged documents confirming his true identity and purpose.

A Cambridge Cassandra

When World War Two broke out Richard Stone (1913–91) was working at Lloyd's, which led some in Whitehall to assume, quite wrongly, that he knew all about shipping; so he was directed to the Ministry of Economic Warfare to monitor the movement of strategic imports into neutral countries. Stone personally interpreted this to mean that he should focus on the movement of tankers, especially Italian ones. In May 1940 he noted that all known Italian tankers were suddenly diverting from their usual routes and guessed they were under orders to make for home or neutral ports in anticipation of an Italian declaration of war. Estimating that all the ships would have reached their assumed destinations by 10 June 1940 he predicted that Italy would declare war on that date. The very suggestion caused outrage among the Italophiles of the Foreign Office, who interpreted the Italian build-up of kerosene stocks as entirely explicable by the need to keep a devoutly Catholic nation well supplied with altar candles. Needless to say, Italy did declare war on 10 June. Richard Stone eventually returned to Cambridge to become the founding father of applied economics in the university, receiving the Nobel Prize for his efforts in 1984.

Boffins

The First World War had demonstrated conclusively the fundamental significance of science and technology for the successful prosecution of modern warfare. For the first time, the British state had seen the need for a strategic science policy and had cobbled together the machinery to formulate and administer it. The onset of conflict in

1939 therefore led to a far more systematic and successful mobilisation of the nation's intellectual talents.

With shipping space at a premium, nutrition experts Robert McCance (1898–1993), Reader in Experimental Medicine, and his collaborator, Elsie Widdowson (1908–2000), set out to establish how far the nation's dietary needs could be met from food grown in Britain, rather than imported. The standard weekly ration they devised consisted of one egg, one pound of meat or fish, six ounces of fruit, five ounces of sugar, four ounces of cheese and four ounces of fats. The bulk of the diet was to consist of unrationed vegetables and brown bread, supplemented by a quarter of a pint of milk a day. To prove the viability of their formula, McCance and Widdowson and two student volunteers, James Robinson (1914–2008) and Andrew Huxley (1917–2012), followed it rigorously for three months. To test their fitness McCance and Robinson then cycled to the Lake District in less than three days. The four then spent 10 days hiking across the fells. On one day McCance and Huxley climbed 7,000 feet and covered 36 miles in less than 12 hours, burning off 4,714 calories in the process. McCance and Widdowson also conducted a series of experiments on the body's absorption of calcium from bread. As a result, every wartime loaf was reinforced with a supplement of calcium carbonate – and still is to this day. McCance and Widdowson's definitive study, *The Chemical Composition of Foods* (1940) became the nutritionists' Bible; the sixth edition was published in 2002. McCance went on to conduct experiments investigating shipwrecked sailors' survival at sea and became CBE and FRS. After the war Widdowson helped rehabilitate malnourished orphans in defeated Germany and eventually also achieved long overdue recognition as FRS, CBE and CH. James Robinson became a distinguished physiologist in New Zealand. Andrew Huxley won a Nobel Prize and became FRS, OM and Master of Trinity.

Viennese-born Max Perutz (1914–2002) arrived in Cambridge in 1936, aged 22, and joined the staff of the Cavendish Laboratory. The German annexation of Austria in March 1938 changed him from a guest to a refugee, banned from paid employment. Desperate to re-establish his status, Perutz showed his work on using X-rays to investigate the structure of haemoglobin to Professor Bragg, who immediately arranged a grant from the Rockefeller Foundation, which enabled him to appoint Perutz as his research assistant, thus saving his scientific career. It also enabled Perutz to bring his parents to England, rescuing them from the Holocaust. Like so many other refugees, however, in May 1940 Perutz was nevertheless rounded up as a security risk and sent to the Isle of Man and then to Canada before being called in to the bizarre Habbakuk project, a fantastical plan to create a permanent aircraft carrier out of ice and wood shavings, to be anchored in the mid-Atlantic. Perutz was in fact uniquely qualified to contribute to the venture as his pre-war work in crystallography had included a definitive study of how snow is turned into glacial ice. After the war Perutz would return to Cambridge, where his time was more usefully employed in uncovering the structure of haemoglobin, which gained him a Nobel Prize for Chemistry in 1962. He was subsequently furnished with a CBE, OM, CH and FRS. His last publication was a volume of essays intriguingly entitled *I Wish I'd Made You Angry Earlier* (1998), on the pursuit of scientific knowledge.

The code-breakers

The activities of the Government Code and Cypher School at Bletchley Park in Buckinghamshire remained secret for some 40 years after the end of the war. As late as 1982 the publication of *The Hut Six Story* by Gordon Welchman (1906–85), a former maths don at Sidney Sussex, was sufficient to cause official concern and cost the author his affiliation to the US security establishment. Welchman, who was primarily responsible for cracking the German army's fiendishly complex Enigma code, was only one of a crucial cadre corralled into Bletchley, more coming from Cambridge than from any other university. In a brief chapter of fewer than six pages devoted to the Second World

War, the official *History of the University of Cambridge* merely notes in passing that 'a notable contingent was recruited for the celebrated intelligence think-tank at Bletchley' and then passes on to its major preoccupation with the freezing of professorial posts.

One of the youngest Cambridge recruits to Bletchley Park was Harry Hinsley (1918–98), who had only just finished the second year of his history degree. In 1943, aged 24, he was sent to the USA to negotiate the first agreement between British and American code-breakers. In 1946 he served as secretary to the top-secret conference which agreed to perpetuate this cryptographic alliance. He went on to become Sir Harry Hinsley, Vice-Chancellor, Master of St John's and Professor of the History of International Relations.

Dillwyn Knox (1884–1943), a King's classicist with a lifelong addiction to puzzles, had served in the Admiralty's Room 40 during the Great War, when his ear for metre had helped to break the German admirals' flag code by recognising repeated snatches of poetry which established a crib from which the rest of the code could be unravelled. At Bletchley he broke the Italian naval code and was thus directly responsible for enabling Admiral Cunningham (1883–1963) to be forewarned through intercepts of the movement of an Italian battle group which he devastated in a decisive night action off Cape Matapan in 1941. Another brilliant stroke of intuition led Knox to predict correctly that many of the four-letter settings used by German signallers for the Enigma cipher machine would be swear words or girls' names. Dying of cancer, Knox worked from his bed to the last, only getting up to dress for investiture with the Order of St Michael and St George (CMG) by a Palace emissary.

Philip Hall, FRS (1904–82), a maths don at King's, worked on the Italian and Japanese diplomatic codes. Maxwell Newman, FRS (1897–1984), another mathematician, from St John's, made a crucial contribution to the designing of the proto-computer known as Colossus. Other recruits included Chess Master Hugh Alexander (1909–74), who worked on German naval codes and went on to head the Government Communications HQ at Cheltenham, and Geoffrey

Barraclough (1908–84), an expert on medieval German history, who monitored Luftwaffe traffic during the Battle of Britain.

The most celebrated of all was Alan Turing (1912–54), another King's maths don, who, as a postgraduate, had already demonstrated a precociously brilliant interest in the possibilities of machine computing. Having helped to break the German naval cipher and design vital components of the machinery for handling high volumes of decoded data, Turing after the war went on to make foundational contributions to the emerging field of artificial intelligence. A prosecution for homosexuality cost him his security clearance, and arguably had a connection with his death two years later from cyanide poisoning. A verdict of suicide was recorded and in 2009 Prime Minister Gordon Brown issued a public apology for the 'appalling way he was treated' by the government.

Jet set

The jet engine was developed too late to exert a decisive influence on the conduct and outcome of World War Two; but it was a product of that war nonetheless and, indirectly, of Cambridge – not so much the birthplace of the jet as its nursery.

Born the son of a factory foreman in the engineering city of Coventry, pint-sized Frank Whittle (1907–96) only succeeded in joining the RAF as a boy apprentice at the third attempt but, as early as 1928, he claimed that it would be feasible to construct an entirely new type of aero engine, capable of unprecedentedly high speeds at high altitudes. In 1930 Whittle filed a patent for an engine driven by jet propulsion. Although he was promoted to commissioned rank and became a test pilot, his ideas were dismissed with derision by the Air Ministry.

Entering Peterhouse in 1934 as a mature student of 27 to read mechanical sciences, Whittle met with encouragement rather than scepticism and in 1936 joined with two former RAF officers to found Power Jets Ltd. The following year, in which he was awarded a First, Whittle performed a successful ground test of his first prototype jet.

Roy Lubbock (1892–1985), Whittle's Peterhouse tutor, arranged a year's postgraduate study for Whittle to enable him to work full time on his engine, in contrast to the niggardly six hours a week allowed by the Air Ministry. The onset of war reversed the negative attitude of officialdom and made funds available for rapid development work, leading to the first jet-powered flight in May 1941. In 1944 Power Jets Ltd was taken over by the government and the jet-powered Gloster Meteor took to the skies to intercept German V-1 flying bombs.

In 1948 Whittle left the RAF with the rank of air commodore and was knighted. He subsequently received a tax-free government gratuity of £100,000 and, in 1986, the Order of Merit, in recognition of his work. At the age of 70 Whittle was appointed a research professor at the US Naval Academy at Annapolis. The Whittle Laboratory at Cambridge was opened in 1971.

They also served

K H Roscoe (1914–70) of Emmanuel College, a keen sportsman and sapper in the pre-war university Officer Training Corps distinguished himself with the Welsh Guards in a rear-guard action at Boulogne before spending five years as a PoW, during which time he taught himself French and German and escaped and was recaptured three times. Roscoe eventually broke free from a 'death march' column fleeing before the advancing Americans and was belatedly awarded the Military Cross. Returning to Cambridge he became the founding father of the study of soil mechanics and a lieutenant colonel in the Officer Training Corps.

Former antiquarian book-dealer Alan 'Tim' Munby (1913–74), another five-year PoW, penned verse in the style of Betjeman, ghost stories in the style of M R James and a prison-camp guide in the style of Baedeker. Munby returned to found the Cambridge Bibliographical Society (1949) and compile a definitive guide to Cambridge college libraries (1960). As librarian of King's, Munby would be entrusted with the care of the personal papers of Rupert Brooke, E M Forster and J M Keynes. He also built up an outstanding collection of the works of Macaulay and pioneered the use of booksellers' and auction catalogues as historical sources.

Between 28 and 31 March 1944, Trinity College was taken over for a comprehensive, top-secret briefing for leading commanders of the projected invasion of Europe. St John's Combination Room housed 'a beautifully constructed model of Normandy and its beaches'. Four days after D-Day, Lt Gen Bucknall (1894–1980) found time to write appreciatively to G M Trevelyan, the Master of Trinity – 'I hope that some day I might be able to explain to you fully how the plans laid at Trinity helped to mould the course of history', concluding his missive with the laconic understatement that 'We have a stiffish fight coming.'

As Britain's leading economic guru, J M Keynes sacrificed his health and ultimately his life for the war effort. Following a severe heart attack in 1937 he had cut back on his many commitments but answered the call to become a Treasury adviser, devising policies to pay for the war and control the threat of inflation. Allied co-operation obliged him to make six visits to the US in as many years, most notably to the 1944 Bretton Woods conference which devised the post-war monetary system and at which the delegates gave him a standing ovation. His last contribution was to negotiate a crucial but controversial US loan, which enabled the exhausted UK economy to make the challenging transition from war to peace. Despite these many trials Keynes also championed the Council for Encouragement of Music and the Arts, which later evolved into the post-war Arts Council.

Another angle

Brian Thompson's painful but hilarious memoir of a fractured upbringing, *Keeping Mum: A Wartime Childhood* (2006), recalls Cambridge from the perspective of a new interwar suburb. Following Brian's birth in 1935 in Lambeth, Thompson's parents rented one of the 'Homes for the Future', uncertainly located in a social limbo between Drummer Street bus station and Cherry Hinton, then 'a bucolic village decorated with straw wisps'. Gypsies still left their coded marks on the doorposts of hostile houses but modernity was represented by a cement works, a commercial apple orchard and Marshall's airfield. For the small boy, Cambridge was 'simply a town', its colleges only significant as places where neighbours worked in the kitchens.

The outbreak of war gave Thompson's misanthropic but ambitious father, a Post Office engineer, the chance to reinvent himself. Courtesy of the RAF, this 'very, very gifted man without a real idea in his head' disguised his colour blindness to fly as a navigator on 28 missions, including D-Day and Arnhem, and eventually emerged as a pipe-smoking, moustachioed member of the officer class. Deprived of her husband's regulatory presence, the boy's mother, meanwhile, drifted rapidly into a chaotic non-routine of domestic neglect, until a shaft of sunlight arrived from across the Atlantic. 'After 1942 the streets were stiff with Yanks, ambling along ... fitter and cleaner than the miserable bundles of khaki they occasionally encountered.' For Peggy they represented a 'good time', cartons of Lucky Strikes and a repetitive illusion of romance; for Brian a resented intrusion, unmitigated by placatory offerings of candy bars, an unwanted baseball bat and a school atlas to enable a current escort to indicate the whereabouts of Indiana.

Shuttled between relatives in various run-down parts of blitz-battered London, Brian Thompson eventually returned to a small, private boarding school near Fenner's cricket ground, where he subsisted on whale meat and potatoes cooked with the skins on. Near his home there was a camp where Italian PoWs sunbathed and played bowls with home-made woods. Out on the road to Newmarket he explored a scary graveyard for the scorched and shattered skeletons of B-17 bombers. When the hostilities ended, Brian's still warring parents opted for a semi-detached marriage while he proceeded to grammar school, supplemented by self-education courtesy of Gustave David's Saturday market 'stall of waifs and lost souls'. It tickled him to think, as he purchased Penguin No 48 *A Passage to India*, that 'for all I knew E M Forster ... may have been standing next to me in the flesh when I passed my money across.' Eventually, very much against the odds, Thompson read English at Cambridge and went on to become a playwright, film-maker and biographer – in Oxford.

In memoriam

Of the more than 100 US airfields in East Anglia, a dozen were within ten miles of Cambridge. The US Eighth Air Force, thousands of whose members lie buried at Madingley, sustained more than 26,000 casualties during the war, almost half of the total USAAF losses. At the end of the war the Eighth was granted the Freedom of Cambridge. An entire gallery at the Imperial War Museum, Duxford, is devoted to their story. The ceiling of the back bar of the Eagle pub in Bene't Street still bears many of their squadron numbers and nicknames, flamed onto its smoky surface with Zippo lighters or candles – in Clive James's memorable words:

> ... a portent, doubly hideous for its innocence, of their own fate, and a grim token of the fiery nemesis they were bringing every night to the cities of Germany. Unwittingly they created a hall of fame, a temple of the sacred flame, a trophy room for heroes.

It is still there. Look for 222 Squadron, which flew out of Duxford.

Cambridge fatalities in the Second World War were far fewer than in the First. Nevertheless, Peterhouse, a small college, lost 60, Christ's 115, Queens' 116, Pembroke 149 and Trinity 389. Supplementary panels bearing the relevant names were appended to previous college memorials. Many expressed similar sentiments to those of the Pembroke inscription – 'With the same courage and the same love of their country these also laid down their lives.' Trinity opted for a more poetic quotation from 1 Samuel 25:16: 'They were like a wall around us night and day.'

LOOKING THE PART: A SARTORIAL INTERLUDE

Members of the medieval university were required to affirm their status in clothing and appearance. Peterhouse statutes of 1338 ordered that 'the scholars of our house shall adopt the clerical dress and tonsure ... and not allow their beard or their hair to grow contrary to canonical prohibition, nor wear rings upon their fingers for their own vain glory.' King's College statutes of 1443 banned 'red and green shoes, or secular ornaments or fancy hoods ... or swords or long knives ... or girdles and belts adorned with gold and silver'.

Such restrictions survived the reformation of religion. In 1575 Law Professor William Soone (c.1520–80), advised a foreign friend that 'the common dress of all is a sacred cap; (I call it sacred, because worn by priests); a gown reaching down to their heels, of the same form as that of priests.' In fact, university regulations a decade later were much more prescriptive and detailed than that, prohibiting the wearing of then-fashionable stuffed garments, which exaggerated the contours of the body, and instead requiring that gowns be made of 'woollen cloth of ... sad colour', with standing not falling collars, and a hood of 'the same or like cloth and colour'. Further prohibitions outlawed the wearing of velvet or silk or any embroidered item or any garment with fancy stitching, lace or slashes to reveal the lining.

Anticipating a visit from William Laud (1573–1645), the authoritarian Archbishop of Canterbury, who had taken a keen personal interest in conditions at Oxford, in 1636 the authorities had a pre-emptive report compiled on *Common Disorders in the University*, including a list of inappropriate current fashions – 'Roses upon the Shoe, long frizzled hair upon the head, broad spread bands upon the Shoulders and long large Merchants' Ruffs about the neck, with fair feminine Cuffs at the wrist'. In the event the inspectorial visit never materialised.

Some undergraduates endured the additional tyranny of continued parental interventions. In 1624 Lady Katherine Paston wrote to her son William at Corpus Christi:

I do send thee a new suit of satin to wear this commencement, as also a pair of silk stockings, points, garters and shoe strings and a silver girdle ... have a great care to wear thy clothes neat and clean, it is a great Commendation to see a young man ... neat, without spots and dirtiness ...

In 1625 she sent a suit of damask and in 1626 another, a girdle, two shirts and two ruffs and gave permission to buy a newly fashionable beaver hat. Other parents had the opposite problem of curbing their offspring's desire to cut a figure. In 1680 one wrote to the Master of St Catharine's:

Let the milliners etc. be forbidden to trust him; he hath clothes enough for a quarter of a year ... watch him for speaking untruths, to which he is so prone; as also to chop and change his clothes so as to cut and alter them to my great detriment...

If metropolitan fashion-consciousness obtruded on provincial Cambridge, officially approved costumes remained *de rigeur* for formal occasions. In 1748 the *Universal Magazine* published illustrations of 24 different modes of academic dress, ranging from a vice-chancellor to a college servant. These showed, for example, that while doctors of divinity wore a mortar-board, doctors of law or physic or music wore a soft cap. There was still a distinctive outfit for the son of a noble-man – 60 years later Byron would exult at the effect produced in Hall when he donned his for the first time and looked, by his own account, 'Superb' – which, at £100, it should have. Another gown, to be worn on festival days only, cost at least another £50. Trinity undergraduates likewise had their own distinctive purple gowns, trimmed in silver or gold. There was even a special dress for a Master of Arts *in mourning*.

Sporting colours

Sartorially speaking, sport remained a casual concern, as testified by a cricketer who played in the first match against Oxford in 1827 – 'We had no colours ... we wore pretty much what we liked ... Knee-breeches and thin gauze silk stockings, doubled up at the ankles, formed a popular costume'. 60 years later it would be very different, as newcomers were advised that 'in the matter of hats, there is safety in the ordinary hard round felt; even a straw hat should not be brought up, as the colour of the straw and of the ribbon will depend on the College Club which is eventually joined.'

There was one sport which, even in late Victorian times, had no dress code – literally, as Gwen Raverat remembered:

> All summer, Sheep's Green and Coe Fen were pink ... for bathing drawers did not exist then ... to go Up River, the goal of all the best picnics, the boats had to go right by the bathing place, which lay on both sides of the narrow stream. These dangerous straits were taken in silence, and at full speed. The Gentlemen were set to the oars ... and each Lady unfurled a parasol, and, like an ostrich, buried her head in it ... until the crisis was past and the river was decent again.

Dandy dons

In the city itself, by contrast, the strictest propriety was maintained and as late as the eve of the Great War the official *Students' Handbook* made it clear that 'on Sundays cap and gown must be worn in the courts and grounds; but students going for a country walk may wear ordinary dress provided they do not pass through the streets' – quite how this was possible was unexplained.

Dons' eccentricities – manifested in a bewildering variety of mannerisms – often extended to their dress. A C Benson thought that a don should wear the 'style-before-last' and himself favoured shapeless flannels. Professor Arthur Quiller-Couch (1863–1944), by contrast, was accused of giving lectures 'rather too carefully dressed for Cambridge'. In his off-duty hours 'Q' favoured full riding gear – 'a suit of emphatic checks and a brown bowler hat and brown leather gaiters'. According to Bertrand Russell, Aldis Wright (1831–1914), Vice-Master of Trinity, never appeared outdoors 'without a top hat. Even once when he was roused from sleep at three in the morning by a fire, the top hat was duly on his head.' Philosopher George Edward Moore was a caricature of the absent-minded professor – 'his gown was always covered in chalk, his cap was in rags or missing ... He would go across town to his class with no more formal footwear than his bedroom slippers'. The economist A C Pigou favoured white gym shoes with black laces and at High Table wore 'a double-breasted lounge jacket filched from a parcel of clothes that his aunt was sending to a Church Army shelter.' The critic F R Leavis famously did not wear neckties and dressed, if the word can be used at all accurately with reference to one so fastidious of language, like a rather slovenly gardener.

There were, of course, also undergraduate poseurs. The exquisitely tailored future avant-garde novelist Ronald Firbank (1886–1926) affected imported ties and antique rings and, anxious to remain slim, 'used to starve himself, go out for runs in all weathers etc.' The poet Rupert Brooke 'dressed in a coal-black flannel shirt, with a bright red tie and a suit of grey homespun', calculated to throw 'the fine colouring of his head into strong relief'.

Female fashions

The advent of female undergraduates and the permission for dons to marry inevitably brought a novel dimension to the Cambridge fashion scene but, according to Noel Annan (1916–2000), this was inhibited by a residual, moralistic evangelicalism:

> A fashionably dressed wife would not only have been an extravagance but an act of submission to worldly vanity: and the Pre-Raphaelite cloaks and dresses which had been donned as a homage to beauty and a protest against the world of upper-class fashion degenerated in some cases into thick woollen stockings

and flannel petticoats ... worn as a badge of financial and spiritual austerity.

Gwen Raverat, who lived very near Newnham, thought its inhabitants wore deliberately dull clothes to show they were serious students. Dora Black (1894–1986) of Girton, future wife of Bertrand Russell, denied this – 'we ... did not wear severe shirt blouses with formal ties, nor did we drag back our hair; we were most fashion-conscious, much given to saucy hats, designed to impress male colleagues at lectures'. Frances Partridge (1900–2004) of Newnham recalled the challenge of the 1920s dance craze. She had only one, rather old, evening dress, trimmed inexpertly to make it look different for special occasions – 'being impatient by nature I cut and stitched away at random, adding a bit of ribbon for a belt, elastic in the hem to give the fashionable "Turkish trouser" look ... I must have looked a perfect fright and was lucky not to come to pieces in mid-tango'. Finally, in desperation, she dyed the dress an unfashionable black 'and removed most of the front and all the back down to the waist, so as to give a startling décolletage which I vaguely shrouded in some pieces of gauze rather like wings. In this getup I was reported to look very "fast"'.

Shabby chic

The aristocratic Russian émigré Vladimir Nabokov, writing of the same era, was considerably underwhelmed by the masculine 'style' of the day:

> The usual attire of the average Cambridge undergraduate, whether athlete or leftish poet, struck a sturdy and dingy note: his shoes had thick rubber soles, his flannel trousers were dark grey, and the buttoned sweater, called a 'jumper', under his Norfolk jacket was a conservative brown. What I suppose might be termed the gay set wore old pumps, very light grey flannel trousers, a bright-yellow 'jumper' and the coat part of a good suit.

Formal academic dress remained spectacularly anachronistic, much to the delight of outsiders. When Rudyard Kipling (1865–1936) was made a Fellow of Magdalene in 1932 he wrote to his daughter that 'if you had seen your Dad in a fair white linen surplice (most becoming) with his red D Litt hood trailing down his back, you'd have been impressed ... I look very beautiful at meals in a simple black gown with ample sleeves'. As late as 1955 the American poet Sylvia Plath (1932–63) could still write excitedly to her mother that she was 'quite loving wearing my black gown, which makes me feel so wonderfully part of this magnificent place! Sort of like Sacramental robes!'

During World War Two, when civilian living standards fell by 50 per cent, shabbiness was patriotic. Cambridge, chilly at the best of times, witnessed a revival of the medieval habit of wearing gowns and even overcoats indoors. Corduroys, formerly the sturdy garb of the working man, came into favour for their warmth and durability. Sir James Beament (1921–2005), a Fellow of Queens', observed:

> It seems surprising that, with clothes rationed, gowns were still made and had to be worn at night, but squares (mortar boards) were abandoned in 1942 because they became trophies grabbed in the black-out by US airmen with whom the streets of the city abounded. And, because gowns made us identifiable, a few of the pubs most frequented by the said airmen were out-of-bounds to the University ...

Austerity was not to last. In the mid-1950s the official *Student Handbook* underlined the resurgence of full-fledged sartorial snobbery with its strident admonitions:

> Throw those corduroys away; this is not Nottingham University. If you want to wear undergraduate uniform (which we don't particularly recommend, and which does not include any part of Army uniform!) it consists for lectures of sports jacket and flannels. Eminently preferable is cavalry twill trousers, and a

blazer, but don't, repeat don't, wear a pullover with a blazer; it looks like Balham Tech if you do. Otherwise suits on high days and holidays and duffles any time at all. No macintoshes – this is NOT Balham Tech.'

The same publication insisted:

DO wear a gown after dusk or when in the University Library or Church, or in the Senate House, also in lectures and when paying calls on University officials. The gown must be worn 'in decent order and in the proper manner'. It is not worn thus if worn over a sweater or by ladies in trousers ...

As late as 1967 the unwary were advised that they would be committing a breach of discipline if seen smoking while wearing academic dress and equally if wearing a coloured blazer (i.e. not plain dark blue or black) 'except on the way to or from a dinner at which blazers are worn with evening dress'. A glimpse of another world ...

The sartorial wind was, however, already blowing in a quite different direction. In 1962 bespoke tailor Pratt, Manning and Co closed down, pronouncing its own sniffy epitaph – 'thirty years ago students were proud of their dress and bought four suits at a time. Now they shuffle around in jeans and sweaters and do not have two ha'pennies to rub together.'

The banner of elegance is still flown, however, at robemakers Ede and Ravenscroft, whose premises at the corner of Trumpington Street and Silver Street are as stylish as their window displays. Founded in London in 1689, the company's website cautiously claims that it is 'thought to be the oldest firm of tailors in the world'. Having provided the robes for the coronation of William and Mary in the year of its foundation, the firm has held royal warrants from 13 successive monarchs. Apart from tailoring and the manufacture of academic, judicial and ceremonial robes, Ede and Ravenscroft also make wigs and offer dress hire and photographic services, aimed particularly at graduating students in all their (temporary) finery. At the other end of King's Parade, by Great St Mary's, Ryder and Amies, self-proclaimed 'University Store' for 120 years, also offer a comprehensive range of armorial plaques, college ties, bow ties, scarves, cufflinks, caps, sweatshirts, T-shirts and even 'hoodies'.

11

Town Into City

Post-war Cambridge still retained an aura of antiquity and austerity. For John Vaizey (1929–84), from south London, it was like going 'to live in the country. Each ... winter day began with the river smell, mixed with the scent of damp leaves and ... bonfire smoke.' Luxuries like running water and gas fires were still only 'gradually coming in' for many undergrads and 'coal was still rationed to a sack a term'. As ever, changes came hesitantly. As late as 1966 Corpus Christi could inform its alumni that 'improvements are being made in the provision of lavatory and washing facilities on various staircases: the college takes the view that some abatement of the rigours of life is not a sign of decadence'. In 1951, rather out of nowhere, King George VI conferred on Cambridge the status of a city. In 1958, however, when Hardy Kruger and Sylvia Sims came to film *Bachelor of Hearts,* it was because Cambridge still provided a suitably antiquated backdrop for romance.

In the 1950s a new engineering laboratory opened in Trumpington Street and a new Veterinary School off Madingley Road. Not until the 1960s, however, did Cambridge, for better or worse, begin to acquire the sort of modern 'cityscape' which, if allowed to go too far, will eventually mean that it looks just like anywhere else, as architecturally inconsequential office blocks colonise street-corners and national chain stores infiltrate the streets around the Market Square.

The University Arms radically changed its frontage to provide integral parking for guests *a l'Americain*. In 1961 Bradwell's Court was opened as the city's first shopping arcade. (It was demolished in 2006). A large public swimming bath was opened at Parkside in 1963. In 1964 parking meters began to appear on the streets and in 1965, yellow lines. In the same year the requirement that undergraduates should wear gowns after dark was abolished, rendering nocturnal roisterers marginally less identifiable to the authorities. Also in 1965, as if to reaffirm the validity of its heritage, Cambridge became twinned with the German university city of Heidelberg.

Familiar landmarks, however, continued to disappear. The centuries-old outdoor fishmarket which had given Peas Hill its name (from Pisces, Latin for 'fish') closed in 1949. The Corn Exchange ceased trading in 1965. In 1962 Addenbrooke's began to move out of Trumpington Street to its new location at the south-eastern edge of the city. The 'retail mix' of the city centre was steadily diluted by the closure of traditional or specialist outlets for bespoke tailoring, smoking requisites, bookbinding and the repair of shoes and watches. Hints of future change included the opening of a Tesco supermarket on St Andrew's Street and a Fine Fare in Mill Road in 1963, the takeover of British manufacturer Pye by the Dutch combine Philips in 1967 and the closure of the city's last independent brewery, the Star, in 1972.

In 1950 the doyen of British town-planners, Professor William Holford (1907–75), had recommended against the further expansion of Cambridge itself in favour of the development of a circuit of outlying 'necklace villages'. As a consequence, Bar Hill, to the west of the city, was developed in the 1960s as a new community of some 5,000 plus. During that same decade, Arbury and King's Hedges on the north side of the city came to be included in its boundaries. Within Cambridge itself the expansion of the university – reflecting national trends to open higher education to an ever-growing proportion of the population, to enlarge postgraduate teaching and to devote greater resources to cutting-edge research – created new pressures on both the physical space for accommodation and on established institutional arrangements. A decade after the war almost half of the 800-plus teaching staff were without fellowships, especially in subjects only studied by postgraduates. Further pressure came from the rising proportion of support staff in the form of administrators, librarians, curators, technicians and, later, providers of computing services. Unless the collegiate system was to be abandoned, it had to be enlarged by the creation of entirely new colleges – which is what happened. The university itself built a Graduate (now University) Centre in 1964–7 in Granta Place, off Mill Lane, offering social and recreational facilities, primarily for research students and support staff – and even their children.

New Hall

In 1947 Cambridge finally assented to the admission of women as full members of the university. The then Queen Elizabeth, consort of George VI, was the first female to receive a degree – honorary – that year. Degrees were conferred on women on a regular basis from 1948 onwards. In 1997 the university would invite back coachloads of Girtonians and Newnhamites in their eighties and nineties to award them the full diplomas formerly denied them. This final acceptance of females led to the founding of further colleges for women.

Opened in 1954 as a women's college with just 16 undergraduates, New Hall represented the combined efforts of members and supporters of the existing women's colleges, led by Dame Myra Curtis (1886–1971), principal of Newnham. It acquired its name by default, for want of any better. Its first home was at The Hermitage and the Old Granary on Silver Street, now part of Darwin College, moving to the Huntingdon Road in 1964–5, thanks to generous donations from the Wolfson and Nuffield Foundations. The work of Chamberlin, Powell and Bon, builders of the Barbican complex in London, the architecture of New Hall attracted much comment, the assertive dome over its hall reminding onlookers variously of a mosque and a peeled orange. 'In architectural history the line between grandeur and folly is a thin one. Is a poverty-stricken college of learned women the place to indulge in Byzantine whims?' the editors of *Cambridge New Architecture* enquired portentously. The *Blue Guide* criticised the paired arrangement of undergraduate rooms, the upper level reached by ladder-like steps, 'a novel, if hardly practical, idea', and found the overall impression 'faintly reminiscent of the Taj Mahal'. Pevsner, unusually, was reduced to conjecture, opining that 'the total whiteness was ... probably chosen as something feminine'. For Cordelia Gray, heroine of P D James's murder mystery, *An Unsuitable Job for a Woman* (1972), the white brick had an 'obtrusive femininity', the shallow pools of the gardens a 'mannered prettiness', the cumulative effect giving the impression of 'a harem... owned by a sultan with liberal views and an odd predilection for clever girls'. New Hall has subsequently come to be recognised as an ideal setting for an outstanding collection of some 200 sculptures and paintings by women artists, from Cambridge resident Gwen Raverat to international icons Dame Barbara Hepworth (1903–75) and Dame Elisabeth Frink (1930–93).

Following a donation of £30,000,000 from former New Hall undergraduate Ros Edwards and her husband, New Hall in 2008 changed its name to Murray Edwards College in honour of its first President, Rosemary Murray, and the generosity of the Edwards' benefaction.

Churchill

Churchill College is the national memorial to Sir Winston Churchill (1874–1965) and, as such, the first Cambridge college to be named after a person in their own lifetime. In 1959 Churchill came in person to plant an oak tree, symbolic of endurance and continuity. The college scarf and boats sport Churchill's personal racing colours of chocolate brown and pink.

Churchill regarded himself as a self-educated man. At the Royal Military Academy, Sandhurst, he had excelled at tactics and history but struggled with mathematics. As First Lord of the Admiralty during the First World War and as Prime Minister during the Second,

Churchill had become keenly aware of the vital role of technology for strategic security and economic development. Inspired by the Massachusetts Institute of Technology, the founding statutes of Churchill College required that 70 per cent of the students should be enrolled in mathematics, science or engineering courses. The first Master of the college was Sir John Cockroft, FRS, OM, Churchill's own nominee and a leading figure in the international scientific community. The establishment initially consisted of 60 fellows and 540 students, a high proportion of them postgraduate.

Built on 42 acres of former farmland on the Madingley Road, the architecturally 'uncompromising' new college occupied the largest site in the university. Even the modernist aficionado Pevsner conceded that the dining hall block represented '1960 at its most ruthless'. The design, however, incorporated such traditional motifs as the arrangement of rooms around staircases and of blocks into interlocking courts. Architectural historian James Lees-Milne (1908–97) thought the result a 'beastly building, like an enormous public lavatory' – and believed Churchill himself would have loathed it. A more whimsical description, invoking Churchill's own majestic birthplace, hailed it as 'the Blenheim of the Welfare state'.

Churchill's chapel is – literally and institutionally – detached, symbolic of the separation of science and religion. The proposal to build a chapel in a new college primarily devoted to science provoked controversy. Francis Crick (see below) refused a fellowship in protest, allegedly sending a cheque for £10 for the provision of a brothel, on the grounds that no fellow needed to use that *either* unless he chose to. The building is therefore carefully referred to as the chapel *at*, rather than *of*, Churchill College. A Danish benefaction funded the Moller Centre for Continuing Education, designed by Henning Larsen. Churchill's grounds feature Oscar Nemon's massive bust of Sir Winston (1961), Barbara Hepworth's *Four Square Through* (1966), Bernard Meadows's *Pointing Figure with Child* (1966) and Dhruva Mistry's *Diagram of an Object* (1990).

In 1972 Churchill became the first all-male college to admit women.

Whether despite, or because of, its recent foundation Churchill soon acquired its own distinctive character, evidenced in the guidebook for intending entrants produced by its own students in 1973:

> the facilities are luxurious ... the rules are not severe ... students ... are generally highly politically involved ... Perhaps because newness breeds insecurity, the college places considerable emphasis on good exam results (if you don't pass you're sent down) ... therefore the proportion of public school entrants is much lower than in the rest of Cambridge.

Churchill College also houses the Churchill Archives Centre, built in 1973, a major source for historians, which also includes the papers of many of Churchill's war-time colleagues, and of eminent scientists including Frank Whittle as well as the papers of Baroness Thatcher.

Secrets of life and the universe

Whereas in the first half of the century Cambridge scientists led the world in investigating the nature of the atom, in the post-war period attention was focused on the field of molecular biology – the understanding of how living things function. By the 1950s it was understood that genetic information, such as what determines the colour of a person's eyes, was held as a chemical code in the complex giant molecule deoxyribonucleic acid (DNA) – but quite how it worked remained a mystery. The code was finally cracked in 1953 by the American James Watson (1928–) and his British collaborator, Francis Crick (1916–2004), who demonstrated that the DNA molecule formed a double helix. When cells divided, the DNA copied itself by unzipping its interlocking strands to create a perfect copy of all the genes in the new cell. Allegedly, Crick and Watson celebrated at their favourite lunchtime rendezvous, the Eagle in Bene't Street, by ordering pints of beer instead of halves. A golden helix can be seen hanging above the front door of Francis Crick's former home in Portugal Place. Crick and Watson were awarded the Nobel Prize for Physiology in 1962, the year in which the scientists of the Medical Research Council moved out of the historic Cavendish Laboratory to a new Laboratory of Molecular Biology off Hills Road.

Only belatedly, however, was it acknowledged that Crick and Watson's world-changing breakthrough owed much to experimental X-ray work undertaken at King's College, London by Rosalind Franklin (1920–58), herself a graduate of Newnham, who died tragically young of cancer at the age of 37. A recent (1995) building at Newnham perpetuates her name.

A second area of scientific strength developed in the field of radio astronomy, using the faint radio waves emitted by stars and galaxies to study them. On a disused railway track south of Cambridge, Martin Ryle (1918–84) ingeniously devised the equivalent of a radio telescope with a dish five kilometres across by using a series of movable small dishes. Using this apparatus Ryle's colleague, Anthony Hewish, discovered pulsars and quasars.

The two cultures

A man of many incarnations, C P Snow (1905–80) would probably have been gratified to know that the *Dictionary of National Biography* categorised him as an author – less happy with the additional soubriquet 'and publicist'. The archetypal provincial 'scholarship boy', Snow entered the Cavendish Laboratory in 1930 to undertake doctoral research. His first novel, a detective story, was published just two years later, by which time he was a fellow of Christ's. During World War Two, Snow played a key role as a government adviser on the recruitment and deployment of scientific manpower. Taking its title, *Strangers and Brothers* (1940), from the first novel in a sequence of eleven, Snow's *magnum opus* charted the chequered career and private life of academic lawyer, Lewis Eliot. Drawing on the author's eclectic knowledge of contrasting professional worlds, different volumes dealt with Cambridge Combination Room politics (*The Masters,* 1951), the evolution of Britain's nuclear deterrent (*The New Men,* 1954) and the relationships between politicians and senior civil servants (*Corridors of Power,* 1964, whose title added a phrase to the language). Like Trollope, Snow was 'an acute observer of both public and private stress'; like H G Wells, Snow was an enthusiast for science and its potential for good.

In 1959 Snow gave the Rede Lectures, taking as his theme *The Two Cultures and the Scientific Revolution.* Claiming a foot in both camps, Snow argued that science and the humanities had become so specialised and separated that even highly educated members of a Cambridge high table scarcely shared a common culture, with a real danger that 'unscientific' minds could easily become 'anti-scientific' ones. Snow's argument provoked widespread public discussion, as he had hoped. F R Leavis belatedly attacked with venom and relish in 1962, dismissing Snow himself as

> portentously ignorant ... intellectually undistinguished as it
> is possible to be... *The Two Cultures* exhibits an utter lack of
> intellectual distinction and an embarrassing vulgarity of style
> ... He can't be said to know what a novel is. The nonentity is
> apparent on every page of his fiction.

Intentionally or otherwise, this typically toxic outburst rather underlined Snow's point – but not, perhaps, quite as he might have wished.

A clutch of new colleges

The years 1965–6 were marked by a remarkable proliferation of new college foundations, largely in response to the expansion in the university's postgraduate population. Jointly promoted by Caius, St John's and Trinity, Darwin College was established in 1965 as the first entirely postgraduate college in Cambridge. It occupies three adjoining properties formerly associated with members of the Darwin dynasty – The Hermitage, the Old Granary and, between them,

Newnham Grange (1793), the childhood home of Gwen Raverat. The Hermitage was built in the 1850s and enlarged in the 1870s; its name supposedly recalls pre-Reformation hermits who served a chapel hereabouts and collected tolls from users of the small bridge nearby. The Old Granary was associated with the mill which stood on the other side of the pond to the rear. As the first application for membership was submitted by a woman – before details of qualification had been finalised – Darwin became the first mixed college in Cambridge more or less by accident.

Lucy Cavendish College was founded as Britain's first college for mature women. Named after the daughter-in-law of the founder of the Cavendish Laboratory, a Victorian campaigner for women's education, it evolved from a Dining Society established in 1951 by Dr Anna Bidder (1903–2001), a Newnham zoologist, who became first President of Lucy Cavendish. Others were gradually recruited to the 'guild' until they achieved institutional recognition in 1965, and in 1970–6 the college found a permanent home in three adjacent houses built on Lady Margaret Road for Victorian married dons. The nautilus in the college crest recalls its first President's special area of expertise.

Wolfson College, originally University College on its foundation in 1965, was an initiative of the university itself but, following a grant of £2,000,000 from the Wolfson Foundation, changed its name to acknowledge its benefactor in 1973. New buildings were constructed in 1972–7, designed to fit around an original domestic property, Bredon House. Apart from accommodating graduate students, Wolfson College also accepts a proportion of mature undergraduates and organises short courses for industry and government.

Clare Hall was established in 1965, with American backing from the Ford and Old Dominion Foundations, as Clare College's own facility for visiting scholars and their families. Built to the designs of Ralph Erskine (1914–2005), a British-born but Sweden-based architect best known for his massive Byker Wall housing complex in Newcastle, what Pevsner called 'this curious hill-villagey compound' on

Herschel Road combined bedsits, flats and terraced houses and had its own day nursery.

In 1965 St Edmund's House received recognition as an 'approved society'. Tracing its origins to 1568, when the English College at Douai was founded to train Roman Catholic missionaries to be smuggled back into Anglican England, the institution was eventually repatriated to become St Edmund's College at Ware in Hertfordshire. Its Cambridge incarnation was established in 1896 as a lodging for Roman Catholics. St Edmund's finally achieved collegiate status in 1975 and is now non-denominational in its intake of graduates.

Like St Edmund's, Fitzwilliam was the reincarnation of a Victorian lodging. Established in 1869 as an institution for students not attached to any college, from 1874 this hostel occupied rooms at 31 Trumpington Street, opposite the Fitzwilliam Museum, whose name it informally adopted to become Fitzwilliam Hall, and from 1922, Fitzwilliam House. Temporarily disbanded during World War Two, in 1946 it had an intake of 400 students, making it the fifth-largest undergraduate institution in Cambridge. The present college, formally recognised as such in 1966, relocated to Huntingdon Road to premises built in 1961–7 to a strict budget by the prime exponent of concrete 'brutalism', Sir Denys Lasdun (1914–2001), architect of London's Royal National Theatre – and of the uncompromising and unloved New Court (1966–70) at Christ's, a severely raked, terraced accommodation block reminiscent of an Aztec pyramid for human sacrifice, but nicknamed 'The Typewriter' by its inhabitants. Even Pevsner thought that Lasdun had 'not done himself justice at Fitzwilliam'. Another critic thought the college had 'all the charm of a motel'.

Architects and architecture

The teaching of architecture at Cambridge began tentatively in 1912. A degree was established in 1922 and a home for the department in Scroope Terrace in 1924. But the subject really took off with the appointment in 1956 of (Sir) Leslie Martin (1908–2000) as the first professor. Formerly head of the Architects' Department of the London County Council and best known as the designer of the Royal Festival Hall, Martin collaborated with Colin St John Wilson (1922–2007) to create Harvey Court for Caius College in 1960–2, a squashed brick ziggurat off West Road ('the most sensational new building up to that date in Cambridge' – Pevsner). Martin also shoe-horned the eight-storey William Stone Building into a confined site at Peterhouse.

In the year of Leslie Martin's appointment, Sir Hugh Casson (1926–99), himself a Cambridge architecture graduate and design mastermind of the 1951 Festival of Britain, began, in collaboration with Neville Conder (1922–2003), to sketch out a plan for something almost every university in the world has but Cambridge had not – a campus. Located 'over to the West and across the Backs', it would cover the former Caius' sports ground and be known as 'the Sidgwick Site'. The original Casson and Conder concept envisaged a series of raised buildings around courtyards. Only one of these, appropriately known as the Raised Faculty Building, now home to the Faculties of Modern and Medieval Languages and Philosophy, was actually built.

A defiantly discordant note was struck by the History Faculty Building, designed by the youthful iconoclast James Stirling (1926–92) and completed in 1968. Entirely rejecting the traditional court-yard concept, it has been variously described as like an open book, a waterfall and 'a glass house posing as a brick building'. Pevsner didn't know what to make of it – 'actively ugly ... avoiding anything that might attract ... But never mind, it hits you'. *Cambridge New Architecture*, by contrast, hailed it as embodying 'the inexplicable obvious-ness of a great work of architecture'. Despite being locally loathed as much as it was acclaimed by the architectural profession, the build-ing was awarded the Gold Medal of the British Institute of Architects in 1970. Over the course of the following decade, however, its users complained that it was freezing in winter and boiling in summer, with dodgy acoustics and problems of leaking and condensation which threatened the books in the Seeley Library. Great architecture it might or might not have been, but it was a rotten build. In the 1980s complete demolition and replacement were seriously debated but rejected as even more expensive than the major refurbishment that had to be undertaken at the cost of *millions*. With a masterly manipulation of the past, the website of the History Faculty merely notes that its home has been considered 'notorious' by some. In 2000 Stirling's creation was granted Grade II listed status. A couple of years later historian David Cannadine still excoriated it as 'part bunker, part factory, part greenhouse, all folly ... ugly, strident, unpopular, aggressive, unwelcoming'. Why not pop across and see what all the fuss was about?

PLAYING THE GAME: A SPORTING INTERLUDE

> Every Cantab takes his two hours exercise *per diem,* by walking,
> riding, rowing, fencing, gymnastics etc. ... In New England
> ... the last thing thought of is exercise ... unlike the Cantab's
> constitutional of eight miles in less than two hours ...
>
> A C Bristed, *Five Years in an English University* (1852)

The contrast with his home country likewise struck French composer Camille Saint-Saens:

> Each college has splendid grounds, where the students take their
> leisure, not to speak of the river ... where the famous oarsmen
> train. This open-air life, in which physical exercise plays a major
> part, is very different from our French students ...

At the installation of a new Chancellor in 1811, the Regius Professor of Modern History celebrated Britain's greatness as the product of its laws, its religion, its valour, its freedom but, above all, 'from hardy sports, from manly schools'. Playing, in other words, was a serious business.

Some thought the cult of sport excessive. Jesus College was, for example, once referred to as 'nothing but a boat club'. This was not fair. Jesus men excelled at many sports. Of 29 freshmen entering Jesus in 1895, 17 would represent Cambridge in rugby, football, cricket or rowing. It was only in examinations that the college lacked distinction.

Many, indifferent to competitive sport, still felt called to exercise. As Charles Bristed observed, 'the staple exercise is walking', his friends often covering 'not once, but repeatedly, fifteen miles in three hours, without special training, or being the worse for it next day.'

Harold Abrahams (1899–1978), a graduate from Caius in 1919, whose successful pursuit of Olympic gold in the 100 yards at the 1924 Paris Olympiad inspired the Oscar-winning film *Chariots of Fire*, has been taken as the personification of the Cambridge athlete. Abrahams had already set a unique record with eight inter-Varsity victories in the 100 metres, 440 metres and the long jump. He went on to become a successful barrister, broadcaster, civil servant, sports administrator and doyen of sports statisticians. But another, more versatile, candidate might be the Welsh oarsman, J G Chambers (1843–83) of Trinity, champion walker, founder of the Amateur Athletic Association and the Thames Regatta, and pioneering sports journalist. Chambers coached four successive winning Boat Race crews and devised the rules of boxing, which he had the nous to realise had a much better chance of being adopted if his friend, John Sholto Douglas, 9th Marquess of Queensberry (1844–1900), lent them his name.

Apart from promoting physical fitness and building 'character', sport buttressed collegiate spirit and enabled participants to cross social and even racial boundaries. The cerebral Leslie Stephen (1832–1904), future editor of the *Dictionary of National Biography* and father of Virginia Woolf, recalled that 'the college boat club was a bond of union which enabled me to be on friendly terms with young gentlemen whose muscles were more developed than their brains.' Even the devoutly unathletic A C Benson was impressed by the sight of 'an elegant African black undergraduate, slim and nimble, playing lawn tennis with Englishmen' at Emmanuel in 1907.

Victorian Britain transformed both traditional and new sports through the invention of clubs, codes and competitions. Railways for the first time made it possible for teams to compete regularly with rivals from more than a few miles away. Beginning with rowing in 1827, Cambridge University clubs were founded for athletics (1857), cycling (1874), lawn tennis (1881) and hockey (1890).

In football, rugby and boxing Cambridge proved instrumental in establishing rules and conventions adopted worldwide. University sport has, since then, lost some of its cachet. Chris Brasher (1928–2003) is probably more widely remembered as the founder of the London Marathon than as a pace-maker in the world's first successful four-minute mile, just as actor Hugh Laurie is not widely known for having rowed in the University Boat Race, nor Oscar-winner Sam Mendes for playing cricket for Cambridge.

Country pursuits

The statutes of King's College in 1443 decreed that 'fellows and scholars ... are expressly forbidden to throw or shoot stones, balls ... arrows, or anything else, or to play any games ... within the college or its close or gardens.' Medieval college statutes generally banned students from sparring with swords or baiting bulls or bears. Hunting was likewise frowned on, with bans against owning dogs, hawks, ferrets or nets and, from 1577, 'stone-bows'. Easily hidden and silent, these miniature crossbows fired pellets at birds and small game. University authorities were outraged by the 'late great destruction of dove-houses' and because 'much pewter vessel hath been consumed and molten for the maintenance of pellets, and great hurt done in Glasse of churches, chapels and College Halls'.

The marshy areas around Cambridge supported plentiful snipe and plovers, some partridge and bitterns and the occasional pheasant or hare. Henry Gunning (1786–1854) confessed that as an undergraduate in the 1780s his passion for shooting 'consumed more time than all my other employments put together'. As late as 1902 university regulations still banned students from pigeon-shooting or taking part in a steeplechase or horse race.

Virtually devoid of rules or restraint, football was deemed particularly hazardous, especially if townsfolk were involved – the sport was considered 'fitter for clownes than schollers'. In 1580 the Vice-Chancellor decreed that

> no scholar of what degree or condition so ever ... should at any place or at any time hereafter, play at football, but only within the precincts of their several colleges, not permitting any stranger or scholars of other colleges or houses to play with them or in their company, and in no place else.

Handball, however, was permitted – away from stained-glass windows – as were archery and 'real' (i.e. royal) tennis, still a regular Cambridge pastime – 'the king of racquet sports'. Tennis in the 16th century was for the social elite, requiring an expensive court and equipment. Its popularity reflected the changing social profile of the Tudor student body, with increasing numbers of a 'gentle' status. By the 1590s Cambridge had no fewer than 10 tennis courts, more than there were in all of London. The name of Tennis Court Road, at the rear of Pembroke, recalls a court depicted on a site plan of 1592 and not demolished until 1880. The present courts in Grange Road were built for Trinity in 1866 and Clare about 30 years later.

The lure of the green

Bowling became a donnish pastime in Tudor times when traditional 'ninepins', played on any patch of ground outside an alehouse, gave way to a new version with a jack ball as a target for asymmetrically weighted 'woods', biased to follow a curving arc; these needed velvet smooth turf to achieve the best effect. Favouring patience and cunning over speed or strength, this game suited older rather than younger players. At Cambridge, moreover, it was held 'to teach men's hands and eyes mathematics and the rules of proportion.' At Emmanuel College, where 'they preached up very strict keeping and observing the Lord's day' the devout Lancelot Andrewes (1555–1626) of Pembroke discovered that, discreetly screened behind a locked door, 'these hypocrites did bowl in a private green at their college every Sunday after sermon'.

Rowing

Competitive rowing, perhaps regarded as the university sport par excellence, only emerged two centuries ago but nevertheless came to epitomise sport itself as undergraduates were differentiated between 'reading men' and 'rowing men'. St John's and Trinity both formed boat clubs in 1825 but it was observed in 1826 that

> the only idea of encounter they had was that each should go, as it were casually, downstream and lie in wait, one of them, I believe, sounding a bugle to intimate its whereabouts, when the other coming up would give chase with as much animation as might be expected when there were no patrons of the sport or spectators of the race.

To remedy this unsatisfying situation the first inter-collegiate bumping races were inaugurated in 1827. As the Cam was too narrow for boats to compete side by side, they set off at timed intervals after one another to 'bump' the boat ahead, each bump entitling the crew to move one place up a ladder of competitive excellence, from 1888 onwards culminating in the exalted status of 'Head of the River'.

Rowing soon acquired a passionate following. In February 1837, the reclusive swot Alexander Gooden recorded that

> the boat races have begun and excite much interest, many bets and considerable quantity of sweating in general and drunkenness in particular. The evenings of the race days are generally devoted to festivity, which universally ends in the overthrow of the parties' sobriety.

In 1863 a Town Rowing Club was established and by the 1890s women were rowing as well.

The first Inter-Varsity Boat Race against Oxford was rowed in 1829 at Henley-on-Thames, the second not until 1836, on the Thames in London. The now traditional course from Mortlake to Putney was first raced in 1845. Except during the two World Wars the race has been held annually since 1856, soon establishing itself as not merely a university but a national occasion, attracting supporters from classes and communities with no contact whatsoever with either university or rowing. In 1877 the two crews rowed to the only dead heat so far recorded. Cambridge set the record time – 16 minutes 19 seconds – in 1998. The first women's Inter-Varsity Boat Race was rowed in 1927. Television coverage of the Boat Race began in 1954.

Australian-born 'Steve' Fairbairn (1862–1938) was the most celebrated of Cambridge rowing coaches. Having rowed four times for Cambridge, qualified for the bar and worked on an Australian sheep station for 20 years, Fairbairn returned in 1906 to spend the rest of his life coaching, notably for his own old college, Jesus. His memory is perpetuated by a major winter time-trial fixture, the Fairbairn Cup.

Most practice nowadays takes place in autumn and winter, between dawn and lectures. Serious rowers – i.e. aiming at the university crew – put in 32 hours a week, as well as time travelling to and from the University Boat Club training base at Ely. Nevertheless, even in the 21st century, when academic priorities are paramount, more than 2,000 students belong to a crew and some 1,500 take part in the May Bumps. When it comes to the Boat Race, however, three-quarters of the crews are postgraduates and only about a third British, the largest foreign contingents being American and German.

Cricket

Cambridge has produced a dozen England cricket captains, although its greatest cricketing son had nothing to do with the university and his near equal was ignored by it until almost too late (see below). Initially the game was played casually on Parker's Piece, the only regular fix-tures being against Cambridge Town and Bury St Edmunds. In 1848 Fenner's ground was let to the University Cricket Club. The first varsity match was played in 1839; by the 1870s it was a national social and sporting occasion, attracting some 20,000 spectators.

Prince of the crease

For two years after entering Trinity in 1890 the first Indian cricketer to achieve international fame – His Highness Kumar Shri Ranjit-sinhji Vihabji, Maharajah Jam Sahib of Nawanagar, better known as 'Ranji' – only played for town teams. Then word of his imperious elegance with the bat reached university cricket captain F S Jackson, who had himself played in India. After playing against Oxford in 1893 Ranji became a permanent member of the Cambridge side. The rest is legend. In 1896 on his Test debut against Australia, Ranji's devastat-ing 154 saved England from crushing defeat. He later became the first cricketer to score 3,000 runs in a season – and to go on to a distin-guished career in politics.

'The Master'

John Berry 'Jack' Hobbs's (1882–1963) only university connection was that his father was the groundsman at Jesus College and Hobbs himself did some coaching there. As a boy Hobbs got up at 6:00 to practise on Parker's Piece before school, playing his first cricket for his church choir team. Recruited by Surrey, in his first major match he made 155 against Essex, who had ignored his letter of application.

From 1907 to 1930 Hobbs played in every Test match for which he was available. Famously self-disciplined and instinctively modest, as an opening batsman, fielder and bowler he was England's No 1 in every sense. Sober, immaculate and a regular churchgoer, Hobbs negotiated the social perils of his ambiguous standing as the hero from a humble home with instinctive restraint, never aspiring to captaincy.

By 1920 Hobbs was second in the season's batting averages and topped the bowling. In 1926 he made his first century against Australia on his home ground, the Oval, enabling England to regain the Ashes after 14 years. In the same year he also made his career best score, 316 not out at Lord's, setting a ground record which stood until 1990. The world's leading batsman between Dr W G Grace (1848–1915) and Don Bradman (1908–2001), Hobbs retired in 1934, after scoring 197 first class centuries, 98 of them after the age of 40. In 1953 Hobbs became the first working-class sportsman and first professional cricketer ever to be knighted. His was a household name even among those who knew nothing of sport, let alone cricket.

Football

When the Football Association was established in 1863 it adopted the rules drawn up at a meeting in Trinity College in 1846 and published in a slim volume chosen in 2006 by Melvyn Bragg as one of the *Twelve Books That Changed the World*. In acknowledgment of the Cambridge ambition '*to make the game as simple and natural as possible*' the university was given a permanent seat on the Council of the Football Association. The first varsity match was played in 1874 and became significant enough to be played at Wembley between 1953 and 1987. Nowadays the sport involves some 1,000 male students and 400 female.

Rugby

Cambridge Rugby Union Football Club has produced more than 320 international players representing the nine 'senior' playing countries and has also played a major historic role in the development and diffusion of the sport. By the 1930s the Varsity match against Oxford was reckoned the second most important domestic fixture after the England–Scotland confrontation. As late as 1995, the year when the advent of professionalism decisively relegated university rugby to secondary status, the game could still draw 70,000 to a mid-week fixture. At the peak of its influence in the 1950s half of the Cambridge side would regularly graduate to the international game.

The first recorded Cambridge rugby match took place on Parker's Piece in 1839 but play remained informal and occasional until the first match against Oxford in 1872. In the following year the Cambridge Rugby Union Football Club (CURFC) joined the newly established Rugby Football Union. The Varsity match of 1875 was a landmark in the history of the game, fixing 15 as the approved number of players for a team and recognising a 'try' as a scoring opportunity. Another landmark was established in 1892 when the referee superseded the two captains as sole adjudicator of play.

By the 1880s 'Blues' were being awarded for representing the university, and ex-Cambridge men were introducing the game to Australia, New Zealand and South Africa. In 1899 E B Clarke (1875–1934) of Corpus introduced rugby at Keio University in Japan. A century later the club would support the development of women's rugby in Cambridge.

By 1896 CURFC was wealthy enough to buy its existing grounds at Grange Road. By the 1920s it was generously making loans – many never recalled – to support at least nine other university sports. Intercollegiate competition was soundly established in the same decade. From 1921 onwards the Varsity game was played at Twickenham, the home of English rugby. Long before cheap jet flights took the adventure and expense out of long-distance travel, Cambridge rugby sides encouraged the development of the game overseas by touring the USA (1934), Argentina (1948) and Japan (1953). Paradoxically, the flexibility of university life, freeing players to devote themselves so thoroughly to training and practice, undistracted by the pressures of paid employment or family responsibilities, enabled Cambridge men to become some of the most proficient 'professionals' of the sport's amateur age.

Hockey

Hockey seems to have been introduced in 1883 as a personal favour to the notoriously obtuse Prince Albert Victor, Duke of Clarence, known to his family as 'Eddy' (1864–92), as one of the few activities in which he expressed interest. A university club was founded in 1890, the same year in which a Girton team was established. The men's and women's university clubs merged in 2000 and now field six teams, while the number playing at collegiate level is around 800.

Tennis twins

Reginald (1872–1910) and Hugh 'Laurie' Doherty (1875–1919) were born, very appropriately, in Wimbledon; both were educated at Westminster and Trinity Hall and went on to win the Wimbledon doubles a record eight times, taking the US title twice. Laurie also won the Wimbledon singles title five times (1902–6), Reggie four (1897–1900). Laurie won gold medals in the singles and doubles at the 1900 Paris Olympics, Reggie gold in the men's doubles and mixed doubles, bronze in the singles and in 1908 gold in the men's doubles. All this despite such indifferent health that Reggie died at 38 and Laurie, after wartime service in the Royal Naval Reserve, at 43. 'The Doherty Gates' are at the south-west entrance of the All England Club, Wimbledon.

Envoi?

University sport, it is generally admitted, is not what it was. However, the annual varsity Boat Race still attracts an audience of eight million viewers. Furthermore, Britain's squad for the 2008 Olympics in China did contain nine Cambridge graduates and one undergraduate (a woman fencer) and the 2012 Olympic squad included 14 Cambridge graduates, four of whom won medals (all in rowing). The 21st-century student can also opt for a much wider range of sports than ever before, including lacrosse, water polo, judo, basketball, badminton,

Australian rules football, pelota, petanque and pentathlons. However, while some *colleges* have decent facilities, the university has not only no sports centre but no swimming pool and not even its own courts for fives or squash.

12

Only Yesterday

The changing city

The transformation of Cambridge quickened from the 1970s onwards. Ancient, down-at-heel, but undeniably picturesque, Petty Cury was swept away to be replaced by the Lion Yard shopping centre, library and multi-storey car park, a sacrifice of 'character' to amenity which grieved many. In the words of Charles Mosley and Clive Wilmer, local residents and members of the university's English Faculty:

> few cities, even in those barbarous decades, can have had quite so much of their ancient heart ripped out of them, to be replaced with the tawdry: Lion Yard and the new Petty Cury are already [1998] dated and the City Fathers responsible immortalised their vandalism with their names grandiose and smug on a stumpy, ugly pillar outside St Andrew's church ...

– a self-tribute you can probably afford to miss.

To the south-west, between East Road and Maid's Causeway, a large part of a well-built working-class residential area, known from its outline as 'the Kite', gave way in 1984 to a shopping complex, the Grafton Centre. After more than a decade of neglect, the Corn Exchange was refurbished as a concert venue in 1986. Despite the opening of the Elizabeth Bridge (1971) and the rebuilding of

Magdalene Bridge (1988) and Victoria Bridge (1992), traffic and parking remained seemingly intractable problems, although cycle routes were established and the pedestrianisation of Sidney Street diminished hazards to shoppers in a busy retail area.

In 1990 The Junction opened as Britain's first purpose-built youth venue, and in 1999 the Parkside pool was rebuilt. The much-loved Cambridge landmark department stores Joshua Taylor and Eaden Lilley closed in 1992 and 1999 respectively, although the building of the Grand Arcade allowed their old rival, Robert Sayle, to survive. Heffer's, another business named after its founder, had been established in Fitzroy Street in 1876 by a Fen farmworker's son, William Heffer. Originally selling hymn books and stationery, it had moved to Petty Cury and diversified into printing and publishing. Reuben George Heffer, grandson of the founder, built up its specialist output in medicine, phonetics and oriental studies. The destruction of Petty Cury forced a move to No 20 Trinity Street, but it remained a family business until 1999, when control shifted to another family business – Blackwell's of Oxford.

Tourist trail

Writing of the summer of 1760, the Pembroke poet Thomas Gray had observed that 'Cambridge is a delight of a place, now there is nobody in it.' His friend and fellow poet Christopher 'Kit' Smart (1722–71) disagreed:

> At length arrives the dull Vacation,
> And all around is Desolation.

Not any more. Although modern Cambridge was unconcerned to promote itself as a visitor destination, tourism has continued to expand until its contribution to the local economy accounted for in excess of 5,000 jobs. The visitor presence – and 'spend' – also significantly revitalised such areas as Green Street, King Street and the quayside around Magdalene. Shops increasingly began to cater to visitors' whims rather than students' needs. The Cambridge Festival (1961–92), Folk Festival (from 1965), Beer Festival (from 1974) and Film Festival (from 1977) may have boosted numbers. A corps of professionally trained Blue Badge guides developed to steer visitors deftly through colleges and courts. Open-topped tourist buses began to circumnavigate the streets from 1987 onwards and in 1991 a Holiday Inn opened on Downing Street. Between 1975 and 1997 the annual number of visitors more than doubled to pass 3,500,000. 60 per cent were from overseas, half of those from Europe. Their passage was usually fleeting, two out of three visiting for a single day or part of one. Research revealed that the great majority of visitors never ventured more than a quarter of a mile from Market Hill, leaving Kettle's Yard and the Fitzwilliam to the adventurous – or those who had bothered to read a guidebook.

Contrary to widespread local perception, fewer than 10 per cent visitors arrived by coach. Half came by car, further aggravating the chronic problems of congestion and parking. Fortunately, however, the tourist influx reached its peak between July and September, when undergraduates were absent, although their rooms were usually occupied, as colleges belatedly began to capitalise on the appeal of their architecture, accommodation and facilities by hosting conferences and summer schools during the vacations. Another significant sector of employment and expenditure emerged with the proliferation of language schools teaching English.

'Monstrous regiment'?

In the early 1970s females accounted for less than 10 per cent of the undergraduate body; nowadays they make up almost half. The exclusive Apostles admitted its first female members in 1971. In 1972 Churchill, Clare and King's became the first all-male colleges to admit women as undergraduates. Realising that they were denying themselves students of real quality, the rest of the 'men only' colleges followed, though Magdalene held out until 1988. Colleges accordingly found themselves faced with challenges with regard to the provision of bathrooms, the acceptance of sexual relationships between students and the novel issue of female drunkenness.

In 1978 Girton likewise began to admit men. Newnham resisted the trend to co-education. Instead it achieved another feminist landmark with the first university building designed by a woman, Elizabeth Whitworth Scott (1898–1972). Her Fawcett Building was named for Philippa Fawcett (1868–1948), who gained the highest marks in the mathematics examinations of 1890, despite the fact that her gender would deny her an actual degree. The Cambridge Union remained an all-male bastion until 1963, but then changed swiftly to elect its first woman president, Ann (now Baroness) Mallalieu, in 1967. (By 2005–6 the office had been held by three women in succession.) Rosemary Murray became the university's first female Vice-Chancellor. In 1992 the city elected Anne Campbell as its first female Member of Parliament. In 2003 anthropologist Alison Richard, a former Newnham undergraduate, became the university's 344th Vice-Chancellor and the first female to hold the post full time. The last unquestioned male citadel crumbled when Jesus appointed a woman, Helen Stephens, as a porter; she subsequently became Deputy Head Porter at Trinity and in 2009 made history yet again by becoming the first female Head Porter, at Selwyn.

Revolting students

Compared to some other universities, post-war Cambridge experienced only minor disorders in terms of student activism. In 1967 a protest banner against the Vietnam War was suspended from the roof of King's College Chapel. In 1968 a visit by the Defence Minister was accompanied by fistfights. In 1969 a visit by the US Ambassador prompted a 'sit-in' at the Old Schools. In 1970 a city-wide 'Greek Week' to promote tourism to that country – then under the rule of a military junta – culminated in a dinner at the Garden House Hotel which attracted a crowd of some hundreds of protesters. The occasion was disrupted. Diners were jostled. Damage and violence may not have been intended but occurred. The police made arrests. The sentencing of half a dozen undergraduates to prison terms was generally regarded as disproportionately heavy-handed. In the same year the recently established Student Union addressed an issue of more widespread concern by organising protests against the college practice of charging for meals that one might not eat and closing their gates at night. The changing demographic profile of the student body was underlined in 1975 by a sit-in at the Senate House as part of a campaign for nursery provision. In 1976 there was a sit-in at the University Library to agitate for longer opening hours.

More new colleges

The expansion of the university continued. By 2007 the 8,500 undergraduates of 1976 had become 11,000. Over the same period the university's operating budget increased from £27,000,000 to £600,000,000, one-third of the latter generated from research contracts. Specialised centres of expertise were established, devoted to such diverse areas of investigation as the Study of Human Evolution, Mongolian and Inner Asian Studies, Psychometrics, Atmospheric Science, Autism and Brain Mapping.

The archetypal reclusive millionaire, Sir David Robinson (1904–1987) left school at 15, worked in his parents' bicycle shop in Cambridge, made a fortune from the TV rental business and put up £18,000,000 for a brand new college, opened by the Queen in 1981. Ranged along a road, rather than around a courtyard, the buildings still featured such traditional features as a gatehouse, complete with tower and 'drawbridge', and were built of hand-made brick. Robinson was the first college to be founded specifically for both men and women, and with the acknowledgment that it would play a major role as a conference centre during vacations. David Robinson also put up half the £6,000,000 cost of a state-of-the-art maternity hospital for Cambridge, named Rosie after his mother, which opened in 1983.

Homerton and Hughes Hall, former teacher-training institutions, were absorbed into the university in 1977 and 1985 respectively. Homerton was by 2001 the largest college in Cambridge, achieving full collegiate status in 2010. In 1992 the city's former polytechnic achieved university status as Anglia Ruskin, with outlying campuses at Chelmsford and Colchester in neighbouring Essex.

The Cambridge phenomenon

While Cambridge was never a particularly industrial town, over the course of the 20th century it spawned some significant industrial enterprises, including the Cambridge Scientific Instrument Company (1881), Pye and Co (1896) and Marshall's (1909). These companies were all technology based, drew at least partially on university expertise and were located around the fringes of the city. University scientists had also created specialist businesses whose unvarnished names implied a deliberately downbeat, almost self-deprecating, approach to the market-place – Aero Research, Metals Research, Cambridge Consultants Ltd.

National Institutes for Plant Breeding, Agricultural Botany, Animal Physiology, Animal Nutrition and Welding also existed around the urban periphery. In 1968 the government decided on Cambridge as the appropriate location for a national Computer-Aided Design Centre. A favourable national context was also emerging. By the 1960s East Anglia was Britain's fastest-growing region in terms of population. The opening of the M11 motorway to London in 1980 and the subsequent upgrading of Stansted to become London's third airport banished the traditional isolation of the Fen-bound city.

These trends prompted a change of heart within the university and the city. Whereas they had formerly endorsed Holford's block on urban growth and the 'intrusion' of industry – to the extent of rejecting outright major initiatives from Tube Investments and IBM – in 1969 the Senate approved a report from future Nobel Laureate Nevill Mott (1905–96), head of the Cavendish Laboratory, which proposed the encouragement of links between the university and science-based industries.

The pioneering initiative came, however, not from the university itself but from Trinity College. Pre-eminent in science, wealthy and well-connected, Trinity proposed to develop former farmland three miles from the city centre which had been owned by the college for four centuries and last used as a tank-proving ground during World War Two, but had since lain derelict. Led by Dr (now Sir) John Bradfield, a Cavendish zoologist and Senior Bursar of Trinity, the college in 1970 committed itself to creating a 130-acre Science Park just off the A14, north of Chesterton. The first tenant, Laser-Scan, a computer graphics company formed by three Cavendish research-ers, moved onto the site in 1973. The businesses that followed – on Trinity's site and elsewhere – were also locally established, capitalised on university research and skilled personnel, attracted foreign capital and entrepreneurial expertise and used cutting-edge technologies to exploit new niche markets, not only in computer-related areas but also in pharmaceuticals, plant genetics, printing, drilling, vaccines, lasers, freeze-drying and precision imaging. By 1975, 30 acres of the Trinity site had been occupied; by 1982, 86 acres; by 1996, all of it. The site was later extended by incorporating adjacent land owned by Trinity Hall.

Trinity's initiative was warmly praised in 1979 by the newly elected Prime Minister Margaret Thatcher, herself a former postgraduate research chemist. The phrase 'Cambridge Phenomenon' was coined by Peta Levi in an article in the *Financial Times* in 1980. In 1985 Oxford economist Nick Segal published a book-length account of *The Cambridge Phenomenon*, which by then had attracted some 260 technology-based firms employing 13,700 people. By 1987 Trinity's Science Park alone had 65 tenants and Cambridge as a whole almost 500 technological companies. In 1988 St John's opened its own Inno-vation Centre – opposite Trinity's venture – on land it had owned for six centuries.

Throughout the post-war period Cambridge University Press

benefitted from the expansion of higher education in the English-speaking world, from Commonwealth demand for school textbooks and from the worldwide hunger to master the English language, which now accounts for a third of its global turnover. A masterly reorganisation of the Press by chief executive Geoffrey Cass secured it a charitable status, relieving it of significant taxation. Closing the London premises to relocate all operations to Cambridge enabled Cass to house the entire publishing staff in imposing new buildings on Shaftesbury Road in 1981. In 1992 CUP took over the corner shop at No 1 Trinity Street, where books have been sold since 1581, making it the oldest bookselling site in Britain. Not content with these successes, by 1996 the company had expanded to the point that it could boast more than 20,000 authors in 98 countries; its all-time best-seller was no longer the Bible but Murphy's *English Grammar in Use*, which had sold over 16,000,000 copies by 2009.

In 1990 former Cambridge graduate Paul Judge, creator of Premier Foods, put up £8,000,000 to establish the Judge Institute of Management Studies. The Italianate Addenbrooke's Hospital of 1864–5 was converted by James Outram to become its home. As Wilkinson and Ashley observe with a hint of a lifted eyebrow in *The English Buildings Book*: 'a rather sober building became intoxicated in the process.' The first intake, primarily graduates, entered in 1995.

In 1992 the Isaac Newton Institute for Mathematical Sciences opened on Clarkson Road as the largest mathematical campus in the world. By 1996 Cambridge was home to a thousand companies, employing 35,000 staff. In 1997 billionaire Bill Gates donated £12,000,000 to the university for a new computer laboratory. By 2010 Trinity's initiative – now known as the Cambridge Science Park – was celebrating its 40th anniversary and its self-proclaimed standing as 'Europe's longest-serving and largest centre for commercial research and development', complete with conference facilities, fitness centre and nursery. A complementary website – www.cambridgephenomenon.com – claimed that the city now had 1,000 technology and biotech companies, plus 400 further companies providing financial and other support services, collectively employing 40,000 people. Seven miles west of Cambridge, Cambourne was developed as a 'super village' from 1999 onwards. By 2011 it was estimated that the daily commuter population of Cambridge had passed the 40,000 mark.

Happy birthday to us

In 2001 Cambridge celebrated the 800th anniversary of its charter and its 50th year as a city. In 2009 the University of Cambridge celebrated the 800th anniversary of its foundation and took the opportunity this offered to launch a worldwide fundraising campaign. By June 2010 this had raised more than a billion pounds, making Cambridge the first-ever university outside the USA to raise such a sum – two years ahead of schedule. In the same year Cambridge also became the first non-American university to achieve first place in the World University Rankings. In 2011 it came first again – and also topped the national rankings for student satisfaction.

The Royal Mail marked the university's landmark 800th birthday by issuing a series of stamps celebrating the achievements of the university's staff and alumni – William Harvey's description of the circulation of blood, Newton's *Principia*, Darwin's theory of evolution by natural selection, Macaulay's *History of England*, Crick and Watson's discovery of the structure of DNA, the Boat Race, Footlights and the Festival of Nine Lessons and Carols – which is where we began.

Onward and Outward?

Five centuries after the foundation of the university the population of Cambridge was still only about 5,000 – about a sixth of the size of Norwich, the regional capital of East Anglia. Since then the population of Norwich has grown sevenfold: of Cambridge by a factor of 30. By the time of the first national census in 1801 the Cambridge figure had doubled to around 10,000. By 1851 that had almost tripled, but the pace of demographic expansion then slowed so that in the second half of the century Cambridge added just 10,000 to its population. Then came another growth spurt, adding almost 50 per cent to the population between 1901 and 1921. Between 1921 and 1951 growth continued but more slowly, increasing from 60,000 to 80,000, passing the 100,000 mark in the 1990s. Since then growth has once again become spectacular, raising the population from 108,000 in 2001 to 146,000 in 2021.

Much of this growth was fuelled by the establishment and rapid expansion in and around the city of research and development hubs, devoted especially to life sciences and, more recently, the exploitation of artificial intelligence. In 2016 AstraZeneca moved its global headquarters to Cambridge. Five years later its Discovery Centre was opened by the Prince of Wales. Cambridge has become home to more than 200 start-ups and scale-ups, giving it, relative to its population in per capita terms, more than anywhere else in the United Kingdom. Reflecting the close collaboration between the university and enterprise, this has made Cambridge, in the words of one enthusiastic investor, 'the safest place to grow high-risk businesses'.

The University of Cambridge and business have not been the only drivers of growth. The Cambridge School of Art, founded in 1858, became the Cambridge College of Arts and Technology and, in 1992, a full-fledged university, which in 2005 adopted the name Anglia Ruskin to honour the influential Victorian author, art critic and social theorist John Ruskin. With more than 35,000 students, its enrolment is considerably larger than that of the University of Cambridge, although its six campuses are variously located in Cambridgeshire, Essex and Greater London. ARU has its own international business school and has special strengths in fields ranging from optometry to nursing, sports, computing and music. Spectacular developments have also occurred within the University of Cambridge. In 2013 it opened its first research centre outside the UK, in Singapore. (The founding father of the modern independent city state, Lee Kuan Yew, was a Cambridge alumnus). In 2010 Homerton College, a former teacher-training establishment, was charted as a full college of the

University of Cambridge. With 600 undergraduate and 800 post-graduate students, it is now the largest in terms of student enrolment in the university.

In 2015 Pembroke College received a bequest of £35,000,000 from the estate of American alumnus Ray Dolby, inventor of Dolby surround sound, the sound system almost universally used in the world's cinemas. This was the largest single donation to a college in the history of the University of Cambridge. The gift turbo-charged Pembroke's ambitious £75,000,000 development programme, which is focused on the redevelopment of the site opposite the college's main entrance, featuring a performance space in a former church, teaching facilities and accommodation in Ray and Dagmar Dolby Court. In 2017 the Dolby estate gifted a further £85,000,000, this time to the university itself. This primarily funded the establishment of the Ray Dolby Centre for advanced research and development, particularly in physics, at the Cavendish Laboratory. This was completed in 2024.

Growth has brought growing pains. Cambridge over the past twenty years has achieved the unenviable distinction of being one of the least affordable places to live in Britain, with local house prices at 10 times average local annual incomes. Cambridge property prices rose by a staggering two-thirds between 2011 and 2021 alone. Unsurprisingly this has pushed many workers outside the city to become commuters, with as many people coming into it to work as actually work and live within its boundaries. To service their needs, an entire new railway station, Cambridge North, was opened in 2017. It has, however, been discovered that many Cambridge workers are willing to cycle much further to work than had been generally expected; indeed, no less than one worker in three commutes by bicycle.

Planners anticipate that by 2031 Cambridge will have generated 44,000 new jobs. To accommodate their housing needs, 33,500 homes are scheduled to be built – some in and around Cambridge itself and 2,500 in Camborne, 10 miles west of the city. At Bourn Airfield, a whole new village of 3,500 houses is planned: at Northstowe and north of Waterbeach, two whole new towns of 10,000 and 11,000 houses respectively.

In Victorian times there was a 'Varsity Line', a railway link, between Cambridge and Oxford. Its reinstatement is projected. When, if, this is ever achieved, it will complete a 'Golden Triangle' – Cambridge–Oxford–London – embracing a potential powerhouse of world-leading technological and medical advances and economic expansion.

Further Reading

Guides

Castillo, Eathan E., *First Timer's Guide to Cambridge Adventure* (2024)

Clark, Ross, *Cambridgeshire* (1996)

Davies, Grahame, *Real Cambridge* (2021)

Doig, Sarah E. and Scheuregger, Tony, *A–Z of Cambridge: Places – People – History* (2019)

Glover, Sarah, *Cambridge UK Travel Guide* (2022)

Home, Gordon and Clark, J W, *The Victorian Traveller's Guide to Cambridge* (2014)

Horton, Rosalind and Simons, Sali, *111 Places in Cambridge that You Shouldn't Miss* (2024)

Payne, Sarah, *Down Your Street: Cambridge Past and Present*, vols. I and II (1983, 1984)

Sargent, Andrew, *Secret Cambridge* (2018)

Scarfe, Norman, *Cambridgeshire: A Shell Guide* (1983)

Walking Tours

Brown, Clive, *Walks for All Ages: 20 Circular Walks in Cambridgeshire* (2017)

Kershman, Andrew, *Walking Cambridge: 1,000 Years of History in 8 Walks* (2020)

Meyer, Ruth, *A–Z Cambridge Hidden Walks* (2023)

Sinclair, Jo, *Cambridgeshire: 40 Town & Country Walks* (2021)

Cambridge Illustrated

Bennett, Emma, *The Cambridge Art Book: The City Through the Eyes of its Artists* (2017)
Durrant, John, *Cambridge Past and Present* (2007)
Fitzwilliam Museum, *Cambridge Portraits: From Lely to Hockney* (1978)
Gaunt, Richard, *In and Around Cambridge in the 1960s* (2017)
Gregory, Nancy, *Cambridge Inscriptions Explained* (2006)
Petty, Michael J, *Images of Cambridge* (2006)
Rawle, Tim, *Classic Cambridge* (2019)
Reeve, F A, *Victorian and Edwardian Cambridgeshire from Old Photographs* (1976)
Sheldon, Ian, *Cambridge Footsteps: A Passage Through Time* (2009)
Slack, Sue, *Cambridge: Images of England* (2005)

History

Boyd, Stephanie, *The Story of Cambridge* (2023)
Chrimes, Nicholas, *Cambridge: Treasure Island in the Fens* (second ed. 2012)
Cobban, Alan, *The Medieval English Universities: Oxford and Cambridge to 1500* (2017)
Garrett, Martin, *Cambridge: A Cultural and Literary History* (2004)
Howarth, T E B, *Cambridge Between Two Wars* (1978)
Sager, Peter, *Oxford and Cambridge: An Uncommon History* (2006)
Taylor, Alison, *Cambridge: The Hidden History* (2001)

The University

Black, Michael, *A Short History of Cambridge University Press* (second ed. 2000)

Evans, G R, *The University of Cambridge: A New History* (2010)

Fox, Peter (ed.), *Cambridge University Library: The Great Collections* (1998)

Hunter-Blair, Andrew, *The Colleges of Cambridge University* (2012)

Leedham-Green, Elisabeth, *A Concise History of the University of Cambridge* (1996)

Macfarlane, Alan, *Cambridge University and its Colleges: A Personal Exploration* (2019)

Pagnamenta, Peter, *The University of Cambridge: An 800th Anniversary Portrait* (2009)

Parkinson, Stephen, *Arena of Ambition: A History of the Cambridge Union* (2009)

Taylor, Kevin, *Central Cambridge: A Guide to the University and Colleges* (second ed. 2008)

The City

Bryan, Peter, *Cambridge: The Shaping of the City* (second ed. 2008)

Elliott, Chris, *Cambridge: The Story of a City* (2001)

Parker, Rowland, *Town and Gown: The 700 Years War in Cambridge* (1983)

Cambridge People

Annan, Noel, *The Dons: Mentors, Eccentrics and Geniuses* (2008)

Deacon, Richard, *The Cambridge Apostles: A History of Cambridge University's Elite Intellectual Secret Society* (1985)

Harman, Peter, and Mitton, Simon, *Cambridge Scientific Minds* (2002)

Lubenow, W C, *The Cambridge Apostles 1820–1914* (1998)

Mason, Richard (ed.), *Cambridge Minds* (1994)

McWilliams Tullberg, Rita, *Women at Cambridge* (1998)

Shils, Edward and Blacker, Carmen, *Cambridge Women: Twelve Portraits* (1996)

Slack, Sue, *Cambridge Women and the Struggle for the Vote* (2018)

Architecture

Bradley, Simon and Pevsner, Nikolaus, *The Buildings of England: Cambridgeshire* (2014)

Rawle, Tim, *Cambridge Architecture: A Concise Guide* (second ed. 1993)

Ray, Nicholas, *Cambridge Architecture: A Concise Guide* (2008)

Autobiography and Memoirs

Beard, Mary, *It's a Don's Life* (2009)

Fry, Stephen, *The Fry Chronicles: An Autobiography* (2010)

James, Clive, *May Week Was In June* (2008)

Hawking, Jane, *Travelling to Infinity: The True Story Behind the Theory of Everything* (2014)

Macfarlane, Alan, *The King's Community: A Personal View* (2019)

Raverat, Gwen, *Period Piece: A Cambridge Childhood* (2018)

Humour

Gill, Anton, *How to be Oxbridge: A Bluffer's Guide* (1985)

Hewison, Robert, *Footlights!: A Hundred Years of Cambridge Comedy* (1984)

Johnson, Gordon, *University Politics: F. M. Cornford's Cambridge and his advice to the young academic politician* (second ed. 2008)

Lifestyle

Batey, Mavis, *The Historic Gardens of Oxford & Cambridge* (1989)

Billows, Karen, *The Cambridge Cookbook* (1995)

Bird, Richard and Haycraft, Dona, *The Gardens of Cambridge* (1994)
Knight, Frida, *Cambridge Music* (1980)
Stubbings, Frank, *Bedders, Bulldogs and Bedells: A Cambridge Glossary* (1995)
Whipplesnaith, *The Night Climbers of Cambridge* (2007)

Anthologies

Fowler, Laurence and Helen, *Cambridge Commemorated: An Anthology of University Life* (2009)
Moseley, Charles and Wilmer, Clive, *Cambridge Observed: An Anthology* (1998)

Fiction

As Graham Chainey noted in *A Literary History of Cambridge* (1986), very little fiction treats the city 'as a serious place with intellectuals living there' or concerns itself with the realities of student life, although the first half of Sebastian Faulks's *Engleby* (2007) does just that. In Frederic Raphael's *The Glittering Prizes* (1976), Cambridge becomes 'Fame-Bridge', the gilded gateway to worldly success – but not infallibly. In Tom Sharpe's *Porterhouse Blue* (1974), the arch-reactionary college porter, Scullion, by dogged resistance ultimately triumphs over a reforming, politically correct master, accidentally killing him and being elected in his place, despite being stricken paralytic and *non compos mentis*. (Sharpe went to Pembroke College – draw your own conclusion.)

Margery Allingham was educated at the Perse School and made her cerebral sleuth, Albert Campion, a Cambridge graduate; her *Police at the Funeral* (1931) features a fictional, donnish dynasty, the Faradays, who live in Socrates Close, off Trumpington Road. In T H White's *Darkness at Pemberley* (1932) the master of the mythical St Barnabas College (Queen's'?) is a cocaine addict. Kwame Anthony Appiah's *Avenging Angel* (1991) revolves around threatening letters

– in Latin. Ivo Stourton's *The Night Climbers* (2008) exploits the university's most spectacularly peculiar pastime.

By far the largest category of fiction set in Cambridge revolves around crime, often in a historical setting. In Ariana Franklin's *Mistress of the Art of Death* (2007), the 12th-century Jewish community is collectively accused of child murder. Prolific author Susanna Gregory has written more than 20 books featuring Matthew Bartholomew, a physician in 14th-century Cambridge, starting with *A Plague on Both Your Houses* (1996) and *An Unholy Alliance* (1996). Charlie Cochrane's dozen-strong *Cambridge Fellows* series features a pair of gay dons in the Edwardian period. Alison Bruce's *Cambridgeshire Murders* (2005) are retellings of actual crimes. Glenda Goulden's *Foul Deeds and Suspicious Deaths in and around Cambridge* (2006) focuses on the city itself. Kate Atkinson's *Case Histories* (2004) introduced Jackson Brodie, former police inspector turned private detective, and was praised by Stephen King as 'the best mystery of the decade'. Alison Bruce's Gary Goodhew is a Cambridge-based police detective, while James Runcie's Sydney Chambers, central character of *The Grantchester Mysteries*, is the troubled vicar of a picturesque village on the edge of Cambridge. Dozens more Cambridge crime titles are listed at www. cambridgecrime.com.

Glossary

Cambridge 'jargon' can be indecipherable to an outsider. For a comprehensive guide visit the Queens' College website: www.queens.cam.ac.uk

'Arch and Anth'   Archaeology and Anthropology
BA   Bachelor of Arts; normal undergraduate degree awarded at Cambridge, regardless of subject
(The) Backs   The much-photographed area between Queens' Road and the rear of the colleges backing onto the River Cam, from Queens' round to St John's
Bedder   Member of college staff (now nearly always female) who cleans students' rooms and makes their beds (see Gyp)
Bedell   University heralds, originally employed as guardians of ceremonial and as messengers. Two Esquire Bedells retain their ceremonial function, carrying maces as their insignia of office
Blue   Light-blue blazer and scarf awarded for playing in an official match against Oxford; a person who has been given such an award
Boat Race   Annual contest against Oxford, rowed on the Thames between Putney and Mortlake, a distance of 4.25 miles (6.8 km)
Bull   A written mandate from the Pope

Bulldog	University constable, usually recruited from college porters, to assist proctors in enforcing discipline
Bumps	Races between college crews to decide which becomes 'Head of the River'; rowed in the spring and summer terms
Cantab	Abbreviated form of Latin *Cantabrigium*, denoting 'of Cambridge', indicated after a degree, as in BA Cantab
Chair	Professorial post; most are permanent but some may be created for a specific person
Chancellor	Official head of the university, now largely a ceremonial post. Elected by the Senate, the Chancellor holds office until death or resignation. HRH the Duke of Edinburgh was Chancellor 1977–2011
College	An endowed, self-governing community of scholars; the establishment occupied by such a community, consisting of residential accommodation, library, chapel, dining hall and gardens
College Nicknames	Catz (St Catharine's), Corpus (Corpus Christi), Emma (Emmanuel) Fitz (Fitzwilliam – but *The* Fitz denotes the Fitzwilliam Museum), Tit Hall (Trinity Hall)
Combination Room	Cambridge term for a Common Room
Congregation	A meeting room of the Regent House
Council (of the Senate)	Since 1856 an executive body, elected by the Regent House, which links the university and colleges for the purposes of strategic planning and finance
Court	Inner courtyard of a college, known as a quad in Oxford

CUSU	Cambridge University Student Union
Dean	Traditionally a priest responsible for the chapel and religious life of the college
Don	A university teacher or researcher, from the Latin *dominus,* meaning master
Fellow	Tenured member of a college, with privileges of dining and residence, usually matched with responsibilities for teaching and administration, unless the status is otherwise qualified (e.g. Research, Visiting, Honorary or Emeritus Fellow)
Fellow-Commoner	Pre-modern wealthy student, privileged to dine with Fellows at High Table
FBA	Fellow of the British Academy
FRS	Fellow of the Royal Society
FSA	Fellow of the Society of Antiquaries
Finals	Final examinations leading to the award of a degree
First	Top-class honours degree; truly exceptional candidates may be awarded a 'starred' first; followed by Upper Second/Two One (2.1), Lower Second/Two Two (2.2) (a.k.a. a 'Desmond', as in Archbishop Desmond Tutu) and Third (3rd).
Fresher	Freshman, first-year undergraduate
Going up	To come to study in Cambridge; leaving is 'going down'
Grace	Proposal put to the vote in the Regent House
Grads	Graduates; the University Centre was initially tagged the 'Grad Pad'
Gyp	Male 'bedder', replacing sizars from the 18th century onwards, now abolished
Gyp room	Small kitchen for student use, equipped for preparation of snacks
Hall	Dining hall; formal dining involves waited service and the wearing of gowns

High Table	Dining table reserved for Fellows and their guests; in older colleges this is often on a raised dais and at right angles to other tables
Hostels	Halls of residence, varying in size, permanence and wealth, which preceded incorporated and endowed colleges; from the 19th century institutions aspiring to college status might gain transitional recognition as a 'hostel' or 'house'
Jacobite	Supporter of the successors of the ousted (1688) James II (James translates to *Jacobus* in Latin), a convert to Roman Catholicism, resistant to their replacement in 1714 by the Protestant Hanoverian dynasty of George I and his successors; Jacobitism lingered semi-secretly at Oxford until the later 18th century
JCR	Junior Combination Room, the undergraduate common room and its elected representatives and officers
King Street Run	Traditional 'pub crawl' requiring participants to drink a pint of beer in each of the street's pubs
Land economy	Study of estate and environmental management and planning
Long vac	Long vacation, i.e. summer break
MA	Holders of the BA degree after two years can style themselves MA (Master of Arts) on payment of a modest fee
Master	Usual title for the head of a Cambridge college
Matriculation	Registration at the beginning of the academic year in October, from the Latin *matricula,* a little roll or list; originally this also applied to college and university servants and required an oath of allegiance to the Crown and assent to the established form of religion

May Week	Post-examination celebratory period of boat races and balls held in June
Mechanical Sciences Tripos	Name used between 1894–1970 for engineering
Moral Sciences Tripos	Name used between 1851–1969 for philosophy
Old Schools	Complex of buildings opposite Great St Mary's, originating as medieval lecture rooms and libraries, now occupied by the central administration
OM	Order of Merit, prestigious honour for distinguished achievement, founded by Edward VII; membership is limited to 24 at any one time
Pensioner	Student paying college fees for teaching and board and lodging
Porter	College security officer, charged with care of keys, post and rebuking unruliness, not carrying baggage
Proctor	University official originally elected to enforce discipline
Professor	Occupant of a chair in a specific subject or head of a faculty
Reader	A senior but sub-professorial Lecturer
Regius Professor	Occupant of a prestigious chair endowed and usually appointed by the Crown; established in Cambridge in 1540, in Oxford in 1546
Reading	Studying
Regent House	Electorate (e.g. for the Council) and consultative body comprising all university teaching and administrative staff (c.3,000)
Residence	Students are required to live inside the university's boundaries, i.e. within a three-mile radius of Great St Mary's

Rusticated	Temporarily excluded for a specific period, from the Latin for living in the countryside
SCR	Senior Combination Room
Senate	Body of all existing MAs with electoral and legislative functions, now almost non-existent
Senate House	Historic building opposite Great St Mary's used for meetings of the Regent House, elections of university officers, conferment of degrees and other official ceremonies
Sent down	Expelled
Sizar	Impoverished student who worked his way through college
Square	Square cap; academic headgear otherwise known as a 'mortar board'; not worn at graduation at Cambridge
Subfusc	Formal dress for degree award ceremonies, from the Latin for dark
Supervision	Weekly teaching session of one hour plus between a student and their supervisor, responsible for teaching the material leading to a particular subject examination
Syndicate	Committee appointed to supervise a university function (e.g. Library) or to consider and propose action on a specific issue
Terms	The autumn term (October to December) is Michaelmas (after St Michael's Day, 29 September), the spring term (January to mid-March) is Lent and the summer (April to mid-June) is Easter; each lasts eight weeks
Tomkins Table	Academic league table since 1980 ranking colleges by degrees awarded

Town and Gown	Rivalry between members of the university and local residents; in the past a serious matter involving entrenched legal privileges of the university; subsequently unspoken understanding of mutual avoidance regarding specific pubs etc.
Tripos	Degree course and associated examinations, named after a three-legged stool examiners once sat on for oral examinations
Undergraduate	A student who has matriculated but not yet passed the BA degree
UL	University Library
Union	Debating society, not to be confused with the Student Union (see CUSU)
Vice-Chancellor	Administrative head of the university; formerly elected annually, usually for two successive years; the post usually rotated amongst Heads of Houses, but is now a permanent appointment for a fixed term of seven years
Wrangler	Student passing the final examinations of the Mathematical Tripos with First Class honours. The student with the highest individual marks was nominated Senior Wrangler, the next Second Wrangler and so on. The person with the lowest marks was traditionally awarded a wooden spoon. These rankings were public until 1909 but not since. Famous Wranglers have included Lord Rayleigh Senior Clerk-Maxwell and J J Thomson (2nd), Bertrand Russell (9th) and J M Keynes (12th)

Chronology

1861	University teachers allowed to marry
1870	Cavendish Laboratory opened
1874	Leys School founded
1883	Footlights founded
1888	First 'safety bicycles' in use
1905	First motor bus services established
1908	Ban on Sunday railway trains lifted
1911	Population 40,000
1932	Atom split at the Cavendish Laboratory
1934	Last Stourbridge fair; University Library built; Guildhall rebuilt
1936	Arts Theatre opened
1947	Women granted the right to receive degrees
1948	Last University MP elected (separate university representation abolished 1950)
1951	Cambridge granted city status
1970	Trinity College establishes Cambridge Science Park
1972	King's and Churchill accept female undergraduates
1995	Judge Institute of Management Studies opened
2001	Population 109,000 (including 22,000 students)
2005	Anglia Ruskin Polytechnic becomes Anglia Ruskin University
2009	Cambridge celebrates 800th anniversary
2017	Cambridge North railway station opens, reflecting the city's expansion

College Foundations (with full and alternative names)

1284	Peterhouse (College of the Scholars of the Bishop of Ely, St Peter's College)
1317	(The) King's Hall (merged into Trinity, 1546)
1321	University Hall (refounded as Clare Hall)
1324	Michaelhouse (merged into Trinity, 1546)
1326/46	Clare Hall (Clare College)

1347	Pembroke Hall (College, House or Hall of Valence Mary, Pembroke College)
1348/9	Gonville Hall (1351 Hall of the Annunciation of the Blessed Virgin Mary; 1393 took over Physwick Hostel (merged with Trinity 1546); 1557 re-founded as Gonville and Caius College)
1349/50	Trinity Hall (College of the Scholars of the Holy Trinity of Norwich)
1352	Corpus Christi College (College of Corpus Christi and the Blessed Virgin Mary, St Bene't's, Benet College)
1428	Buckingham College (1542 re-founded as Magdalene College)
1439	Godshouse (1505 refounded as Christ's College)
1441	King's College (Royal College of St Mary and St Nicholas)
1446/8	Queens' College (Queens' College of St Margaret and St Bernard, refounded 1465)
1473	Catharine Hall (St Catharine's College)
1496	Jesus College (College of the Blessed Virgin Mary, St John the Evangelist and the Glorious Virgin St Radegund)
1505	Christ's College (incorporating Godshouse)
1509/11	St John's College (College of St John the Evangelist)
1542	Magdalene College (formerly Buckingham College)
1546	Trinity College (College of the Holy and Undivided Trinity – merged from King's Hall (1317) Michaelhouse (1324) and Physwick Hostel (1393))
1584	Emmanuel College
1594/6	Sidney Sussex College (Lady Frances Sidney Sussex College)
1731	Homerton College (1895 moved from Hackney to Cambridge, in 1977 'adopted' by the university)
1800	Downing College (from a bequest of 1717)
1869	Girton College (1872 moved from Hitchin to Cambridge) Fitzwilliam House (1966 Fitzwilliam College)
1871	Newnham College

1882	Selwyn Hostel (1923 Selwyn College; 1957 full collegiate status)
1885	Hughes Hall (Cambridge Training College for Women; 1985 'approved foundation)
1896	St Edmund's House (1965 St Edmund's College; 1975 'approved foundation')
1954	New Hall (2008 Murray Edwards College)
1960	Churchill College
1964	Darwin College
1965	Lucy Cavendish College
	University College (1973 Wolfson College)
1966	Clare Hall
1977	Robinson College (1985 'approved foundation')
2010	Homerton College chartered as a full college of the university
2013	Cambridge opens its first research centre outside the UK, in Singapore
2015	Pembroke College gifted £35,000,000 bequest from the estate of Ray Dolby
2016	600th anniversary of Cambridge University Library
	200th anniversary of the Fitzwilliam Museum
	AstraZeneca moves its global headquarters to Cambridge
2017	Dolby estate gifts £85,000,000 to the University of Cambridge
2019	Launch of Cambridge Zero programme to maximise the university's contribution to achieving a zero-carbon world
2021	Launch of Foundation Year programme in Arts, Humanities and Social Sciences – a free, one-year pre-degree course for educationally disadvantaged students
	Prince of Wales opens The Discovery Centre (DISC) of AstraZeneca
2023	Cambridge ranked second in QS World University Rankings (MIT first, Oxford fourth)
2024	Ray Dolby Centre for research and development completed at the Cavendish Laboratory

Index